CONTENTS

INTRODUCTION

AIMS

This book aims to:

- examine creativity and perception in management
- introduce creative approaches to management
- examine the impact of cognition, intuition and perception on action
- illustrate the concepts of mind-set and metaphor
- differentiate between a variety of personal styles and note their implications for creativity, problem solving, communication, decision making and role preference
- understand the impact of cultural values and certain historical habits of thought on management and organization
- consider the nature of personal, organizational and global development
- understand the main ways in which management can enable organizations to be more sustainable and responsible.

OVERVIEW

We are at a time of change – the increasing pace of change is forcing companies to be more responsive and flexible. In their effort to survive amidst ever-increasing competition organizations are turning to creativity to add value, especially in high-wage economies. At the same time IT and globalization are changing the nature of business. Parallel to these economic upheavals, deeply ingrained habits of Western thought are being challenged on a number of fronts. Something of a paradigm shift seems to be under way, that is legitimizing new ways of organizing and managing.

This book begins to elaborate some of the principles and practices entailed in the new form of management associated with creative and innovative organizations. The text is especially concerned with the role of perception in management, the impact of thought on action, and the role of cognition in creative endeavour. It introduces the topics of creativity, cognition, style, development and sustainability as they pertain to management. It aims to play a part in articulating how neglected aspects of management, such as tacit knowledge, perceptual competencies and cognitive style, feed into the new approach of creative management. The book is divided into five sections: creativity (Chapters 1 and 2), perception (Chapters 3 and 4), style (Chapters 5 and 6), values (Chapters 7 and 8) and sustainability (Chapters 9 and 10).

Chapter 1 *Creativity* shows how our understanding of creativity has changed over time. What was once seen to be a generalizable ability of the chosen few is now seen as domain-specific skill we all possess, given appropriate motivation and experience, expressed according to our particular creative style. This new understanding leaves more room for adaptive or incremental creativity, a form of creativity long nurtured in the East but barely recognized in the West until recently.

Chapter 2 *Creative management* elaborates on the role of the creative manager. It discusses new management competencies, transformational leadership styles, the characteristics of a creative climate, and introduces some features of innovative organizations and organizational change practices that can help organizations become more creative.

Chapter 3 *Cognition* begins by reminding us that Mintzberg has long pointed out the importance of soft data in managerial thought. Recent advances in our understanding of how the mind works now leave us better placed to explain why this is. This chapter explains the critical role of unconscious learning, tacit knowledge and intuitive judgement in effective decision making, and illustrates the fallibility of the rational mind.

Chapter 4 *Metaphors* describes how organizational metaphors are changing, through a discussion of mechanistic, biological, cognitive and systemic metaphors, including the idea of organization as network, brain and complex adaptive system. It goes on to question whether the changes we are seeing in management and organizations represent a fundamental shift in management thinking that is part of a larger paradigm shift in Western thought.

Chapter 5 *Style* presents five key personality traits which seem to have a genetic underpinning and discusses their implications. It goes on to describe inventories that are designed to assess cognitive style, such as the MBTI, KAI and LSI, and illustrate the importance of working with people with diverse styles.

Chapter 6 *Roles* explains the various roles that have been found to be necessary for effective teamwork and to bring innovative projects to fruition.

Chapter 7 *Culture* maps out some of the main differences in cultural assumptions and describes how this has led to fundamentally different forms of management and can lead to inadvertent misunderstandings between managers. It goes on to explain why social capital appears to be important to economic endeavour.

Chapter 8 *Development* discusses how our thinking has been channelled by certain unquestioned assumptions that derive from our particular cultural heritage. In particular, it discusses how Western assumptions that date back centuries have led to particular approaches to both personal, professional and global development and how these are now changing.

Chapter 9 *Sustainability* elaborates on why organizations need to take increasing account of environmental issues, how they can respond to this challenge and what this means for organizational strategy.

Chapter 10 *Responsibility* ends on an optimistic note, documenting some of the ways in which organizations involve themselves in the community and the pay-off for doing so.

In short, the book offers a business psychology text that emphasizes the processes entailed in creative and perceptive management. This approach acknowledges difference, uncertainty and the impact of history, and emphasizes the need to involve stakeholders and to allow space for informal interaction and unconscious ways of knowing. It encourages self-development and pays attention to the context in which work occurs. The book aims to give an indication of how the mind works, to show the variety of styles in play and how ideas are very much a product of their time and culture.

The book's focus on perception shown by the emphasis on tacit knowledge, uncertainty, emergence and participation, also acts as a counter to the more traditional management focus on analysis with its emphasis on rationalism, predictability, planning and control. The notion of adaptive creativity in Chapter 1 challenges the idea that outside experts can know best. The suggestion in Chapter 2 that an open climate is necessary and local knowledge is inherent in a creative organization reframes the idea of management from controlling to facilitating. The stress on intuition, unconscious processing, tacit knowledge, mind-sets and judgement biases in Chapter 3 undermines notions of the pre-eminence of rationality. The metaphor of complexity in Chapter 4 challenges the extent to which planning is possible. The different cognitive styles described in Chapter 5 highlight the need to accommodate very different ways of working. The many different roles and rather haphazard development found in most innovative projects, introduced in Chapter 6, show the importance, not of the lean organization, but of the need to build in redundancy and to allow staff free time to pursue their interests. The Anglo-Saxon management tradition and Western-style MBA teaching often tends to act as if there were one form of management applicable to all settings. Chapter 7 shows the traditions of management in different cultures are not the same and have led to different sectoral relationships and strengths. Chapter 8 shows how, by failing to challenge certain long-standing assumptions and to take adequate account of local knowledge, the West has perhaps failed in its approach to both personal and third-world development. In addressing the need for sustainability, Chapter 9 challenges that fundamental tenet of Western capitalism, the assumption of continued growth. Chapter 10 closes by suggesting that a focus on shared values and social responsibility, rather than solely profit, is perhaps now more likely to lead to long-term organizational survival.

The chapters also have different characters. Chapter 1 *Creativity*, 3 *Cognition* and 5 *Style*, for example are more inward-looking and have a significant personal development component. It will be impossible to learn all that can be picked up from them without giving some thought to the activities suggested there. Chapters 2 *Creative management*, 4 *Metaphors* and 6 *Roles* are more practically oriented. Chapters 7 *Culture* and 8 *Development* contain a substantial theoretical component and Chapters 9 *Sustainability* and 10 *Responsibility* hint at future directions for the forward-looking organization.

The book has a strong developmental and experiential element. The activities form a central part of the material presented; they are gleaned from 20 years' experience offering creativity and development training to managers. They give you the opportunity to examine your experience to see what has worked for you, whether others agree with you or not and how your assumptions affect the way you strategize, frame and interpret others' communications. Examining perceptions in this way can open up important new perspectives.

This text builds on material I wrote for my earlier books on *Perspective* (Open University Press, 1991) and *Creativity, Cognition and Development* (Open University Press, 1999). I would particularly like to thank Geoff Jones for his contributions to Chapter 7, Ian Beadle for material drawn on in section 6.1, Ros Bell, Robert Campbell, Jon Mundy, Ian Williams and Eion Farmer for their comments on an earlier draft of this text, and Les Jones and David Mayle for comments on a specific chapter, and acknowledge that certain examples in section 3.1 are influenced by Guy Claxton's writings.

The sister text, *Creative Management*, 2nd edition (referred to as Henry, 2001) offers readers a series of articles which follow up the themes presented here. Sage also publishes *Managing Innovation and Change* (Henry and Mayle, 2001), which acts as an ideal complement to the *Creative Management* text. All three texts are used on the Open University Business School MBA programme in course *Creativity, Innovation and Change* (B822). For the other related course materials contact the Open University Business School.

Jane Henry
The Open University, Milton Keynes, UK
e-mail: j.a.henry@open.ac.uk
July 2000

Associated materials

J. Henry, *Creative Management*, 2nd edition (London: Sage, 2001)

PART 1
CREATIVITY

This part looks at the need for creativity, and at how our ideas about how to achieve creative action have changed over time. It goes on to consider the types of management, leadership and organizational style that support creative endeavour.

1 CREATIVITY

This chapter argues that the increasing pace of change and globalization has stimulated interest in creativity. It goes on to show how our understanding of what causes creativity has changed over time, and how attempts to engender creative endeavour at work have changed along with our understanding of what brings it about.

1.1 NEED FOR CREATIVITY

Pace of change

Globalization

Technological change

One hundred years ago in the UK a worker could scythe one acre, where today they do twenty.

(Handy, 1998, p.1)

The world is changing fast. Technological innovation has led to an *increasing pace of change*, and new products and services are emerging at a faster rate than ever before.[1] Table 1.1 offers an overview of major technological and social innovations through the ages and illustrates the recent exponential increase in technological invention. Information, communications and biotechnologies are leading to new and previously unsuspected possibilities. Thirty years ago there were no personal computers, mobile telephones, satellite television, bio-engineered plants, cloned animals, micro-surgery or precision missiles able to reach a ventilator shaft thousands of miles away. Handy (1991) suggests that information technology and biotechnology are developing so fast that their output is unpredictable, and that the only solution is to expect the unexpected.

Table 1.1 Innovations with major impact on human history		
Technological inventions	**Approximate date of invention**	**Social inventions**
Tools	1,750,000BC	
	500,000BC	Language
	400,000BC	Hunting
	400,000BC	Immigration
	150,000BC	Shelter
	20,000BC	Religion
	15,000BC	Agriculture
	7000BC	Cities
Wheel	3500BC	
	2800BC	Book
	2700BC	Taxation

[1] Of course past generations have had to cope with technological upheaval. After the invention of the printing press monks predicted the demise of education if people could merely read books rather than copy them out longhand! (A cry rather reminiscent of current concerns over the rise of video and internet usage and decline of book reading.)

	2500BC	School
	2400BC	Courts of law
	2200BC	Mail – letters
	1500BC	Alphabet
	1500BC	Irrigation systems
Boats	1500BC	Number system
	1000BC	
Wind power	1000BC	
	700BC	Coinage
	600BC	Hospital
	510BC	Democracy
Clock and compass	1200	
	1500	Science
	1640	Political party
Engines	1780	
	1800	Labour trade union
Electricity	1810	
Coal and oil for energy	1810	
	1880	Banking and insurance institutions
Car	1890	
Telecommunications	1900	
Aeroplane	1905	
Antibiotics	1935	
Nuclear energy/weapon	1945	Welfare state
Computer	1950	
Extensive use of fertilizer	1960	Supermarket
Satellite	1960	Credit cards
Laser	1965	
Fax	1965	
Moon landing	1969	
Genetic engineering	1970	
Organ transplants	1970	
Bar codes	1970	Open learning
Personal computer	1975	
E-mail	1980	
Mobile phones	1980	
Internet	1985	
Cloning	1995	

(Source: adapted and extended from Makridakis, 1989, pp. 40–1; and Albery and Yule, 1989, pp. 5–6)

Globalization

Two-thirds of the world's trade is managed by 500 corporations.

(Handy 1998, p.69)

Telecommunications now allow instant contact with colleagues around the globe via fax, phone, e-mail or videophone. Anyone who can access a telephone line and computer can gather information on just about anything they want on the web. The combination of telecommunications technology coupled with fast long-distance transport has brought about a *globalization* of commerce. Globalization has generally led to increased competition. The current political trend of deregulation and privatisation has exacerbated the pressure for change. In addition the Internet has lowered the barriers for entry into a number of markets. In short organizations are faced with ever-increasing competition and an increasing pace of change.

Company life

The average life of Fortune 500 companies is 40 years.

To survive, organizations have had to become more responsive, and flexible enough to react quickly to environmental changes and, in high-wage economies, creative enough to *add value through continual innovation.*

It is now creativity, knowledge, innovation and learning that add value, rather than land, labour or capital. At the time of writing, the intangible assets of companies are, on average, in the order of three to four times the value of fixed assets. In the case of knowledge-intensive industries, such as IT or biotechnology, and dot.coms, the ratio is much greater. Microsoft, for example, has a ratio of intangible to tangible assets of more like 100 to 1. OECD estimates half the wealth of advanced industrial societies is intangible assets (Handy, 1998, pp. 160–1).

The recognition of the importance of creative knowledge to organizations and the central role of employees' ideas have led to an interest in ways of drawing out creativity in the workforce. In the 1990s, a number of governments, NGOs and organizations around the world introduced initiatives designed to aid this process. For example in the UK these included the ESRC (Economic and Social Science Research Council) Innovation programme, various DTI (Department of Trade and Industry) Innovation Unit programmes such as Partnership through People, the Technology Foresight programme, the RSA (Royal Society of Arts) Tomorrow's Company and so on. Currently the UK government has a major project examining the so-called 'creative industries' (music, film production, art, literature, museums, antiques, etc.).

The following sections describe how people have attempted to draw out creativity and how the approach taken has changed over time.

1.2 NATURE AND ORIGINS OF CREATIVITY

Activity 1.1

How would you define creativity? What associations does creativity have for you? Write down any words and phrases that it suggests to you.

Creativity seems familiar enough, but it is also a term that can mean different things to different people. Asked for their understanding of the term, groups of managers typically volunteer a list of words that includes the following: new, novel, original, invention, imagination, insight and intuition. Formal definitions generally incorporate at least two defining characteristics: *newness* and *appropriateness*.

Newness, indicating unusualness and originality, comes as no surprise. However, it is worth pointing out that this is not just originality in the sense of an idea that is new to the species, but also *relative novelty*, i.e. any idea that is novel to the perceiver. (West and Farr (1990) argue strongly for attending to this aspect of creativity.) The second quality, appropriateness, may be forgotten initially but it is important. It emphasizes the quality of the idea or invention. Truly creative ideas have lasting impact and are perceived to be worthy by others: being different is not enough – you must also be apt.

Creative ideas are new and appropriate.

Theories of creativity

Activity 1.2

What do you think causes creativity, and where do new ideas come from?

To be in a position to draw out creativity in the workforce, one needs some idea of what conditions favour creativity. A quick examination of the various explanations that have been put forward shows that historically these have changed considerably over time. Table 1.2 gives an overview of the main theories.

Table 1.2	Theories of creativity
Focus	**Assumed cause**
Grace	Muse
Serendipity	Luck
Association	Insight
Personality	Trait
Skill	Mental flexibility
Experience	Expert recognition
Motivation	Persistence
Culture	Nurture
Emergence	Interaction

(Source: adapted from Henry, 1994)

Creativity was traditionally seen as an unfathomable mystery, but more recent theories of creativity can be loosely associated with different decades. For example, in the 1950s creativity was thought to be an *ability* granted only to the gifted few; in the 1960s it was seen more as a skill of *mental flexibility* that could be learnt. In the 1970s the role of *relevant experience* was more fully appreciated by researchers, and in the 1980s attention was drawn to the key role of *intrinsic motivation* (doing things because you want to). All these theories locate the source of the creativity in the individual; recently managers and researchers have begun to turn their attention to the part played by the social context. In the 1990s organizations became conscious of the effect work *climate* and environment have on the potential for creativity on people in organizations. We are beginning to get a better understanding of the extent to which organizational creativity is an emergent phenomenon that builds on what has gone before and arises from ongoing interactions. This newer perspective considers the part played by *social context*. I will discuss each of these approaches to understanding creativity in turn.

Traditionally, like its sister *intuition*, creativity seemed so mysterious that possessing it was attributed to an act of *grace* on the part of the muse. When we think of Shakespeare's plays, Leonardo da Vinci's drawings, Mozart's music or

Einstein's theory of relativity, we can understand how such powerful creative acts may seem to owe something to the supernatural.

An alternative perspective assumes creativity results from *serendipitous* good fortune, a case of being in the right place at the right time. This approach presumes that Fleming was just lucky to notice the odd reaction on one of his Petri dishes, an observation that led to the discovery of penicillin.

1.3   INDIVIDUAL CHARACTERISTICS

In the right place at the right time

Many people never realize that they are standing in a propitious space/time convergence, and even fewer know what to do when the realization hits them.

(Csikszentmihalyi, 1996, p. 47)

Activity 1.3 _____

Think of two or three people from the worlds of science, art, music, business, sport, literature or any other field of your choice and note what you think is creative about:

(a) the people

(b) whatever they produce.

Depending upon whom you chose, your ideas may differ from what follows, but often what emerges is a surprising commonality in many of the characteristics identified. Try it with your family or friends. As you might expect, creative people do the unexpected and are *original,* but it is often observed that they also have a dream or *purpose* to guide their activities. Sometimes creative people are perceived to be very single-minded and *determined* in their main interest, verging on the obsessional. They may also be seen as difficult people to work with.

Activity 1.4 _____

Think of some people known to you personally whom you believe to be creative. Select:

(a) a creative colleague (or better still superior, peer and subordinate colleagues)

(b) a friend, a relative or a child, who seems fairly creative to you.

In both cases write brief notes on:

(a) the sort of people they are

(b) the way they do things.

If you find it difficult to think of anyone at work who is really creative, choose someone who is more creative than most.

This exercise may produce a few surprises. A quality that often, but not invariably, features when considering creative colleagues (at least in the UK) is a combination of adaptability and *flexibility:* for instance, in the way in which a creative person manages to make use of the people and resources available. Creative friends and colleagues are often judged to be receptive and have a *positive* outlook. The effective ones may well be seen as good listeners with appealing personalities, a characterization that is quite at odds with the idea of the crazy genius in the attic.

Ability

Ability

Creative *ability* has always been valued and, over the years, psychologists have attempted to identify what abilities are involved. Guildford's (1959) list concluded that originality, flexibility, idea fluency, problem sensitivity and redefinitional skills were all critical to creative performance. Perkins's (1981) study stressed the importance of intrinsic motivation, a personal aesthetic or sensitivity to form, a capacity for objectivity, the ability to take risks, mental mobility, including tolerance for ambiguity, and problem-finding skills. Many studies have tended to come to similar conclusions, regardless of the domain they are studying. One common finding is that creative people seem to possess *problem-finding* abilities – the art of recognizing the important question. They are also able to tolerate ambiguity and thus can avoid premature closure by not settling on a solution too soon.

Trait

In the 1950s it was assumed that creativity was a *trait* possessed by some people but not others, a special ability possessed by the gifted few. In this view, Fleming's discovery of penicillin was not accidental but a reflection of his exceptional creative ability.

A consequence of this perspective is that managers are best advised to try to identify who the creative and innovative staff are. Over the years there have been various attempts to develop tests that measure creativity. One approach aims to measure 'divergent thinking ability', the ability to come up with many uses for a particular object, for example. (It is now questioned whether in fact this is an adequate measure of creativity.)

Style

All individuals, however, have the capacity to be creative: for example, we have all learned to speak and utter creative and unique sentences every day. The alternative and more modern perspective focuses less on who is and is not creative and more on the different *styles* of creativity they display. Kirton (1989) suggests there is a case for differentiating between the innovative approach to creativity, which involves reframing problems and coming up with radically new approaches, and the adaptive approach, which involves improving on existing practice. He suggests there is a continuum, with some people favouring a creative approach involving doing things differently and others preferring to do things better. This distinction is elaborated in Chapter 5, section 5.4. In Western societies we tend to associate creativity with innovative breakthroughs, but most innovations come about through a series of incremental improvements. The adaptive style of creativity, building on what has gone before, has received little attention in the West until recently.

Mental skill

Many people associate creativity with insight, and assume that this arises when applying previously unrelated ideas or metaphors from one field to another. The most famous example is Archimedes. While taking a bath, he suddenly realized that his irregularly shaped body displaced a volume of water and that this same principle would allow him to measure the irregular volume of the king's crown. This notion of creative *association* is probably the most common everyday theory of the creative process. (It has been popularized by Koestler's (1969) writings on the idea of bisociation and de Bono's (1971) ideas on lateral thinking.)

Studies of creative individuals reveal that they do indeed tend to possess a certain mental flexibility that allows them to withhold judgement, shift their perspective on a problem, be prepared to redefine the issue and tolerate ambiguity. In the late 1960s and 1970s de Bono (1984) was one of those who popularized the idea of training people in these creative skills. This type of creativity training aims to break through mental barriers and increase mental flexibility to make it more likely that potentially useful insights are not bypassed. In this view creativity is a *skill* which can be taught.

The implication of this approach is that creativity is a transferable skill, a notion that is in keeping with a common current government policy that stresses acquisition of competencies as a route to learning. While many trainers and politicians accept without question the idea that management competencies and creative problem-solving skills are transferable, researchers who have studied the genesis of ideas tend to take the opposite view, showing convincingly that the skill of mental flexibility is only part of the story.

1.4 EXPERIENCE, KNOWLEDGE AND MOTIVATION

Relevant experience

Studies of creative people, whether they are chess players, musicians, businessmen or scientists, have emphasized the role of *relevant experience* and with it the idea that *chance favours the prepared mind*. Studies show that creative experts tackle problems differently from novices. It seems that, as they build up their experience, they organize their knowledge in ever more sophisticated chunks which means they can access key cues more quickly. Consequently they are better placed to recognize important problems. For example, Fleming may have stopped to question the unusual reaction in a Petri dish, that subsequently led to the discovery of penicillin, because years of work had alerted him to irregularities that were likely to be significant problems (i.e. his experience had led to superior problem-finding skills).

Chance favours the prepared mind.

Many great industrial inventors, just like their counterparts in science and music, have worked in particular fields for many years before apparently stumbling upon their inventions, and have taken many years afterwards to develop their ideas. For example, Edward Land took three years to develop the polaroid camera after his initial insight (Westley and Mintzberg, 1991).

Weisburg (1986) argues that you need to work in an area for ten years before you are capable of achievement of exceptional creative worth. Many of the business people who have successfully turned around their industry have indeed been working in their area for many years. For instance Jan Carlzon, who rejuvenated Scandinavian Airlines, was a travel veteran, and Lee Iacocca, who revitalized Chrysler, had been brought up in the car industry.

In this view, creativity is largely a matter of *expert recognition*. The implication is that creative competencies are 'domain dependent' and not necessarily transferable skills. A consequence is that the wise manager is well advised to think twice before downsizing by letting experienced staff go. Younger staff may be cheaper but they will not have the experienced staff's know-how.

Intrinsic motivation

Amabile[2] (1983) argues that neither the possession of mental flexibility nor relevant experience are sufficient for creativity to flourish. Rather creativity emerges when there is a combination of these factors along with *intrinsic motivation*, i.e. people are doing what they want to do. So, while chance may favour the prepared mind, motivation seems to be an equally important factor, and the *love people feel for their work* may be just as good a measure of their level of creativity. The argument here is that you need to be intrinsically motivated to drive the persistent effort needed for a creative outcome. Plus, if you really care about something, you are more willing to take risks to achieve it. Both perseverance and a capacity for risk-taking seem to be necessary creative attributes. The implication is that people are more likely to be creative in areas they are most interested in, so employers might be well advised to let them work on projects they are most attracted to.

Many innovative companies do now have policies that allow research scientists to follow their own motivation to some degree. For example 3M, a company with 30% of products developed in the last five years, has a motto '*find the inventors and do not get in their way*'. It allows researchers 15% of their time to pursue their own projects; Hewlett Packard allows 10%. Post-it™ pads and superconductive materials both emerged from projects conducted in researchers' 'free time'.

1.5 THE CONTEXT OF CREATIVITY

Climate

Work climate and culture are important for creativity in several ways. This is not only because an open climate is likely to afford more opportunities for people to work on tasks and in ways that they find motivating, but also because people are more likely to be prepared to explore new areas and try different approaches in a culture where they feel safe and know they will not be punished for this type of exploratory behaviour. So motivation, and through this performance, are affected by the environment.

It is a psychological truism that people rarely take risks unless they feel safe and valued. If people feel threatened they tend to react more defensively. This is

---

[2] See Amabile (1998) on 'How to kill creativity' in Henry (2001).

perhaps one reason why initiatives (like total quality management) that are trying to document and control the process of creative improvement can face an uphill battle: as you cannot legislate for creativity, you have to trust it will emerge.

Studies of creativity at work (e.g. Jelinek and Schoonhoven, 1990; Ekvall, 1991) have emphasized that, by and large, certain organizational climates are much more conducive to creativity than others. The more favourable climates are more open, they give employees freedom and responsibility for their work, tolerate rather than punish mistakes and make a point of nurturing new ideas.

In the West many organizations have accepted the importance of developing conditions that favour creativity through more open organizational climates. In the latter part of the twentieth century numerous companies endeavoured to change their culture and structure to support more open climates that have a better chance of nurturing creative endeavour. The UK Government supported this approach through such initiatives as the DTI Innovation Unit's 'Winning Company' programme.

Not that everything is sunshine and roses in open and creative climates; typically people find they need to allow more time to communicate with each other. Working in multidisciplinary teams with people who do not agree with you and have other concerns is bound to be uncomfortable from time to time. However, it seems there are few other ways to run innovative, creative companies in a number of sectors, including IT.

Social context

With a few honourable exceptions (Barron, 1968), most of the work on creativity to date, especially in the West, has tended to locate the source of creativity within the individual. This view is finally beginning to be questioned and, belatedly, some researchers are turning their attention to the community of practice from which creative endeavour emerges.

Csikszentmihalyi (1996, 1999), for example, looks at three aspects of creativity: the creative individual, the domain of knowledge they are working within (marketing, accountancy, psychology, etc.) and the social field (the norms and gatekeepers that govern the area) within which these endeavours take place.[3] Certain fields at certain times seem to foster and accelerate creative endeavour in particular domains, for example art and architecture in Florence at the beginning of the fifteenth century, the Bloomsbury Set and writing in the 1920s and 1930s, Silicon Valley and the development of computers in the latter part of the twentieth century, pop music and Liverpool in the 1960s and Manchester in the 1990s, new business and the ASEAN countries in the 1970s and 1980s, perhaps Cambridge and biotechnology in the 1990s. Can you think of other, lesser-known examples?

This view draws attention to the extent to which ideas build on what has gone before. A consequence is that managers might be better advised to spend less time looking at the qualities and behaviour of creative individuals and to focus

---

[3] See Csikszentmihalyi's 'Systems view of creativity' in (Henry, 2001).

instead on the system of social relations from which creative endeavour emerges, examining the conditions and systems that nurture and sustain creative endeavour.

In attempting to predict the creative potential of companies it can be argued that the emphasis on research and knowledge are key factors. For example, if you want to predict which of two companies in the same sector is most likely to come up with an effective new product, Csikszentmihalyi (1996) suggests that the company which places more emphasis on research and makes its knowledge available to staff is the better bet.

Activity 1.5

Compare your organization to a competitor.

Which organization has more data about its domain?

Which puts more emphasis on research and benchmarking competitors?

Where is it easier to get resources to test hypotheses and try out new approaches?

Where does industry-specific knowledge gain more respect?

Where is the data better organized?

Which company disseminates information better among its staff?

Emergent creativity

Another approach to understanding creativity borrows from the new science of complexity to stress the idea of *emergent creativity*. Complexity involves the study of complex dynamical systems involving many agents (creatures capable of learning). The theory shows that, if the individual agents go about their business following a few simple rules, patterns of behaviour begin to emerge in the group that enable the group to learn. One implication of this is that even quite complex systems composed of many agents seem perfectly well able to *self-regulate*. Proponents might cite London as a case in point, which managed to feed and transport the vast majority of its millions of citizens without any central authority running the system for some years. (Sceptics will probably point to homeless people, crime and crumbling sewers as cases that seem to have fallen through this *laissez faire* net.)

Though dynamical systems demonstrate learning, the nature of the patterns that emerge in the system is not predictable at the outset. Neural net software based on these ideas is already in use to analyse the stock market. These programs need practice, they start out performing poorly but, as they learn the different patterns that can arise, they gradually match the existing data better than expert systems. Software engineers only apply them for real once they have got to the point where they predict market trends well and repeatedly. A feature of the software is that the programmers are unable to explain exactly how it works, as the interactions involved are too complex.

Creativity can be seen in the same way, as a property that emerges from a social field due to an interaction of factors, but one which is almost impossible to predict. Creativity is more likely in organizations that are neither too stable and ordered (for example, bureaucracies) nor totally disordered. Since no functioning organization can be totally disordered, the suggestion is that creative endeavour is more likely to emerge at the 'edge of chaos', in the mess between order and disorder.

1.6 CHANGING CONCEPTIONS

Historically, creativity and innovation researchers have investigated rather different questions. Creativity research has asked who is creative, how do they set about being creative, and how can we get round the barriers that stop them from being more creative. (A few creativity researchers have argued for work on other areas, for example Simonton (1988) held that persuasion was a key quality for creative individuals.) Innovation research has concentrated on how ideas reach the market-place, and has tended to frame this research within an assumption that ideas are diffused from the top down. The new research on knowledge management recognizes the importance of local knowledge and focuses on knowledge transfer, assuming that the knowledge generated can be transferred.

Creativity

Innovation

Knowledge

Table 1.3 summarizes the assumed causes of creativity in the theories discussed above. It points out the resultant strategy to develop creativity that arises from these assumptions and the implications for whether all or only some of the population possess creative ability, and whether creativity is perceived as a transferable skill or bound up with knowledge of a particular domain.

Table 1.3 Assumed cause of creativity, resulting development strategy and knowledge location			
Cause		**Strategy**	**Implications**
Ability	Trait	Identify creative abilities	Not everyone is creative
	Style	Balance styles in teams	All people are creative
Competence	Skill	Develop creative skills	Transferable skill
	Attitude	Remove perceptual blocks	Transferable skill
Experience	Application	Develop expert recognition	Domain dependent
	Motivation	Build in personal freedom	Domain dependent
Context	Climate	Encourage open climate	All people are creative but are more likely to be so in open environments
	Field	Nurture creative networks	All people are creative but will not be recognised as such unless their idea is accepted by their field's judges and opinion makers

(Source: extended from Henry, 1997)

Creativity has changed its meaning substantially over the last fifty years (see Table 1.4). Whereas creativity was previously associated with radical insights that only a subset of the population could hope to achieve, it is now assumed that everybody can be creative, and greater attention is paid to small, incremental, creative adaptions. It is also applied to any part of the problem-solving process – you can implement, and not just invent, creatively.

Table 1.4 Changing meaning of creativity		
Chosen few creative	–>	Everybody is creative
Radical insight, innovation	–>	Incremental, adaptive creativity
Uniquely new	–>	New to you
Ideas	–>	Implementation

(Source: Henry, 1998)

Developing creativity

But what can you do to be more creative? One strategy is to model yourself on the behaviours exhibited by creative people. These qualities can be summarized under the headings: positivity, playfulness, passion (or purpose), and persistence, as shown in Table 1.5.

Table 1.5 Characteristics of the creative person	
Positivity	Opportunity-seeking
	Tolerance
Playfulness	Mental flexibility
	Risk-taker
Passion	Motivation
	Commitment
Persistence	Experience
	Problem sensitivity

Positivity is an attitude of mind, one that sees even a bad situation as an opportunity for learning rather than failure or terrible trial; in essence positivity entails suspending critical judgement. This requires sufficient tolerance to accept your own and others' failings.

Playfulness refers to an ability to be flexible. It implies a mind that does not cling rigidly to a particular way of viewing the world but is able to switch perspectives, and tolerates or enjoys the ambiguity in understanding inherent in holding several, perhaps conflicting, viewpoints. Such a mind is possessed of sufficient independence of thought to stand outside the mainstream. Independence is often uncomfortable for others, so you need to accept or thrive on the risk this entails. (Bohm and Peat (1991) describe the importance of play in relation to scientific thinking, stressing the importance of what they term 'free play' in thought to realizing truly creative insights. Martin (1991) covers similar ground from a psychodynamic perspective, concluding that a capacity for creative play is central to healthy living.)

A *passionate* interest in the subject of study provides the motivation and commitment to sustain the persistent effort that many new ideas require. Newton is reputed to have worked 17 hours a day during the 10 years of his life that he devoted to physics. Apparently he was so absorbed in his work he forgot to eat and food had to be placed in front of his nose at his desk.[4]

Another ingredient that seems to be critical is *experience* in the particular field. This enables a person to build up a stock of patterns and understandings about a subject, which may be necessary to help develop sensitivity to the relevant problems. This takes *persistence*.

Several well-known innovators and entrepreneurs have demonstrated quite extraordinary persistence in their attempts to achieve their goals. For example, the story goes that when Colonel Sanders hit 65 he realized a pension was not going to be enough to live on. He decided to offer his chicken recipe to restaurants for a share in any extra profits they made. He travelled for two years before the 1008th restaurant he visited agreed to the scheme. Subsequently Kentucky Fried Chicken has done rather well (Robbins, 1990). Similarly, Chester Carlson is reputed to have spent 20 years trying to interest manufacturers in his invention – the photocopier. The small company that took him up, Xerox, had the vision to see the potential but not many resources at the time.

It could be argued that we should add a fifth 'p', *'persuasion'*, when talking about creativity in organizations or entrepreneurship more generally, since this invariably involves interesting others in your ideas.

1.7   REVIEW

This chapter has explained how personality, mental flexibility, experience, motivation, organizational climate and social context all play their part in creative endeavour. It has endeavoured to show how the search for a single cause of creative output has given way to an understanding that multiple factors are involved; similarly, how a concern with seeking creativity within individuals is giving way to strategies that pay more attention to the social community from which creativity emerges.

In terms of policy this has meant that the search to assess those with creative abilities was first supplemented by attempts to teach everybody creative skills. Subsequently many companies have begun to employ management strategies that recognize the need to nurture communities of creative endeavour.

---

[4] From the late 1690s Newton became Master of the Mint. However, he spent the rest of his life devoted to what he regarded as a more serious pursuit than physics – alchemy!

Recommended reading

M. Csikszentmihalyi, 'A systems perspective on creativity', in Henry (2001).

Further reading

J. Henry, 'Making sense of creativity', Chapter 1 in Henry (1991).

2 CREATIVE MANAGEMENT

The end of the twentieth century has seen considerable interest in ways of developing and sustaining creativity and innovation in organizations. There are a number of reasons for this, foremost of which are the perceived increase in the pace of change, globalization and deregulation. This has resulted in increased competition, and in the assumption that the way forward for developed economies is to add value through creativity and innovation. The shift from the industrial to the information age, and the rise of knowledge-based industries, have enhanced interest further.

In addition, we are faced by various national and global challenges. *Global challenges* include global competition, global warming, pollution and the North–South divide. National challenges in the UK include the decline of manufacturing and adapting to the new Europe. These challenges demand all the creative management that we can muster if we are to survive happily in the twenty-first century.

This chapter looks at the creative approaches to management now being adopted by managers and organizations, and introduces some approaches to transforming organizations. Space precludes anything more than an introduction to this area but the themes raised are taken up in more detail in Henry *et al.* (2001).[5]

2.1 MANAGING CREATIVELY

The changing business environment is changing organizations. The accelerating pace of change has increased the level of uncertainty to a point at which we need to develop procedures that can provide appropriate responses in uncharted territory. This seems to demand a more responsive form of management: one that has to do more with self-organization than with management control, and that requires new and different management competencies.

Flexible response

To achieve the necessary *cost reductions, speed of response, and flexibility to enhance their potential for innovation,* many organizations have had to restructure. Initially, companies tried to meet this challenge with more of the old strategies – reducing the cost base by *downsizing* and *delayering,* and *divesting* non-core business to become leaner, more efficient organizations. Many companies have reorganized into more responsive structures by decentralizing production to multidisciplinary teams, which are organized in product- or service-related cells and divisions acting as their own profit centres. The new leaner twenty-first century organization often finds development and growth

Downsize, delayer, divest, deregulate

---

[5] J. Henry *et al.* (2001), 'Innovation, climate and change', Book 3 of *Creativity, Innovation and Change*, Milton Keynes: Open University Press.

now occurs through partnership and alliance with other companies, even old enemies, who can provide the necessary expertise or capital to compete.

Participation

The new decentralized and, to some degree, empowered workforce has more responsibility than hitherto. As a consequence the nature of the manager's job is changing to one that is more concerned with *perception* and *facilitation* than analysis and control. Continual innovation is more likely where the workforce are committed to the project they are working on and are prepared to share their ideas for improvement. This in turn is fostered through a more *participative* approach entailing an open climate, employee empowerment and (often) reward schemes. In effect, there has been a paradigm shift in the nature of management and organization, in which creativity, innovation and knowledge now have a central role.

The interest in creative management approaches can also be seen as part of a reaction against the managerialist paradigm that has dominated management thinking in the US and UK and increasingly many other parts of globe in the twentieth century. Though this seems to have been an effective way to manage mass production in Anglo-Saxon cultures, increasing competition, faster product life cycles and a greater emphasis on niche markets may now require a more responsive form of management that affords managers less command and control. Box 2.1 offers a brief account of some of the key historical factors that led to managerialism dominating management thinking.

BOX 2.1   MANAGEMENT HISTORY

Fifteenth century
Italian manager
collecting the salt tax

The term 'management' seems to have arisen in medieval times and was first applied to stewards who looked after large agricultural estates. The term manager appears in fifteenth-century Italy to describe traders and, by the seventeenth century, both terms are commonplace. However, treatises on management were specific to the industry concerned and it was automatically assumed that if you switched from managing a cotton mill to a shipping line you would have to learn the business anew (Witzel, 1998; Jones, 1998).

The idea of management as a transferable set of practices was unknown until the twentieth century, and derived from American concepts of mass manufacturing. This form of managerialism developed a sharp distinction between management and labour, and concentrated on improving productivity through scientific management and industrial psychology. Though Britain industrialized well before the US, the idea of management as a set of practices that can be transferred across industries was imported from the US to the UK. This now standard Anglo-Saxon approach to management dominates management thinking, is promulgated through MBA programmes the world over and is increasingly applied to public and not-for-profit as well as private-sector organizations. Locke (1996) argues that this kind of command and control management is peculiarly American and suited only for mass production and not other kinds of activity.

In contrast, French, German and Japanese traditions have retained the idea that management knowledge is specific to a particular industry or sector. And, though they have taken on board certain aspects of global management, these have been moderated by cultural conditions. For example, West German managers tend to believe that the knowledge needed to manage is based on practical experience rather functional specialization. Compared to US or UK managers, West German managers are more likely to have engineering than administrative backgrounds and to be able to perform or at least understand the work they are supervising.

The changing business environment has placed traditional command and control management practices under pressure. Increasingly organizations are experimenting with more creative forms of management that rely more heavily on participation, self-organization, facilitation and nurturing. Creative management has come to be associated with these newer forms of management practice.

Creative management is about changing the way organizations are run, by trying to open up their climate and management style, increasing participation and giving employees more freedom as to how things are accomplished. Thus creative management aims to transform the company from within. For staff in such companies this may entail developing a more creative attitude in themselves, paying attention to ways of developing and nurturing creativity in others, and sustaining an open climate or culture that encourages creative endeavour and systems that enable organizational innovation and interorganizational networking.[6]

However, creative and innovative management are used in at least two distinct senses in organizations. The first refers to more creative and innovative ways of organizing companies designed to sustain creative and innovative endeavour through a more participative and open approach, as described above and practised to varying degrees by, for example, Dutton, Semco, 3M or ABB. The second sense refers to managing the innovation process for the introduction of new approaches, products and services. So both participative organizational renewal and new product development are associated with creative and innovative management. There is no consistent usage, but on the whole *creative management* is linked with transforming organizations and *managing innovation* is linked with new product development.

---

[6] *Creativity, Innovation and Change* Audio 1 offers reflections by Charles Handy, Rosabeth Moss Kanter, Henry Mintzberg and Charles Hampden-Turner on creative management and creative organizations (Henry, 2000a).

2.2   CREATIVE LEADERS

Transforming a company generally involves several different roles, notably those of creative or visionary leader, champion, creative manager and committed workforce. Typically the *creative leader* is presumed to have a vision of how things should be and be charismatic enough to inspire others to follow that creative vision. But like new products, new ideas also often need to be embedded within an organization. A vision for the organization may be taken forward and developed into a more tangible strategy by *champions* or sponsors, who advocate the new approach within their area, focusing on the people and processes necessary to get the idea adopted. One of the *creative manager's* roles – like Belbin's (1988) chairperson and team worker – is to attend to the social needs of the group, ensuring a suitably open atmosphere to nurture and sustain the new approach, so that the idea can be brought to fruition.

Vision
Persuasion

Kanter (1991) has argued that the successful creative leader not only formulates a vision but has power to advance the idea and maintain the momentum. She suggests that creative leaders have good perceptual abilities that she likens to kaleidoscopic thinking – a capacity to question, rearrange and see things from a different angle. They are good communicators, have a capacity to build coalitions and work through teams, and are persistent. Creative leaders need persuasive powers to communicate their vision and the ability to inspire and assist others to carry their dreams on into reality. Kanter claims such leaders make a point of recognizing others' contributions. This suggests they also have good social skills.

In the accompanying *Creative Management* Reader (Henry, 2001), Goleman (1998) argues that the difference between good and bad performance among

Table 2.1	Emotional intelligence	
Components	**Definition**	**Examples**
Self-awareness	understand the effect of moods, emotions and drives, on others	self-confidence realistic self-image sense of humour
Self-regulation	control or redirect disruptive impulse and think before acting	integrity accepts ambiguity open to change
Motivation	intrinsic motivation, energy and persistence	drive to achieve optimism organizational commitment
Empathy	understand and treat people according to their emotional reaction	expert talent-builder sensitive client and customer service
Social skill	proficient rapport, relationship and network builder	effective change leader persuasive expert team-builder and leader

(Source: after Goleman, 1998)

leaders is often due to their level of *emotional intelligence*, a term he has coined to describe the self-awareness, self-regulation and motivation needed to manage yourself and the empathy and social skills needed to manage relationships with others. He believes that though these qualities can be developed over time, they often require a programme of individualized training over a long period.

Activity 2.1

Make brief notes on leaders you have known that you admire. What were their qualities?

Of course, not all leaders adopt similar styles. We can for example contrast the *visionary, entrepreneurial* and *transformational* leadership styles. Westley and Mintzberg (1991) describe five very different leadership styles which can be subsumed under these three approaches (shown in Table 2.2 overleaf). They consider Edwin Land, Steven Jobs, René Lévesque (a Canadian politician), Lee Iacocca and Jan Carlzon. Sometimes a *visionary leader*, such as René Levesque the Canadian politician, can carry people with a timely vision. However, most visions are transient and not easy to adapt to changed circumstances, so visionary leaders are often products of their time. Entrepreneurial leadership may involve the creator moving from inventor to innovator, for example, Edward Land and the Polaroid camera; or the entrepreneur, the proselytizer who focuses on the mass-market product. Steve Jobs's role in starting up and promoting Apple Macintosh is a classic case. *Transformational* leadership often involves leaders who are steeped in the industries they transform, for example Lee Iacocca, known for his role in turning round Chrysler, and Jan Carlzon, the charismatic chief executive of Scandinavian Airlines, had both worked on their respective industries for years.

Visionary

Entrepreneurial

Transformational

In addition to the revitalizing styles of transformational leadership, there is a more radical alternative exemplified by Ricardo Semler (1994).[7] Semler offers an account of the *creative leadership* style that he used to empower staff to self-organize in his Brazilian company, Semco. This involved abolishing most rules, norms and procedures, and jettisoning 75% of corporate staff (e.g. doing without quality, training, data processing or personnel departments). Open-book accounting meant financial information was open to all employees. Employees were also able to take many more decisions themselves, from the appointment and appraisal of their managers, to setting their own working hours, titles, salaries, expenses and (within limits) share of the profits!

Self-organizing

Semler's philosophy is to maximize worker participation, decision making and public information, and to minimize management control procedures that can inhibit creativity. Semler's article in *Creative Management* (Henry, 2001) expands on the way he continued to develop the company through self-organization.

A leader does not need to be a charismatic extravert to run a successful creative organization. William McKnight, General Manager, Chief Executive and then

---

[7] See Semler's article on 'Why my former employees still work for me', in the Reader (Henry, 2001).

Table 2.2	Examples of leadership styles					
Characteristic style	Salient capacities	Content	Process	Organization content	Product/ market context	Target group
VISIONARY Idealist (René Levesque)	Imagination, sagacity	Ideals focus	Deliberate, deductive, introspective, incremental	Turnaround, public bureaucracy	Political concepts, zero-sum market	General population 50% market share
ENTREPRENEURIAL						
Creator (Edwin Land)	Inspiration, imagination, foresight	Product focus	Sudden, holistic, introspective, deliberate	Start-up, entrepreneurial	Invention and innovation, tangible products, niche markets	Independent consumer, scientific community
Proselytizer (Steven Jobs)	Foresight, imagination	Market focus	Emergent, shifting focus, interactive, holistic	Start-up, entrepreneurial	Tangible product, adaptation, mass market	Collective market, competitor infrastructure
TRANSFORMATIONAL						
Bricoleur (Lee Iacocca)	Sagacity, foresight, insight	Product/ organization focus	Emergent, inductive, interactive, incremental	Revitalization, turnaround, private and public bureaucracy	Product development; segmented, oligopolistic markets	Government (in Chrysler), union, customers
Diviner (Jan Carlzon)	Insight, sagacity, inspiration	Service focus	Incremental, sudden crystallization, interactive	Revitalization, bureaucracy	Service development & innovation, mass oligopolistic market	Employees

(Source: regrouped and adapted from Westley and Mintzberg, 1991)

Chairman of 3M for over fifty years, was quiet and softly spoken. Sony's Masaru Ibuku has been described as reserved, thoughtful and introspective. Collins and Porras (1995) suggest leaders of successful visionary companies are not focused on selling a great idea or being a charismatic leader, but rather *building a self-sustaining company.* They point out many organizations famous for their creativity started with a series of product failures, including Bill Hewlett and Dave Packard's fat-reduction shock machines, and Sony's initial tape recorder!

2.3 · CREATIVE MANAGERS

Perception
Facilitation
Nurturing

In a fast-changing environment, where the future is necessarily uncertain and creative endeavour is only likely to be forthcoming from committed staff, the nature of the manager's job alters to one where changing perceptions, ways of nurturing empowered staff and encouraging networking become very much more central to the job.

Views on the emerging role of management identify the need for new competencies, partly brought about by the increasing dependence on IT and e-commerce. Morgan (1991) highlights the following competencies as necessary skills for the modern manager:

Reading the environment

Proactivity

Visionary leadership

Human resource management

Remote management skills

Using IT to transform

Managing complexity

Contextual competencies.

Activity 2.2

Imagine yourself as a more creative manager. What would you be doing? How would you behave? Where would you be working? Imagine that your immediate superior practised a more creative style of management. How would he or she be behaving differently? Could you adopt a similar approach with your staff?

Creative management may seem to be a contradiction in terms, if you view creativity as the freedom to do your own thing in contrast to an image of management as the art of getting others to do what you want; or if you envisage a completely unmanageable creative boffin alone in a cluttered office, in contrast to a picture of an orderly manager. However, organizations do now expect their staff to be able to take creative initiatives, so we need a new type of manager who can work in an environment where he or she has far less control than in traditional companies, and who is able to bring out the best in others. The shift to knowledge-based industries means that a committed workforce is often the key to business success, especially as the shortening product life cycle means any product advantage is often short-lived.[8]

Here we argue that creative management entails an essentially facilitative role, involving perceptual, networking and proactive capabilities. Creative managers bring out the creativity in their staff: they stimulate and sustain an open atmosphere where a spirit of collaboration prevails, and they see part of their job as protecting a team from unnecessary obstacles (i.e. facilitating rather than controlling proceedings). The manager's role is to act as a bridge of understanding, coalescing the team into action around the common purpose, and gaining commitment to bring out the best in the team. Creative managers respond to, nurture and act on ideas offered by team members, have an ability to anticipate environmental changes, and are ready to act quickly. Skills of communication and facilitation, together with perceptive abilities such as anticipation and flexibility, are probably more central to this role than the more traditional control, analysis and measurement functions.

[8] By the 1980s, 60% of patented innovations had been copied four years after their introduction (Mansfield et al., 1981, p. 213).

Perception

Perspectives

A key creative
competency (and the
beginning of wisdom)
is the ability to view
situations from
different *perspectives*.

Much has been written on the development of interpersonal skills, but perceptual and attitudinal skills – such as anticipation, recognition and envisioning – have received much less attention.[9]

A key creative competency (and the beginning of wisdom) is the ability to view situations from different *perspectives*. This requires a certain mental flexibility, which includes the ability to take an *overview*. Handy (1991) talks of helicopter thinking that takes in the broad view; Senge (1991) explains the importance of taking account of mental models and the broad perspective offered by systems thinking, and of the ability to view situations from *different perspectives;* Kanter (1991) uses the analogy of a kaleidoscope.

> The metaphor of a kaleidoscope is a good way of capturing exactly what innovators, or leaders of change, do. A kaleidoscope is a device for seeing patterns. It takes a set of fragments and it forms them into a pattern. Kaleidoscope thinking, then, involves taking an existing array of data, phenomena, or assumptions and being able to twist them, shake them, look at them upside down or from another angle or from a new direction – thus permitting an entirely new pattern and consequent set of actions.

Practice in this art may be had by trying to empathize with, and argue, positions at odds with your own.

Activity 2.3

Choose an issue which you believe in strongly (political, religious, sporting, etc.).

(a) Make a list of the three best arguments in favour of this view.

(b) Note the best objection to each, and then think how you would counter each of these objections.

(c) Return to the original proposition, and prepare to argue the opposite case. Note the three best arguments in support of the opposite case.

(d) Compare these with your arguments for the case, and the objections that you noted against each of these.

The arguments raised in favour of the opposing case often include new evidence that was not anticipated when arguing for the original case. You can take this exercise a stage further, and prepare answers to the points you expect the opposing side to raise.

Organizations have also seen a switch in focus from an internal to an *external orientation*, necessitating perceptual skills of anticipation and reading the environment, and a switch from measuring outcome to *facilitating the process* (Morgan, 1991b).

---

[9] De Bono (1971) is one of those who argue that this is due in part to the failure to teach thinking skills, and that practice in thinking skills really can increase flexibility of thought. Writers such as Ivan Illich have advocated more radical programmes to assist people to reach beyond the conditioned thinking inculcated by school and society.

This means creative managers need perceptual skills in their relationships with *people*. Organizations have always relied on groups of people to achieve their aims, and good managers have always been sensitive to their staff's concerns; but the creative organization, with its faster-acting empowered workforce of multi-disciplinary teams, relies less on procedure and more on an awareness of the different perspectives held by different stakeholders. Being able to adopt different perspectives is not just a matter of looking at a problem from different angles. Understanding the logic and concerns behind different *stakeholders' positions* is equally important. This involves developing the capacity for empathy – the ability to see and feel the situation from the other person's perspective.

Stakeholders

THE SAME PIECE OF TROUBLE CAN BE BIG OR SMALL, DEPENDING ENTIRELY ON WHOSE IT IS.

The following activity offers practice in this competency.

Activity 2.4

(a) Imagine a situation at work or elsewhere in which several parties disagree as to the way forward.

(b) Select the three or four main players and/or representatives for key sectional interests (e.g. union, boss and customer, or expert, general manager, office worker and client).

(c) Jot down a few points that summarize the views of each party on the issue in question. Also note what you think are their main concerns and personal priorities, so that you obtain a feel for how important this issue is to them and thus their likely motivation to resolve any dispute.

It helps if the situation is one with which you are familiar, and the players are real people. Try to make each position statement as close as you can to how you think the real person would respond.

Facilitation

Flatter management structures, with shorter communication lines, lead to new roles for management. Managers become part of the team, working with equals rather than being the bosses. Instead of relying on the position power of a hierarchical role, the manager is denied much of his or her traditional supervisory function and instead becomes a resource to co-ordinate, *facilitate and nurture* the team's creative endeavours – the conductor rather than the captain. Where power is distributed, more co-ordination and communication are required. Management becomes a more subtle and complex task, especially when people are members of several teams and no longer report to a single line manager, and perhaps are physically remote from each other.

Amabile (1998) suggests that part of the skill here is allowing staff sufficient autonomy in the way they set about tasks, so that they are more likely to feel engaged with them. (Clearly the task also has to present an appropriate level of stretch and challenge, and be neither too dull nor too demanding for the individual involved.) Kanter (1997)[10] argues that the manager is more likely to attract and retain the commitment of good staff if they are offered learning opportunities within the job that they see could enhance their reputation in the long term.

SouthWest Airlines seem to have achieved a level of commitment from their staff most organizations only dream of. The airline offers a no-frills service and has many competitors, but has won the triple crown for best passenger service (best timekeeping, fewest lost bags and complaints) nine times, and manages to turn around flights in 15 minutes instead of the industry norm of 45. (It also gave the best return on stock – 21,775% from 1972 to 1992.) Its success seems to have been at least partly due to the way managers work with staff (Pfeffer, 1994).

Evans and Russell (1989) assert that inner values play an important part in the creative management style, arguing that the creative manager has a different way of being rather than doing. This involves developing an attitude that perceives every situation as an opportunity, that asks 'What is this teaching me?' rather than cataloguing shortcomings and blaming others.

Activity 2.5

You might like to consider how creative a manager you think you are and how creative you believe your organization is. Rate yourself and your organization on a scale from 1 to 10 for each of the following items.

	1 ...	5 ... 10
Climate		
Organization	Those around me 'Yes but ...' new ideas	Those around me encourage new ideas
Self	I tend to criticize ideas	I encourage myself and others to have new ideas
Customer		
Organization	We are oriented to providing what we want	We provide what the customer wants
Self	I'm inclined to see things from my point of view	I'm good at seeing things from others' points of view
Mentality		
Organization	Our organization is problem-focused	Our organization is opportunity-focused
Self	I am problem-focused	I am opportunity-focused
Motivation		
Organization	Many of our people are not interested in their work	Our people are well matched to their jobs
Self	I don't care about my work	I love my job
Procedure		
Organization	A certain rigidity in procedure disempowers	Individuals show lots of initiative
Self	I feel disempowered	I take a lot of initiative
Communication		
Organization	We ensure secrecy	We are encouraged to share ideas
Self	I keep my head down	I make a point of networking to keep in touch

(Source: adapted and extended from Brown, 1988)

---

[10] Also in Henry and Mayle (2001).

Interestingly many individuals score themselves higher than their organizations in this type of inventory, yet the organizations themselves are collections of individuals.

Proactivity

Creativity, learning and development are all now taking far greater prominence in the role of the modern manager:

> In the information society the management of an organization's human resources will become increasingly important. Managers will have to find ways of developing and mobilizing the intelligence, knowledge, and creative potential of human beings at every level of organization. Traditional economics has taught us that the important factors are land, labour and capital. But, in the modern age, knowledge, creativity, opportunity-seeking, interpersonal skills, and entrepreneurial ability are becoming equally important.
>
> (Morgan, Chapter 21 in Creative Management, Henry, 1991)

Creativity often involves considering future possibilities and dreams. Part of this skill entails switching attention from worrying about how to react to present crises to contemplating longer time spans, so that the mind is more occupied with comparing the present with possible futures.

Activity 2.6

Imagine yourself in five years' time. How do you see yourself? Will you be in the same employment or elsewhere? What will you be working on? Will you be living in the same place or not? Who will your friends be? What time will you spend with your family?

Try and be as concrete and realistic as you can. The sharper and clearer your focus, the better.

A favoured way of contemplating the future for a business is to consider alternative scenarios in which you map out possible futures based on different assumptions. In his classic article Wack (1991) describes the use of scenario-planning at Shell. This process reputedly left the company better prepared to recover from the worst effects of the 1973 oil crisis, because it had considered apparently improbable scenarios such as a large rise in the price of crude oil (which subsequently became reality).

Scenarios

Activity 2.7

You can try speculating about the effect of different futures by drawing up some scenarios and thinking through their consequences for your business.

(a) Think of the factors that might impact on your organization in the future, say five or ten years hence – for example, *social* factors such as changing values and lifestyle, *economic* factors such as changing performance and costs, *political* factors such as restrictive practices or new European standards, and *technological* factors such as developments in biotechnology or IT. You could also consider the likely impact of *environmental* concerns and *legal* factors.

(b) Make assumptions about each of these STEEP (social, technological, economic, environmental and political) or STEEPL (adding legal) factors. You could draw up three or four alternative scenarios with different assumptions – perhaps optimistic, pessimistic, wild and conservative versions.

(c) Consider what impact these scenarios could have on your industry and your organization.

(d) What business opportunities do they suggest? Are any of these opportunities common to more than one of the scenarios?

(e) Do these opportunities suggest some new direction or change of strategy with respect to current plans?

Alternatively you can use scenario-planning to ponder the possible impact of future changes on the outcome of a particular decision. In this case, begin by selecting a recent strategic decision: for example, to enter a particular market or invest in a particular innovation. Then proceed through steps (a) to (e) above, noting how the factors chosen in (a) are likely to interact with the consequences of your decision.

THE CLOSEST YOU WILL EVER COME IN THIS LIFE TO AN ORDERLY UNIVERSE IS A GOOD LIBRARY.

Recent history has emphasized the need to consider apparently 'wild' scenarios. The last quarter-century saw the demise of the Cold War, Eastern Europe apparently freed from communist shackles, Germany reunited, much of Russia in a precarious state, Kuwait invaded, financial collapse in much of the Pacific Rim and the global plague of HIV and AIDS. Few people would have predicted these events using conventional indicators. What more could be round the corner? What will the tension between some Arab and Western nations lead to? Doom merchants predict the collapse of financial markets and global warming, and optimists the continuing rise of the ethical consumer, responsible organizations and a new world order.

The use of scenario development cannot guarantee to anticipate future changes; but considering apparently wild scenarios generally leaves participants with more open minds and better prepared to deal with a much wider range of contingencies than they would previously have contemplated.

Networking

Our understanding of where ideas come from is now much better than it used to be. In particular we appreciate that ideas emerge from a social ground, and that they take time to develop. It follows that networking with colleagues is normally an important factor in nurturing the process of idea development, not a luxury for when the organization is a bit slack. We also have a better appreciation of the importance of diverse inputs and the need to allow for different styles and ways of working to ensure there is sufficient diversity of perspective. The increase in cross-functional, cross-company and international work groups makes it unlikely managers will ever be in a position to understand all the work that goes on in their team. This, plus the shift to knowledge-based work, means professionals have to be given more freedom. With more short-term and temporary working, and less job security, employees' loyalty may be to the industry or the project rather than the firm. Yet, as expertise and know-how become more central, the cross-organizational network of professional relationships becomes a more and more important part of what people bring to their job (Kanter, 1997). The creative manager makes time to team-build and encourages staff to mix informally.

Nonaka and Takeuchi (1995)[11] have argued that the role of the middle manager should be that of the corporate knowledge engineer, bridging the visions of top management and market desires with concepts that can be realized practically. Nonaka suggests a large part of this role involves making explicit the tacit understanding of front-line employees: for example by using metaphors to help them articulate their knowledge and to inspire commitment. Also to facilitate sharing this knowledge across other parts of the organization. For example, when Canon's top management decreed they wished to 'build an excellent company by transcending the camera business', Hiroshi Nitanda and his team worked around an 'easy maintenance' concept which led to the mini-copier. Subsequently the company pursued the idea through to the development of laser printers incorporating disposable cartridges.

2.4   CREATIVE TEAMS

In the West there has been a tendency to glorify named innovators and locate the source of innovation within an individual. However, creativity in organizations is rarely the province of a single mind, and nowadays we have a better appreciation of the extent to which innovations are constructed by teams of individuals building on others' work. There are also many different ways of contributing to the advance of an innovation: for example, a person may have the initial idea, choose to explore ways of realizing this, modify plans to achieve a marketable model or facilitate a project team.

Experimentation

Communication

Recognition

Much has been written about successful and unsuccessful teams. One notion that emerges consistently is that successful teams comprise people with different styles and backgrounds who bring different angles to the issues at hand, rather than 'clones' who are likely to adopt similar approaches. Indeed, nothing is less productive than a group of creative people all pulling in different directions and following one new avenue after another without completing any of them.

An effective creative team will contain a mix of characters. For example, creative innovators often need to work with a 'completer' who will attend to detail and get the task finished, which are not necessarily priorities for the creative innovator. Belbin (1988) originally identified eight characters in the effective teams he studied. These included: two leader figures – the task-oriented shaper and the people-oriented chairperson; one ideas person – the creator or plant; the resource investigator; the monitor-evaluator; the team worker; the implementer; and the completer. He subsequently added a ninth role – the specialist (Belbin, 1988). We shall return to Belbin's analysis in Chapter 6.

[11] See Nonaka and Takeuchi article in Henry (2001) for elaboration.

The mix of character styles is important for creative teams; it offers a variety of approaches to the problem at hand and increases the chance of cross-fertilization of ideas, albeit at the expense of some tension when the inevitable differences arise. Effective creative teams put a lot of energy into their work and, ideally, harness their passion in a group effort. Obviously, this requires a good measure of trust between the participants so that they can communicate freely. The creative team normally has considerable freedom as to what it is working on, or at least how it goes about it.

Activity 2.8

Think of two creative projects in which you are, or have been, involved. Select one that worked successfully and another that failed.

In each case write brief notes on the way that the idea was handled, the people involved and your dealings with others. What were the working relationships like? What was the atmosphere in the group? How did you set about the project and deal with the outside world?

What differences do you notice between these two situations? Do they apply to other successful and unsuccessful projects with which you have been involved? Are there particular ingredients that you associate with creative projects?

Innovations nearly always involve multi-disciplinary teams and nowadays also interorganizational teams. Key roles include the project leader, the technological gatekeeper who keeps his technical knowledge up to date through informal networking, and the product champion or business sponsor who can steer the product through the organization. (Chapter 6 elaborates on this.) Amabile (1998), in Henry (2001), and West and Anderson (1996) elaborate on some of the other factors that reflect innovation in teams.

2.5 CREATIVE ORGANIZATIONS

New product development at Disney World

The creative organization normally has a combination of a number of different characteristics summarized in Table 2.3. (These approaches are explained more fully in Henry *et al.*, 2001.[12])

Open

Outward looking

Informal

Participative

Table 2.3 Characteristics of the creative organization	
Open climate	Challenging
	Trusting
Empowered staff	Take decisions
	Local resources
Flexible structure	Flatter
	Decentralized
Integrated procedures	Multidisciplinary teams
	Parallel development
Knowledge-sharing systems	Suggestion schemes, idea screening
	IT information bank, newsletters
External partnerships	Suppliers, customers
	Competitors

Climate

A key factor seems to be the climate of the organization: this needs to be conducive to the communication of new ideas, so that employees are able to share their creative insights. This may be formalized via suggestion schemes or a staff newsletter, but an informal ambience that encourages communication and networking is more important. The climate should be one in which people feel listened to and where the time to explore ideas is not begrudged. In addition to facilitating open communication, the organization needs to be outward-looking to keep abreast of changes. This kind of climate seems to be easier to maintain in organizations with an element of informality and a participative style of management.

Motivation, it seems, can be dramatically affected by the environment in which creators find themselves. Ekvall (1991, 1997) has suggested some aspects of the organizational climate that can impact on the capacity for innovation of those working within it. These include freedom, trust, commitment and diversity. Freedom refers to employees having the confidence to take initiatives and obtain information. Trust implies an environment that has open relationships and is supportive of new ideas. Commitment requires a group of motivated people. Ekvall also suggests that diversity is necessary, and acknowledges the advantage of people sharing their varying experiences and skills.

Freedom

Trust

Commitment

Diversity

Ekvall uses the dimensions shown in Table 2.4 as an audit to differentiate between more and less creative organizational climates.

[12] J. Henry *et al.*, 'Innovation, climate and change', Book 3 of *Creativity, Innovation and Change*, Milton Keynes: Open University Press.

Dimension	Poles	
	More creative	Less creative
Challenge	Enjoyable	Alienated
	Energetic	Indifferent
Freedom	Independent	Passive
	Initiatives taken	Rule-bound
Liveliness	Excitedly busy	Boringly slow
Openness	Trusting	Suspicious
	Failure accepted	Failure punished
Idea time	Off-task play	Little off-task play
Mood	Happy/humorous	Serious/dull
Conflicts	Handled constructively	Handled destructively
Support	People listen helpfully	People are negative and critical
Debates	Contentious ideas voiced	Little questioning
Risk-taking	Fast decisions	Cautious, safe decisions
	Risk acting on new ideas	Detail and committee bound

Table 2.4   Creative climate dimensions

(Source: based on the work of Ekvall, 1991)

Amabile and Gryskiewicz's (1988) survey of industrial research scientists also identified freedom and control of their own work as environmental stimulants to creativity, along with good project management and some system of encouragement and feedback. Environmental obstacles included lack of support from other departments and lack of organizational interest. An environment that encourages experimentation and accepts failure is likely to help. (See Amabile's article in Henry (2001) for amplification.)

Trust

An open climate is much easier where people know each other, have had time to see colleagues deliver, and so have developed trust in them. In a penetrating analysis, Handy (1993, 1998) points out that in an organizational setting this means that trust is only likely to be possible with perhaps 50 people. And it is only among these trusties and friends that people are likely to feel willing to share their intellectual property. (Handy's article in Henry (2001) elaborates.)

Pearson (1989) argues that innovative firms not only have an open climate but also a clear strategy, so that people are committed to a common, long-term goal. More recently Kanter (1997) has suggested that the glue that holds the modern workforce together is common values.

Commentators such as Kanter and Handy (1998) have argued that today's business environment calls for a different relationship between employer and employee, and foresee an increasing need for an entrepreneurial orientation.

They say that, if information is now king, organizations needs procedures designed to bring out the best in people working with ideas and information. They suggest the rhetoric of hierarchy, control and ownership that permeates management (from the organizational charts to the whole notion of employers, employees and leaders) is now outdated, and that staff and employees would be better termed partners or associates. Both commentators have suggested that organizations need to restructure along the lines of non-for-profit organizations, where managers facilitate groups of professionals working together because of adherence to common values.

Handy has championed the idea of the organization as a community of citizens. He points out that professionals, like cats, are not easy to herd. Mintzberg (1996) adds that most professional knowledge workers, such as doctors, are already empowered and need support, and freedom to experiment. Kanter (1997) suggests that the answer is to tempt preferred staff with opportunities for development in their chosen area, offering them considerable say in what they work on, a lot of freedom as to how they set about their work, and plenty of opportunity to network with others working on related areas of interest inside and outside the firm.

Psychodynamic interpretations of organizational culture have portrayed bureaucracy as instilling a dependent stance in employees, who are told what to do in a way that inhibits their capacity for initiative. They also paint a picture of bureaucracy as impersonal, and therefore lacking the personal involvement that is necessary to breed trust and commitment. They argue that much management procedure acts as a psychological defence against the anxieties inherent in the job, and serves to calm managers into a false sense of purpose and security. In contrast to the standard bureaucratic organization's attempt to minimize uncertainty by controlling strategy, procedure and culture, Stacy (1996) has argued that creative and innovative organizations display a capacity to accept ambiguity and uncertainty. On this view creative organizations may be psychologically more mature, staffed with people who can live with ambiguity and uncertainty, and allow them to serve as a stimulus to creative work.

After creating a climate in which creative ideas are communicated, and a more responsive structure, the creative organization needs some procedures for 'sorting out the wheat from the chaff' and nurturing potentially useful inventions to the point where they are marketable innovations. This may involve idea champions and innovative teams and, in large organizations, some kind of 'idea office'. It also helps to have procedures for identifying and sharing good practice. Csikszentmihalyi (1999) has pointed out that though many organizations (like Motorola) which depend on technological innovation use substantial resources to ensure their engineers can think creatively, this is all to little avail unless the managers who have the power to judge embryonic innovations are open-minded enough to accept the risks they entail, facilitate their implementation and, where appropriate, manage the process of getting the new approach accepted by the industry.

Until recently a lot of analysis of creativity has focused on the individual, while work on innovation has focused on the team and organization. It is now clear, however, that a better focus for examination might be the networks though which both these endeavours arise. These networks usually operate cross-sector or domain, rather than within an organization.

Activity 2.9

Since a key element in creativity is networking with others, you might like to try to draw a map of the people you relate to at work. One approach is as follows:

(a) Start by drawing lines between yourself and the various individuals and groups that you communicate with, e.g. your manager, customers, colleagues, suppliers, specialists responsible for computer support, financial control and research and development, counterparts, professional bodies, etc.

(b) Use arrowheads to indicate whether the communication is two-way or one-way, and whether it is bottom-up or top-down.

(c) Colour the channels of communication that you think work well in green, and those in which communication is not very effective or unnecessary in red.

(d) Mark the channels that you think are most important in another colour, such as black or purple.

(e) Finally, indicate those channels that you think are most in need of improvement.

Ask a colleague to produce a similar map. Explain your maps to each other, noting where your maps overlap and where they are different.

See also Krackhardt and Hanson's article on 'Informal networks' in Henry (2001). This suggests ways of mapping advice and trust networks in organizations. The authors claim that such maps can aid managers determine who will lead particular project teams most effectively.

2.6 ORGANIZATIONAL CHANGE

In an attempt to become more responsive and creative, organizations often try some kind of organizational change programme, such as continuous improvement, benchmarking, quality, learning, development, knowledge-sharing initiatives, and/or the introduction of focus groups.

Quality management, the learning organization, re-engineering and self-organization are four recently fashionable approaches which aim to develop and sustain organizational innovation. Their underlying philosophies and focus, however, are very different. Table 2.5 contrasts the way in which they approach change. Whereas business process re-engineering and quality improvement focus on procedures, the learning organization and self-organization approaches focus on people. And, while business process re-engineering and self-organization attempt radical change, quality improvement and the learning organization tend to rely on an incremental approach.

Table 2.5	Types of organizational change	
	Radical	**Incremental**
Procedures	Re-engineering	Quality improvement
People	Self-organization	Learning organization

Total quality management focuses on the customer and advocates a process of continuous improvement. However, in practice, quality management systems such as ISO 9000 are rather bureaucratic processes, which emphasize paperwork and adherence to procedures, and this can stifle creativity.

Working on the assumption that change has to be a way of life, and that all employees need to learn continuously, the idea of the learning organization places less faith in procedures and more faith in developing individuals. (See, for example, Senge, 1991.)

Re-engineering emphasizes the need to be prepared to redesign the entire operation, perhaps quite radically, around the key processes. As Hammer says regarding the exploitation of IT to best advantage, 'Don't automate, obliterate' (Hammer and Champy, 1994). However, the approach has become synonymous with downsizing and has lost considerable credibility.

Semler's (1994, 1996) book *Maverick* offers a different, but equally radical, approach to creative organization. Here not only is there an open climate and flat structure, but bureaucracy is reduced to a minimum and employees are trusted to make many more decisions than is normal about all aspects of their work. In effect, this book advocates creativity through participative self-organization.[13]

A high percentage of organizational change efforts fail: Pascale (1999) suggests this is the case for 80% of change programmes. Argyris (1998) argues that the demise of many modern change efforts is inherent in their design. He points out that change programmes often put out mixed messages: for example, a programme theoretically designed to empower the workforce is often based on top management's vision and strategy, leaving the staff little scope for creating some part of the programme they might identify with and commit to. One of the reasons for this is managers' unwillingness to face and air potentially difficult and discordant views.

Activity 2.10

Think of an organizational change initiative you want to implement.

Imagine you could talk to whoever you need to, to achieve this. Envisage a meeting with them.

---

[13] Part 3 of Henry *et al.* (2001), 'Innovation, climate and change', Open University Press, Book 3 of the *Creativity, Innovation and Change* course, discusses these and other approaches to organizational transformation.

Take a piece of paper and note on the left-hand side what you would say to them to try and achieve your goal and on the other side how you anticipate their replies. Write this down as a dialogue.

On the left side note things you might be feeling as each statement is spoken, but are likely to choose not to reveal.

Argyris suggests that most managers try to persuade, sell and influence their colleagues, but avoid areas of upset that might cause disagreement. He argues that in the longer term a more honest form of communication that can openly admit disagreements and difficulties provides a better route to building trust and commitment and so is more likely to achieve the original goal. (The Argyris article on Empowerment in Henry (2001) elaborates.)

2.7 REVIEW

Care
Collaboration
Commitment

This chapter has looked at some of the parts played by creative leaders, facilitative managers and empowered staff in open cultures.

It seems that creative organizations present a more human face, they appear to *care* for employee development. They listen and trust employees to explore ideas that might one day prove useful to the parent organization. The creative team *collaborates*, each member working to his or her strengths, mutually respectful of what others have to offer and daring to explore because they know mistakes are accepted. Creative people seem above all to be *committed* to their ideas and to finding outlets for their curiosity. The best managers are creative, and they are not likely to stay in an organization that does not give them the freedom to explore. Creative organizations tend to have an open climate, together with ways of eliciting and progressing ideas and procedures for managing innovation. They are enjoyable places to work and people work hard in them. They radiate life.

However, creative people are not yes men or women, so a creative environment is bound to be full of ideas in tension with each other. Much of this tension will be expressed at team level. It takes time, goodwill, commitment and maturity to sort out the inevitable differences in perspective and approach, and this attitude is linked to ways of thinking as much as to ways of managing.

Recommended reading

T. Amabile, 'How to kill creativity', in Henry (2001).

R. Semler, 'Why my employees still work for me', in Henry (2001).

C. Argyris, 'Empowerment: the emperor's new clothes', in Henry (2001).

Further reading

D. Krackhardt and J. R. Hanson, 'Informal networks: the company behind the chart', in Henry (2001).

D. Goleman, 'What makes a leader', in Henry (2001).

PART 2
PERCEPTION

This part looks at the cognitive processes that underpin management thinking, and at the impact of metaphor and analogy on the way we construe situations.

3 COGNITION

Truth waits for eyes unclouded by longing.

(Tao Te Ching)

This chapter addresses cognition and its relationship with creative perception. The first section looks at how the brain and mind works, in particular the part played by unconscious information processing and tacit knowledge. The second section looks at the role of intuitive management. It examines some accounts of what managers actually do and how they make decisions. It considers the part intuitive thinking plays in this and raises the question of fallibility in human judgement. The third section discusses mind-sets and conditioned thinking. It highlights the influence of values and beliefs on perception and subsequent action. You are encouraged to examine some of your key beliefs and to try reframing them. The fourth section introduces the idea of deconstruction.

3.1   TACIT KNOWLEDGE

Traditionally Western management has had little respect for tacit knowledge and unconscious ways of assimilating knowledge, even though most managers admit that in practice they rely quite heavily on hunches to make decisions and choose direction. And it is not just management; education too eschews unconscious ways of knowing. This is perhaps not surprising, given that Western culture has placed its faith in explicit, rational modes of analysis for several hundred years. In addition, the success of science has enhanced the value placed on logic, precision and evidence. The counter to this is that intuition, apprehension, and tacit ways of knowing have all but been forgotten as means of apprehending, accessing knowledge and making wise decisions. The pathological connotation now associated with the idea of the unconscious (from the conception of the nasty, dark unconscious introduced by Freud) has probably also retarded our willingness to accept, at least publicly, that the unconscious can offer valuable ways of knowing.

At the present time, the need to manage knowledge across organizations is gaining prominence. Some of the people who have popularized this view point out that, in many cultures in the East, there has always been a greater acceptance of the importance of the tacit knowledge glimpsed implicitly through intuitions, images and metaphors (Nonaka and Takeuchi, 1995, in Henry, 2001). Some management educators are beginning to wonder if, despite a rhetoric that espouses explicit rational plans, it is the neglected unconscious know-how and local knowledge that play the key role in innovative endeavour.

This section gives a brief background to the way the brain operates, and a flavour of the recent work on the intelligent unconscious and tacit learning that is changing our ideas about how the mind functions. It describes some of the studies that are arousing great interest among psychologists, as they suggest that the unconscious plays a far larger role in thinking, learning and decision making than had been anticipated.

There are several reasons why this matters for managers. First, this work goes some way towards explaining the effectiveness of the rather inarticulate hunches and feelings that many managers use to guide their actions and secretly feel are important, but cannot explain. More significantly, they suggest that intuitive, tacit ways of knowing are particularly critical when handling messy, ill-defined, ambiguous and uncertain situations – just the sort of situation managers face day in and day out. So tacit knowledge and intuitive ways of knowing may be especially important management capabilities.[14]

The brain

First a quick lesson in how the brain works. The brain comprises around a hundred billion neurones, each of which is interconnected with numerous neighbours via electrical discharges mediated by chemical neurotransmitters. Each neurone branches out into a tree-like structure of dendrites, illustrated in Figure 3.1.

Plasticity

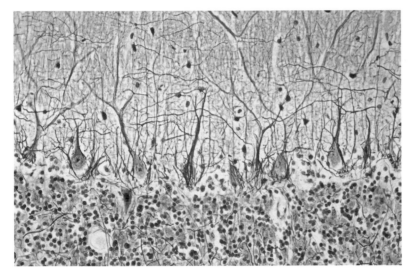

Figure 3.1   Neurone, axon and dendrites

A critical feature of the brain is that it is *plastic* or malleable. When a particular group of cells are excited enough to fire off to their neighbour, this makes it slightly easier for the signal to go along that particular path next time (much as when a groove is worn deeper it is easier for water to flow along it). Where these 'grooves' develop over time is very different for each individual, so each brain ends up being organized very differently, in ways that reflect its particular owner's life experiences. This effect can be so strong that brain scans show how

[14] Guy Claxton elaborates on this theme in 'Complexity and the unconscious', *Creativity, Innovation and Change* Audio 2. A number of the examples in this section came from Claxton (1979).

different individuals can make use of different parts of the brain when answering the same problem. (Claxton (1997) suggests that creativity is associated with low-focus neuronal activity.)

Nor is this individualized brain a passive recipient of information from its environment. Rather it is *actively involved in constructing* everything the mind sees, remembers and interprets.

Active perception

Many people assume that our *perceptions* offer an accurate reflection of what is going on around us. However, it is now clear that this picture is far from the truth. In fact different cells are responsible for capturing different features of an image: for example the colour, movement, shape, and size of an object. How they all manage to link up again to produce a single image is not completely clear. Yet not only are images constructed from numerous separate analyses of parts of the image, but the picture constructed is very much affected by what we expect to see. Show us something unexpected and we will interpret it in terms of patterns and images that are familiar to us – we make the strange familiar. Something may not even be seen if it is not expected. This is one reason why it is very easy for magicians and psychologists to trick the mind with visual illusions.

I once had a vivid demonstration of this. At dinner one night a close-up magician, about a half a metre away from me, made a handkerchief disappear. His sleeves were rolled up so I was amazed he could do this without my seeing how, and I asked him to repeat it. Still I could not see how he did this. My companions, who were in on the trick, burst into fits of laughter and pointed out the plastic thumb he was wearing on top of his own thumb (where he was able to hide the handkerchiefs). Once pointed out, this rather poor quality plastic thumb was glaringly obvious, but my brain had quickly recognized the shape and colour of the one thumb and four fingers it expected to see and had filled in the gap between the plastic and thumb.

Another widespread but unwarranted conception is the assumption that the brain captures and stores an image much as a film does, so each *memory* is located in one particular area of the brain. This is not how the system works. Though it is clear that different parts of the brain are involved with particular types of memory (for example, the cerebellum is involved in remembering skills, and the amygdala and hypothalamus in emotional memories), memory seems to be distributed throughout the brain. Many psychologists now picture memory as more like a neural net since, despite years of searching, they have not found particular locations for particular memories.

Recreate memories

It seems that, far from recalling a mental film from the brain's 'film library' when we remember, we *recreate images* of past events anew on each occasion. So it is no surprise that historians find that people's recollection of past events, say a war, do indeed change as the years go by (i.e. they will be recalled differently at ages 30, 40 and 50). Another interesting feature of memory is that it is state-specific – we will find it easier to recall memories laid down in a particular state (e.g. relaxed) when we are in that same state or a very similar one.

What this means is that our brains are storing information in very different ways, which can lead to varied understandings and insights about the same phenomena. In addition, our perception and memory of events are affected by what we expect to see. This means they are a lot less reliable than we might imagine, and are likely to change over time in ways we are unaware of.

Unconscious information processing

A series of experiments have shown that the unconscious is much cleverer than scientists had previously realized. We now know that the unconscious processes information, learns and make decisions often without our knowledge, and in ways we would be unable to replicate consciously.

Most of us assume we are in control of our lives and that we consciously decide what we will do, but are we in control of our brains, and who or what really makes the decisions that determine our actions? For example, who turned the page you are now reading? Did you do this consciously or did your unconscious mind do it automatically for you? (By unconscious, I am referring to information processing that we are not aware of, not Freud's sublimated urges.)

Several everyday experiences attest to the fact that the unconscious is often *quicker* off the mark than the conscious. For example, we jerk our hand off the hotplate before we are aware it hurts and, fortunately, we usually slam our foot on the brake long before we consciously realize that there is a stalled car in front of us. Experimental evidence now suggests that conscious recognition is about half a second behind unconscious processing (see point 1 in Box 3.1 below).

The smart unconscious

Not only is the unconscious quicker off the mark than the conscious mind, but experiments show that it knows things the conscious does not. An example is subliminal perception, i.e. where subliminal information below conscious awareness is registered and acted on.

Activity 3.1 _____

Write several letters on a card, and hold the card just far enough away from someone looking at the card so that they cannot quite read it. Ask them if they can read any of the letters. Then ask them to guess what the letter might be.

_____

Generally, if you move just far enough away so people cannot consciously read the cards, they will definitely deny that they can read any of them. But ask them to guess what the letters are and they will be most surprised at the accuracy of their guesses.

The unconscious may also have a more accurate grasp of reality. For example, when you are out walking, ask a companion to estimate the steepness of a hill, whether it is 10 or 30 degrees, etc. Then ask them to point their hand to indicate the angle of the hill. Typically, the hand reflects the angle of the hill with perfect accuracy, but the conscious mind considerably overestimates the degree of incline. What is more, couch potatoes reckon the angle is steeper than do fit athletes, so a conscious perception's estimate seems to take account of the effort it would entail to walk up the hill!

In certain circumstances it is also possible to trick the conscious mind more easily than the unconscious.

Activity 3.2

Which of the two central blocks below is the larger?[15]

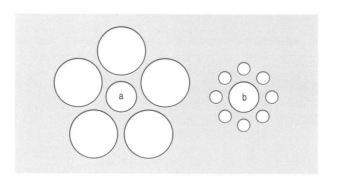

People usually say the one inside the smaller circles is larger but, offered a three-dimensional version of the blocks, these same individuals open their hands equally wide. This shows the body is not so easily fooled by optical illusions as the mind. Your unconscious often knows more than you do.

Box 3.1 describes four more experiments which show the unconscious mind's superior information processing abilities and how our conscious awareness can be quite unaware of this tacit knowledge.

BOX 3.1   THE INTELLIGENT UNCONSCIOUS

1   The tardy conscious

Libet (1993) asked people to move their hands at will while he recorded their brain impulses. He noted that their brain impulses began about 350 milliseconds before they were aware of their intent to move. However, there was a window (of about 150–200 milliseconds) after they became aware of their intent to move, in which people were able to rescind their original decision and stop the arm movement.

[15] Ebbinghaus illusion (Zimbado *et al.*, 1995, p. 210).

The implication is that the intent to move arose in the unconscious not the conscious mind, and that we do not have free will so much as free won't, i.e. our conscious mind can inhibit unconscious intentions if it chooses to do so.

2 Unconscious recognition

Marcel (1993) used a series of weak light flashes and asked participants to acknowledge each flash of light either by blinking, pressing a button or saying yes, or a combination of blinking and saying yes or no. Marcel found blinking produced the highest number of correct guesses and words the least. When asked to blink and answer verbally, people often blink yes and say no, and it is the blink that is much more likely to be correct.

Here the unconscious outsmarts the conscious and the conscious does not even realize that this is happening.

3 Unconscious learning

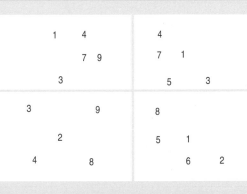

Lewicki et al. (1992) presented subjects with an array of numbers across four quadrants. Lewicki asked subjects to identify which quadrant a particular number appeared in by pressing a button, allowing him to measure how long it took them to get the right answer. He repeated this task in sets of seven trials, and rigged the situation so that the position of the seventh number could be estimated by the position of the numbers shown in the preceding first, third, fourth and sixth trial. Not surprisingly, people did get faster at predicting where the seventh number would be; but not only did they not realize they were doing so, they were quite unable to recognize why they were doing so. Lewicki tried to prompt the poor slow conscious mind by telling people that there was a pattern. He involved his clever academic colleagues, gave them unlimited time and financial incentives but, even so, they were never able to work out what the pattern was.

Here the unconscious mind has learnt an effective strategy which it is unable to articulate, and the conscious mind is completely unaware that this has happened.

4 Conscious mind lags behind unconscious strategy

Most of us have ideas about the relationship between people's features and gestures and their character: for example that fat, smiling faces indicate happy people, downturned eyes can indicate sadness, thin-mouthed people might be mean, people who look away are shifty, and people who look down are weak. Lewicki elicited a number of these rules of thumb from various individuals. He then set them a task where they had to guess the character of individuals from a series of photographs, and provided feedback on the accuracy of their guesses. However, unknown to the participants, Lewicki had fixed the feedback so that some of it was based on assumptions about features that were the opposite of those originally held. The unconscious mind quickly learnt the new rules and judged character according to assumptions opposite to those they originally adhered to. However, remarkably, people did not know that they had changed their behaviour and, when asked about features and personality, people continued to espouse their original beliefs seemingly unaware that they had learnt and were applying another set of rules.

Here the conscious mind continues to espouse beliefs that the unconscious has ceased to use, seemingly unaware that the strategies it is now using have altered. So an individual's conscious and unconscious can practise two quite different strategies, and conscious learning can lag way behind unconscious learning.

(Source: adapted from Claxton, 1997)

Unconscious learning

Darwin

The number of tree doodles in Charles Darwin's notebooks suggest his unconscious was fascinated by this visual metaphor years before he eventually drew on this same metaphor to explain his theory of evolution.

This work suggests that it is the unconscious rather than the conscious mind that does most of our thinking, learning, decision making and problem solving. It also seems that the unconscious mind can learn how to perform well in situations in which the conscious mind cannot begin to recognize, never mind articulate, what it knows. Berry and Broadbent's simulations of management tasks suggest that the smart unconscious is just as active in organizational work as elsewhere (see Box 3.2). These simulations show that the unconscious mind learns how things work much faster than the conscious mind, i.e. our implicit understanding is streets ahead of our ability to make explicit what we know.

BOX 3.2   THE SUGAR FACTORY

Berry and Broadbent asked people to try to control output in a sugar factory simulation, by manipulating variables such as the size of the workforce, financial incentives and level of output. The relationship governing the variables was not revealed, but with practice people became quite expert in producing the required sugar output. However, their explicit knowledge about how the factory worked advanced at a much slower rate than their ability to control the sugar output. It seemed people unconsciously learnt how the system worked but were slow to work out why.

Dienes went on to do a refinement of this experiment which suggested people were good at producing the correct output in cases very similar to those they had come across previously, but no better than chance at combinations that were new to them. This suggests the participants were merely remembering instances that worked (Berry and Dienes, 1992).

In real life, managers also make decisions, based on intuitive expertise, that they may be unable to justify. Interestingly people's confidence in their ability to do a task tends to correlate with their ability to explain what they are doing. Not surprisingly people's confidence in their ability to master the sugar factory problem lagged way behind their performance.

These and many other experiments show that the unconscious can identify, learn, remember and apply things the conscious mind cannot begin to grasp. People gain this unconscious know-how by picking up subtle patterns through repeated exposure to specific instances.

Unfortunately this intuitive know-how is often very firmly tied to the situation in which it was first learnt. For example, if people well practised at the sugar factory problem are presented with essentially the same problem but in another setting, such as traffic flow, they perform no better than novices. Their know-how does not transfer readily to other settings.

Similarly, Brazilian street children and bookmakers (people who take bets at horse races) perform highly complex arithmetic calculations in their heads perfectly, while being unable to obtain even a rudimentary score on essentially the same problems in intelligence tests. Correspondingly Western children can fail at problems that look like school maths when these draw out an inappropriate deliberate approach, but succeed at executing the same task if it is dressed up as a video game, where this draws forth the intuitive mind-set needed to attack the problem. Our memory for how to do things is often tied to the situation in which it was learnt. The now well-attested implication is that knowledge is situated and does not transfer easily.

Unconscious decision making

While business schools spend their time teaching students rational approaches to decision making, real-life studies suggest experienced professionals base numerous decisions on hunch and intuition. Experimental evidence suggests that professionals would be well advised to continue respecting unconscious decision making and, in certain circumstances, be wary of rational decision making. For example, Schooler (1997) asked people to make various decisions, from choosing a course to selecting a poster. He asked half of one group to think through their decision rationally and the other half to decide intuitively. He found that those who had been asked to think through their decisions were more likely to go back on the decision than those who had followed their gut reaction. He also found that the gut decisions were closer to decisions made by experts than those which the novices had to justify.

It seems that intuitive decisions can incorporate information that is too complex to be verbalized, and that in such circumstances intuitive decisions can be more reliable than actions that people have had to justify.

In certain circumstances conscious awareness can interfere with unconscious learning. Experiments suggest that sometimes verbalizing can worsen recall. For example, when trying to identify a burglar from a set of photographs, those who merely had to identify a burglar's face did better than those who had tried to describe the face in question (Claxton, 1997).

Incubation

There is also experimental evidence which demonstrates that people are more likely to come up with the right answer if they are allowed a short break, than if they are forced to guess again immediately. This idea is recognized in the principle of allowing time for incubation. It is also familiar to us all through the mysterious 'tip of the tongue' phenomenon. (This is when we know we know the answer and possibly certain characteristics of that answer, e.g. it has three syllables or starts with 's', but cannot actually recall the word we are looking for at that precise moment. Usually, if you just wait, the answer pops into consciousness minutes, hours or a day later.)

Creativity and intuitive thinking often need periods of incubation to give the brain time to assimilate and reassemble all it knows in a way it can communicate to our conscious minds. This is not the kind of activity you can rush. It is more like tracking, where you have to attend to all the details before you get the picture. Nor is it the kind of thinking that you can affect much one way or the other. Claxton suggests intuitive thinking is similar to gestation and that giving birth provides the perfect analogy for intuitive ideas. The mother provides a home for the developing child but, other than the initial act that produced the embryo, does very little consciously to help the baby develop. Rather she just eats fairly sensibly, perhaps does some exercise and rests more often, but otherwise goes about her business much as usual; and, at the end of nine months out pops a fully formed baby. Of course, the child, like the intuitive idea, still needs lots of care and attention if it is to grow into a fully functioning adult.

However, it is not all bad news for the conscious mind. It does come into its own in some settings. For example, there is an experiment (illustrated opposite) where an individual is asked to tie together two ropes hanging from a ceiling,

that are too far apart to be grasped. They have at their disposal various everyday objects. If the experimenter waits until people find they are stuck and merely says 'Think', they realize more quickly that they can use the staples, scissors or whatever as a weight on the end of one rope to form a pendulum, so they can catch it and tie both ropes together.

So conscious reflection can help jolt you out of being stuck from viewing a problem in one particular way into a more systematic analysis of the options. Note that in this problem there is a nonobvious but correct solution. The rational conscious mind can be better placed to search systematically for perceptual blocks that prevent participants from seeing the solution in circumstances like this, where there is a right answer.

Implications

Though many managers and others do trust and rely on their unconscious intuitions, generally Western culture has not valued this way of knowing. People tend to keep quiet about the fact that their idea is based on a hunch, or feel obliged to justify such ideas.

The kinds of experiment discussed in this section have made psychologists realize that much more mental processing, learning and decision making goes on at an unconscious level than was previously thought. They have also highlighted many situations where the unconscious mind can be more effective than the conscious, notably where good performance depends on grasping the complex interrelationships of many variables – a situation that parallels that facing managers. Such experiments have also shown how the unconscious grasps the relationships implicitly long before the conscious mind is able to describe them explicitly, and that in certain circumstances verbal articulation can interfere with unconscious know-how.

Claxton elaborates on the merits of slower forms of thought in his chapter on the innovative mind in Henry (2001). In the same text, Nonaka and Takeuchi illustrate how Japanese innovators take cognisance of unconscious know-how when developing new ideas and prototypes.

Recommended reading

G. Claxton, 'The innovative mind: becoming smarter by thinking less', in Henry (2001).

I. Nonaka and Takeuchi, 'Organizational knowledge creation', in Henry (2001).

Further reading

G. Claxton, *Hare brain: tortoise mind: why intelligence increases more when you think less* (London: Fourth Estate, 1997).

3.2   INTUITIVE MANAGEMENT

Management thinking

Management schools usually focus on rational approaches to learning and decision making such as planning and problem solving. However, researchers such as Mintzberg (1975, 1996) who have undertaken studies that look at what managers actually do, rather than what management scientists expect them to do, conclude that managers spend remarkably little time 'planning', and stress the part played by intuitive rather than rational thought processes. Similarly, Isenberg (1991) argues that senior managers:

> ... rarely formulate goals, assess their worth, evaluate the probabilities of alternative ways of reaching them, and choose the path that maximizes expected return. Rather, managers frequently by-pass rigorous, analytical planning altogether, particularly when they face difficult, novel, or extremely entangled problems. When they do use analysis for a prolonged time, it is always in conjunction with intuition.
>
> *(p. 44)*

Isenberg adds that senior managers 'devote most of their attention to the tactics of implementation rather than the formulation of strategy', spending time 'thinking about the process for getting others to think about the business'.

Mintzberg (1976, 1994a) argues that there is a fundamental difference between formal planning and informal managing. He points out that planning is associated with an analytical, ordered and sequential approach, whereas management normally involves responding to complex, ambiguous and uncertain situations which may need a different sort of thinking process, one more concerned with a simultaneous, relational and holistic form of knowing. In the light of the recent work in cognitive psychology illustrated in Section 3.1, there is now evidence that the complex, ill-structured problems faced daily by managers do indeed require a different thinking process: one that recognizes the part played by intuition and the superior information-processing capacities of the unconscious mind.

Mintzberg (1976) also highlights the parallels between planning processes and the linear, sequential and verbal thinking associated with the left hemisphere of the brain, and those between the thinking skills required by managers and the spatial, visual and relational thinking associated with the right hemisphere.[16] We can also see these two approaches as embodying the differences between the skills of analysis and the skills of perception. Table 3.1 offers some further differences between the styles of thinking employed in planning and managing.

Table 3.1 Modes of thinking related to planning and managing

Planning	Managing
Analysis	Perception
Linear	Simultaneous
Sequential	Relational
Explicit	Implicit
Analysis	Synthesis
Abstract	Experiential
Reflection	Action
Simple steps	Complex
Clear	Ambiguous
Certain	Uncertain
Known	Novel

Mintzberg argues that the differences between the planning and managing styles are most apparent at policy level. The managers he studied relied more on 'soft' data like feelings and impressions to make strategic judgements and rarely mentioned using explicit analysis. Perhaps this is no surprise as 'half the chief executives' activities observed took place in less than nine minutes'. But again, in light of the work in cognitive psychology on implicit learning (learning without conscious awareness), these executives were probably also wisely allowing their intuition to alert them to important information that was too complex for the conscious mind to tie down into neat quantitative bundles. *Soft data*

Noting that managers need to stay flexible enough to respond to the inevitable changes that arise and to seize new opportunities as they present themselves, Isenberg (1987) suggests management entails an opportunistic resourcefulness which employs an incremental, iterative, non-linear and dynamic approach to management functions, in day-to-day affairs and strategic issues.

At bottom Mintzberg (1987) sees management as an art that develops from deep involvement and intimate knowledge of a particular business. Likewise he has presented strategy as an emergent process analogous to crafting, where thought and action go hand in hand. Mintzberg likens this to the work of a potter who *Management as craft*

[16] Mintzberg links the left and right hemispheres with thinking associated with planning and managing respectively. It is now clear that the neurophysiology of the brain is not this simple. Nevertheless the myth of right and left brain functions offers a useful metaphor to differentiate between different styles of knowing. See Hines (1987) for a review.

senses the way forward through the tacit wisdom gained from personal knowledge, intimate understanding and day-to-day involvement:

> The popular view sees the strategist as a planner or as a visionary; someone sitting on a pedestal dictating brilliant strategies for everyone else to implement. While recognizing the importance of thinking ahead and especially of the need for creative action in this pedantic world, I wish to propose an additional view of the strategist – as a pattern recognizer, a learner if you will – who manages a process in which strategies (and visions) can emerge as well as be deliberately conceived. I also wish to redefine that strategist, to extend that someone into the collective entity made up of the many actors whose interplay speaks an organization's mind. This strategist *finds* strategies no less than creates them, often in patterns that form inadvertently in its own behaviour.

> What, then, does it mean to craft strategy? Let us return to the words associated with craft: dedication, experience, involvement with the material, the personal touch, mastery of detail, a sense of harmony and integration. Managers who craft strategy do not spend much time in executive suites reading MIS reports or industry analyses. They are involved, responsive to their materials, learning about their organizations and industries through personal touch. They are also sensitive to experience, recognizing that while individual vision may be important, other factors must help determine strategy as well.

Mintzberg has contrasted this kind of emergent strategy with deliberate strategies which are planned (Mintzberg and Waters, 1989). He suggests that entrepreneurial strategies are deliberate in the sense that they are the product of a single mind's vision, but that this vision may emerge over time. Westley and Mintzberg (1991) point out that visionary leaders have typically been working in the industries they wish to transform for many years before coming forward with their visions. Similarly, inventors have usually worked in related fields for some time before making their inventions. Bill Gates of Microsoft and Jack Welch of General Motors are cases in point.

Readers who warm to Mintzberg's critical stance may enjoy his article on 'Ten ideas to rile everyone who cares about management' in Henry (2001). Here he elaborates on shortcomings of conventional attitudes to management.

The historical tradition to think linearly has inclined Westerners to view an organization as a hierarchy with a top and a bottom. Mintzberg (1996) suggests we do better conceiving of an organization as a circle with front-line producers at the edge and top management in the middle.

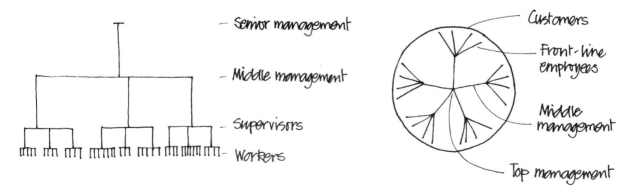

Two views of the organization

Like Nonaka, Mintzberg stresses that we need middle managers to help top management and front-line employees communicate. He is doubtful about the 1990s craze for delayering; while this may create leaner organizations, it risks losing important tacit knowledge held by middle managers and dampening commitment by introducing a climate of fear. Like Claxton, he argues against the tendency to reach for a short-term fix, by finding a leader or consultant with all the answers or getting a consultant to turn around an organization according to the latest fad. He points out that this is based on a misunderstanding of the nature of knowledge. Only people with a deep understanding of the industry are likely to have sufficient understanding and sensitivity of that environment to make accurate judgements about the best way forward. In short Mintzberg has criticized the analytical mentality that pervades management and which places a misjudged reliance on procedure and measurement at the expense of these deeper ways of knowing.[17]

Intuition

It is a feature of a senior manager's life that he or she is necessarily working on a number of different issues simultaneously and that generally these issues are complex, messy and ill-structured, the information is incomplete, the time required to make the decisions is limited and the outcome of the decision is uncertain. We have seen earlier that it is precisely in these conditions that intuitive thinking comes into its own, since it can take account of the superior pattern processing the unconscious is able to provide. What is more, the inevitable time pressures most managers have to work under, and the need to act before a complete picture is available, lead to an intuitive mode of executive action where 'thinking' is inseparable from acting.

Intuition involves apprehending rather than analysing what is going on. The study of processes that underpin this kind of implicit knowledge has mushroomed in recent years, though the integrative skills and perceptive wisdom associated with intuition are still far from understood. Implicit or unconscious learning is likely to be of increasing interest to managers for several reasons: it appears that managers do use intuition, and make decisions based on hunches as much as on cold, hard analysis; the importance of tacit knowledge is at last being recognized by managers; and perhaps some managers also feel that intuition offers the promise of a magical short cut, ideally suited to the present uncertain and fast-changing times.

Apprehension

Isenberg (1987) suggests that managers use intuition in at least five ways:
- to sense when a problem exists
- to perform well-learnt patterns rapidly
- to synthesize isolated data
- to use 'gut feeling' to check results arrived at rationally
- to by-pass in-depth analysis.

[17] Mintzberg extends his critique to traditional approaches to MBA teaching in *Creativity, Innovation and Change*, Audio 1.

Agor (1986) offers a similar list, which includes the use of intuition to explore future possibilities, to synthesize and integrate information, and to check decisions. The executives in his study felt intuition functioned best under situations of uncertainty, where there were no precedents; in unpredictable situations, where there were limited facts and competing plausible solutions; and where there were time constraints.

If Isenberg and Mintzberg are right, then managers need to learn to listen to and develop the apparently mysterious skills of intuition, judgement and timing. Cognitive psychologists have presented a wealth of evidence to suggest that intuition is largely a matter of learnt experience. For example, Simon (1988) claims that 'intuition is no mysterious talent. It is the direct by-product of training and experience that have been stored as knowledge.' He argues that intuition is a speedy form of recognition, based on the ability to remember cues and patterns and to respond appropriately, underpinned by the memory of many thousands of related experiences. It is not just a result of knowing more, rather that through extensive experience people begin to think differently because their knowledge is organized more efficiently, in chunks that relate to patterns of information. Over time, as more and more information is stored in chunks and linked, people are better able to sense patterns and their hunches are more likely to be correct. In this view, intuition is really a matter of expert recognition. Note that this implies that intuitive ability is bound up with subject area experience. Expertise in one area will not necessarily transfer to another – the intuitive doctor is not necessarily an intuitive engineer or architect.

Recognizing intuition

If half the art of intuition depends on having a large stock of patterns based on years of pertinent experience, your work as a manager is adding to this stock all the time, particularly if you reflect on your work experience and learn from it. Workaholics may be at an advantage here!

However, due to the rational bias in Western culture, this form of knowing has not generally been understood or appreciated as much as in the East. It may be that Western managers are not in the habit of attending enough to this form of knowing.

The other side of the coin is sensitivity in recognizing subjective cues (often non-verbal) that alert you to intuitive judgements. Agor suggests that these cues are based on a combination of fact and feeling. Since memory is encoded in specific states, many people find that it is bodily sensations of some sort that alert them to hunches worth attending to.

Recognizing serendipity

Many scientists could have discovered penicillin at the same time as Fleming, had they attended to rather than ignored the unexpected result of bacteria near the penicillin mould being killed.

(Simon, 1988, p. 15)

Isenberg and Simon agree that one way in which people recognize intuition is by attending to feelings of surprise, which perhaps the less intuitive would neglect. The executives studied by Agor reported recognizing intuition through a feeling of excitement, commitment or total harmony: essentially aesthetic rather than logical criteria. They claimed that their intuitive decisions usually turned out to be right. They also reported using their intuition as a guide to what not to do, 'when they sense an impending decision might be wrong', discerned through a sense of anxiety, mixed signals or a sleepless night.

Activity 3.3

(a) For the next week keep a record of any intuitions and hunches you have, and note what led you to recognize them.

(b) Keep a diary of intuitive judgements and decisions you make, and subsequently note whether or not you were proved right.

Judgement

We must insert a word of caution here. Intuitions are not infallible. It can be hard to discriminate between valid intuitions and hunches, and wishful thinking and fantasy or plain prejudice. How do you discriminate between the two? Agor suggests that sound intuitive judgements are more likely when people's egos are not bound up in the decision outcomes, and they are truly open to all possibilities. In other words, the best results occur when people are honest about situations and accept them, rather than projecting elements of their desired outcomes into their thinking about them. Speaking from his years of experience as a captain of industry, Vickers (1984) comes to a not dissimilar conclusion. Good judgement, he maintains, needs a selfless detachment, disciplined commitment and a sensitivity to form. Claxton (1997) and McKim (1980) suggest a state of relaxed attention is the preferred mental state for fruitful incubation. It is probably just as important to attend to factors that block sound judgement. The executives in Agor's study felt that rushing to decide before the time was right, stress or lack of confidence could all inhibit their capacity for intuitive judgement.

Judgement biases

In addition to the problem of wishful thinking, the mind is also subject to various biases which can lead to erroneous intuitive judgements. Some of these come from our use of heuristics – rules of thumb which work as effective short cuts in most, but not all, situations.

Activity 3.4

Imagine you have a rope long enough to go around the circumference of the earth. If you extended that rope by two metres, about how much would the gap be between the earth and the rope?

Most people assume the space would be infinitesimal but actually it's over 30 centimetres. (Appendix B at the end of the book gives the calculation.) In contrast, adding two litres of water to the ocean would raise the water level infinitesimally, as we correctly surmise intuitively. We are misled by applying an inappropriate heuristic, that larger size leads to a smaller change, which we use because it works well in apparently analogous situations.

Similar biases can also be found in everyday situations managers face. For example, Kruglanski and Freund (1983) gave two groups the same information about two applicants for a managerial job. Half the group were given the positive information about the applicants first and half the negative first. Remarkably, those receiving the positive information first rated the candidate as more likely to succeed than those receiving the negative information first. It was as if the intuitive mind decided quickly and took a while to incorporate later conflicting information in ways that could change its initial judgement.

Activity 3.5

Which of the following birth orders is more likely: BGBBGB or BBBBGB (where B is a boy and G a girl) ?

Most people assume that the former is more probable. Actually, both are equally likely. The same would hold true if we had asked about the sequence of tossing coins. This is an example of the *representativeness* bias – our generally poor ability to estimate odds correctly. Box 3.3 lists some common judgement biases.

BOX 3.3   JUDGEMENT BIASES

Human judgement is notoriously fallible. Numerous psychological experiments have shown the extent to which people's judgements are consistently biased. Such is the reliability of this effect that psychologists have named some of the more common biases.

One of these is the *availability* bias. This refers to the tendency to assume events are more frequent if they come to mind easily. Since recent, familiar and vivid events come to mind more readily, we incline to overestimate their frequency. Thus we overestimate the likelihood of accidents from dramatic plane crashes and underestimate the likelihood of undramatic accidents in the home.

There is also a *confirmation* bias. We tend to stick with our initial judgements, noticing confirming evidence and dismissing information that does not fit our beliefs. Thus when each political party accuses the television stations of political bias, it may be that they have simply noticed the items in the broadcasts that were against their positions and paid less attention to those items that supported them.

We tend to be *overconfident* about our own opinions, believing ourselves to be correct much more often than is justified: for example, that lung cancer is more likely to affect others than ourselves. This can lead to us making dangerous decisions.

We also have a *hindsight* bias, believing that we were more certain about judgements initially than we in fact were. This leads to further overconfidence in our own judgements.

We will see in Part 3 that some personality types may be more prone to particular biases than others.

Implications

Studies of how managers think suggest they make much more use of intuitive thinking than management education normally recognizes. However, intuitions are not infallible, and humans are prone to certain judgement biases, so we need to take care differentiating wishes from wisdom.

Further reading

H Mintzberg, 'Ten ideas to rile everyone who cares about management', in Henry (2001).

3.3   MIND-SETS

There is much more information around us than our limited senses can hope to attend to. This means that we cannot absorb the outside world via a process of osmosis: rather we have to choose what we want to attend to, and find ways of construing the world that create the image of reality that we have. We select those things that interest us, that fit in with our world view. In McCaskey's (1982) words, we form a map of reality which 'points out what is to be noticed and valued among the plethora of events in each day'. This is an absolutely essential function to deal with the myriad of information coming our way, but it does mean that our understanding of the world is partial.

We tend to see the world in terms of relatively *fixed ways of thinking*, sometimes referred to as mind-sets. We are all familiar with the effect of a new mind-set on our attention and perception – we buy a new car and suddenly the world seems full of this particular model and colour. We are probably less aware of how this same mechanism can blinker thinking. For instance, we go on holiday and meet but do not recognize the person who delivers our paper back home, because we expect to see him or her on the doorstep and not elsewhere. We may also not notice constraints that have always been there, much as a fish probably has no concept of 'wetness' as this only makes sense in relation to a dryness that the fish has never experienced.

The mind is set to find and create meaning everywhere and anywhere. We invariably impose order on chaos, finding images in clouds and inkblots. In so doing we also tend to simplify complexity and make the inconsistent coherent. The danger is that we see what we expect, not what is there. Those events that do not fit our understanding of what is or what should be, may be ignored, overlooked or assumed to be wrong. The perceiver may unconsciously deny or downplay the event, for information that contradicts cherished beliefs can be disturbing. This tendency can apply to groups and organizations as much as to individuals. American car manufacturers provide an example: they appeared to neglect or deny the growing market for smaller cars in the late twentieth century because their mind-set was oriented to producing large ones. Similarly, IBM seemed to take an unduly long time to adapt to a world where small personal computers rather than large mainframe ones were to be the order of the day.

Tendency to impose order

BOX 3.4 VISUAL PERCEPTION

The figures below offer a visual illustration of the impact of expectation on what is perceived. Look at each figure. Can you see an image there? If you do see something, how long was it before the image became clear?

Figure 3.2

Figure 3.3

If you can't see an image after a few minutes, the answer is in Appendix B at the back of the book. (However, don't look there until you've tried the other puzzles in this section.) Once you have seen the image, you will find it impossible to see the strange mix of black and white that you originally perceived.

In addition, these tendencies to perceive and act in ways that have worked in the past are heightened when we feel a threat to our identity, safety, security or status. So under stress it is usually harder for us to operate outside familiar mental tramlines.

Often we do not have enough information to obtain an accurate picture but, since we are programmed to make meaning, this rarely stops us from jumping to conclusions and defending our resulting opinion, as illustrated by the following Sufi story:

> Five blind men were walking along and encountered an elephant on the path. As it happened they had never come across an elephant before. The first man touched a leg and declared that the object before them was clearly a tree. The second, being at the front of the animal, touched the trunk and realized at once that it was a clearly a serpent. The third being on a slight rise in the path, reached out and touched the ear. He thought his friends mad since it was clear the creature was a large bird with huge wings. The fourth man, further back near the tail, was equally perplexed at his colleagues' stupidity, since on touching the tail, he realized the animal was clearly a large donkey. The fifth man, who was at the side of the elephant, decided it was a large wall clad in leather. The blind men fell to arguing and fighting over who was right, each believing the others were either fools or trying to trick him.
>
> *(Traditional Sufi story)*

Barriers

Our everyday mind-sets show their limitations when faced with the unexpected, as demonstrated by the exercises in Box 3.5 overleaf.

Insight problems are often difficult to solve because we bring to them an existing way of viewing problems, a particular mental set. This leads us to assume limitations that are not present in the problem definition, and to fixate on a particular strategy. The solution is usually found by reframing the way in which the problem was originally perceived.

Mind-sets are conditioned by our values and past experiences. Numerous experiments have shown the remarkable extent to which the way people approach tasks is conditioned by their assumptions about what is required and their experience in related areas. Kaufmann's (1991) list of some of the cognitive tendencies that can be dysfunctional in problem-solving includes: over-reliance on stereotyped responses that have worked previously (see Box 3.6); blocks against using objects in a new way; unnecessary assumptions limiting the range of possibilities considered (e.g. not going outside the perimeter in the nine-dot problem); the tendency to seek confirming and discard disconfirming evidence; and the reluctance to reduce confidence in decisions following disconfirmation. These may all block creative approaches to problem-solving.

BOX 3.5   INSIGHT PROBLEMS

These are problems that are very hard to work out logically step by step, but are more likely to be solved by a sudden insight. For example:

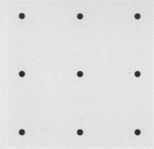

Link up the nine dots above with four straight lines, without taking your pen off the paper or going through each dot more than once.

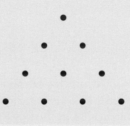

Move three coins (i.e. dots) to invert the triangle.

Draw two squares to give each animal its own enclosure.

(Answers are in Appendix B at the back of the book.)

BOX 3.6   CONDITIONED THINKING

The Luchins water jar experiments provide a classic illustration of the quite extraordinary extent to which we can be conditioned by previous assumptions.

The task presented to subjects was to obtain a set amount of water, given only three containers of different sizes for each problem. After only six trials, where applying the formula

jar B – jar A – 2(jar C)

produced the desired result, 80% of subjects used the same formula for the next two problems, in which jar A – jar C in one case and jar A + jar C in the other would have done the job more efficiently.

Sixty per cent of subjects were unable to solve the problem of obtaining 25 litres of water, given jars where A held 28 litres, B held 76 litres and C held 3 litres. The, by then, apparently conditioned use of the original formula did not work in this case. The required formula was much simpler:

jar A – jar C

Cyert and March (1963) claim that managers exhibit a similar tendency to search in areas close to those in which previous solutions have been found to work. It seems we have a strong tendency to apply rules mindlessly, which means we easily miss new approaches.

The delay in identifying the ozone hole is a case in point. Ozone depletion was first identified by Dr Joe Farman, a long-time member of the British Antarctic Survey, after he noticed a series of unusual readings sent back from Antarctica in 1982. He asked the Americans if they could confirm this finding, and they said not. Two years later, after his paper on ozone loss was published in the prestigious journal *Nature*, the Americans re-examined their raw data, and 'concluded that their satellite had been seeing the same ozone hole for years'. Why then had this important fact not been attended to? The scientists at NASA analysing the data had programmed the computers to throw out abnormal readings, because they were not *expected* to be significant! (Pearce, 1990)

Belated ozone hole discovery

Jones (1984) suggests that, in addition to inhibiting problem-solving strategies, a rigidity in thinking, lack of perception and poor self-image can also block a creative approach. For example, an over-emphasis on traditional ways of doing things can result in an unnecessary conformity that makes unwarranted assumptions, or a tendency to polarize questions into opposites risks overlooking unifying factors. Single-minded, narrow thinking will also restrict the range of options examined. Poor self-image may lead to difficulty in resisting social pressures and fighting for strongly held ideas.

Many creative thinking techniques aim to overcome the blinkering effect of mind-set on perception, to enable us to see an issue from different and more useful perspectives. A number of techniques involve systematic attempts to consider alternative points of view, including those opposite to our own. Mason and Mitroff (1981), for example, advocate a dialectic where two groups develop a case using opposing assumptions and then discuss the conflicting outcomes. Creative thinking is often bound up with the kind of playful attitude that wants to explore alternatives. Kaufmann's review of conditions and procedures that can aid problem-solving includes exploring the problem situation, deferring judgement, separating idea generation and evaluation, the use of conflictual thinking and the place of high motivation and performance. (See the Kaufmann chapter in Henry (2001)).

Beliefs

Changing individual values and organizational mind-sets is hard work, but at least if we are aware of their existence it may be easier to make conscious allowance for them. Brown (1988) illustrates the idea of organizational mind-sets with the example of the Mafia, whose watchwords might be 'loyalty', 'discretion' and 'material gain', contrasting this with a Quaker company in which 'care for employees' and 'local and social responsibility' would be likely to be dominant values. Sometimes companies are quite explicit about their values. Those of Hewlett Packard include trust, openness, management by walking around, enthusiasm and 'small is beautiful'.

Activity 3.6

What would you say are your organization's values? How well do these match your own values?

Some examples of what is meant by 'values' in this case would be: concern with quality, desire to innovate, accountability, paternalism, competitiveness, co-operativeness, friendliness, team work, division into 'us' and 'them', formality, suspiciousness, positive social contribution, partnership.

Self-fulfilling prophecy

Our values and mind-sets about organizations and about the world around us guide many of our decisions in these areas, just as they guide the judgements we make about our own abilities. For instance, if we think we cannot do something we are less likely to try, or we notice failures when we do try and probably give up earlier, our expectations confirmed. Rosenthal (1969) conducted a classic series of experiments that showed the devastating effect of negative belief on performance. For example, teachers were informed that all the children in one group were not expected to do well whereas those in a second group were expected to do well. Children whose teachers believed them less able performed less well than children whose teachers believed them to be able. This effect was not accounted for by any prior difference in ability, as the children's intelligence level was the same in each group. Brown (1971) has reported a similar finding from industry, where foremen were fed false results about new employees' performances on intelligence and dexterity tests. A follow-up showed that the foremen gave opinions about the employees that coincided with the false information, and production figures showed the same trend! In both situations, performance was closer to the authority figure's view of the person's ability than to the person's actual ability. People, it seems, perform close to their labels.

Self-fulfilling prophecy

What positive and negative mind-sets do you hold about yourself, your team or department and your organization?

Activity 3.7

(a) Write down ten beliefs you hold about yourself, preferably ten you really believe to be true, e.g. 'I am a nice person', 'I am no good at figures', 'I am a good manager', 'I am not creative', etc. If these are mostly negative, add at least five more positive beliefs about yourself.

(b) Show these to several colleagues you trust and ask each of them to say whether they strongly agree, agree, are not sure, disagree or strongly disagree with each belief as it applies to you.

This may give you some indication of the accuracy of your self-image.

(c) Select five beliefs about your department or organization that you strongly believe to be true. Imagine what it would be like if the opposite were true.

Reframing

Self-fulfilling prophecies are just as potent in relation to beliefs about ourselves as they are to our perceptions about others. Performance is bound up with expectation: if we think we can do something, we are more likely to achieve it. Take, for example, the four-minute mile. For many years people doubted that it was possible to run a mile in under four minutes. Yet once

Roger Bannister did just that, and in so doing broke the mental set that said it was not possible, a number of other athletes also managed this feat. A positive belief can have a remarkably positive effect on performance.

Transforming negative beliefs into more constructive ones is an example of reframing, and reframing seems to be central to the positive attitude that is often found when we are being creative. One way to do this is to try to reframe unconstructive beliefs into something more positive. For example, instead of saying 'I am stubborn' you might reframe this as 'I am determined'; 'I am weak' could be reframed as 'I am sensitive'. The important thing is that you should feel better about the reframed statement. Try the following test of creativity.

Activity 3.8

(a) List five negative beliefs about yourself. Can you reframe each one into something positive, that you like the sound of better?

(b) When you find yourself talking to people at work who you feel are suffering from low self-esteem, listen carefully to their statements about themselves. Reframe these in a more positive way that you think they will find credible.

It can also be interesting to investigate your mind-sets about other people. As well as genuine grounds for a strong belief or an outstanding grievance, there is often an emotional overlay serving a private need that keeps it alive longer. Take belief in free enterprise as an example of the purpose that a belief can serve. At one level there may be good economic reasons for holding such a belief, but it may also serve more personal needs, such as helping people feel less guilty about others who have less than they do.

Activity 3.9

Think of a belief, attitude or grievance that you feel strongly about. This could be a political belief, or perhaps someone or something that you find hard to forgive, or an attitude you have that you wish to change or lose.

Write down this belief or feeling, beginning 'I am', 'I believe' or 'I should'.

Psychologists say that any belief we hold serves some purpose for us. What purpose could this belief serve for you?

What does this belief prevent you from seeing? Give at least one example.

What does this belief prevent you from doing?

Restate the belief as a goal in the present tense, perhaps beginning 'I want'.

What often happens with this activity is that you realize you are aggrieved because one of your key values has been violated. For instance, you may find it hard to forgive the colleague who made his fame and fortune out of your ideas without acknowledging them, because you strongly believe people should give credit where credit is due; or you may have no respect for an obliging colleague who is always ready to help out because you feel that people should stand up for themselves.

Reframing can become an attitude to life in general, seeing the opportunity and positive side of a situation rather than the problems and negative side: for example seeing what can be learnt from any failure. Handy (1991) gives the example of reframing an enforced short-term move during building work, from being a tiresome inconvenience to an opportunity to experience another part of town. Stress management courses often give the example of a traffic jam as an opportunity to think uninterrupted for as long as it lasts, or to play the music to which you never normally have time to listen. Having to deliver something to another office can be seen as an opportunity for exercise rather than a waste of valuable time. It is all a matter of perspective.

Activity 3.10

For a full day try to see and articulate the opportunity in every problem you face.

Creativity courses may advocate the use of a 'Yes and' mentality rather than a 'Yes but' one. 'Yes but'-ers are nay-sayers who talk down every new proposal by pointing out its weaknesses. 'Yes and'-ers focus on the strengths of a proposal and seek to overcome its weaknesses. The 'Yes and' approach is obviously the more diplomatic and can be used to good effect in meetings.

Yes and

Learning to perceive situations differently is not just about learning techniques or applying rules, for the way we perceive is bound up with our psychological make-up and patterns of thought. Changing deeply held attitudes and values of which we may be unaware involves a degree of honest self-examination.

As Evans and Russell (1989) say:

> Becoming a creative manager is not just a matter of practising new techniques and methodologies – although these certainly help it is also about becoming more aware of our own inner processes. It is about adopting a new style of thinking and perceiving. It is about learning to see ourselves and our problems in a new way.

This involves becoming aware of our patterns of thinking and values. Metaphors, the topic of the next chapter, provide one way of exploring alternative values.

Implications

The sheer information overload that is an inevitable part of life means we all rely on mind-sets as short cuts to making sense of situations. The danger is that these beliefs can become so set that we limit our performance in accord with their assumptions. A conscious attempt to reframe any limiting belief can often be sufficient to open a whole new perspective.

3.4   DECONSTRUCTION

Like any other institution organizations embody certain norms, values and practices. Most managers assume that the way their organization is structured and the procedures they use are rational, but it may be that a large proportion of these practices have become part of the organizational mind-set and are used out of habit.

Discourse

The French philosopher Foucault (1977) drew attention to the way in which professions, such as medicine, psychiatry, and management, construct discourses through which the world comes to be perceived. For example mad people were originally seen as bad – possessed by demons – and in need of punishment. They are now seen as sick people – with biological disorders – that need help. Criminals are still seen as bad people and are held responsible for their actions and hence justifiably punished but, if we came to see criminal behaviour as largely genetically based, the idea of punishment becomes illogical. There are already cases in the US where defendants have successfully argued they are not responsible for violent behaviour as it has a genetic basis.

Stress and bereavement used to be seen as inevitable parts of life and trials which a wise person learnt to endure. They are now seen as psychological conditions needing expert help and counselling (or at least a training course) to aid their removal. Most managers assume that they have to monitor staff regularly, and tend to be fairly secretive about financial matters; but some radical companies have abandoned job descriptions and most of the traditional corporate centre, and allowed staff to take on responsibility for hiring their own managers, assessing their bosses' performance and setting their own salaries (Semler in Henry, 2001).

Management can be seen as just another professional discourse that adopts certain values, norms and practices for social and cultural reasons rather than for good cause and a rational justification (Parker, 1997). It is been suggested that much management practice gets standardized through mimicry. Some ideas, like benchmarking the competition, seem rational; but it is questionable whether a number of other practices taken up by managers are appropriate for all the situations in which they are applied. One reason such ideas are taken up is because managers are not quite sure what will work best, but tend to have faith in the possibility of a quick fix, and hence are prepared to try yet another fad. Another reason is the need to be seen to belong to the management community and to be playing their part.

Legitimacy

Legitimacy

Managers tend to be under pressure to give a good account of themselves. Gaining legitimacy can be important, in that it may make it easier for the manager to access funds or be promoted; but it does not necessarily help the business. Managers may unconsciously imitate practices which do not work, merely to show what good managers they are, and spend a lot of time trying to gain acceptance rather than running their organizations. For example, managers may adopt a company mission statement and declare their intention to follow a strategic plan, without any intention of putting them into practice, largely as a way of signalling to their significant colleagues that they are toeing the line. Managers are also often full of schemes and plans that lie unactioned. Even if these visions and plans do not have much practical value they may fulfil a symbolic need.

Activity 3.11

Thinking of your organization, or one known to you:

(a) Can you recall any managerial programme or initiative that was offered more for public relations purposes than because it was ever seriously intended to be put into practice? Where did the idea originate, who championed it and why? Does your analysis lend any support to the importance of legitimacy as a driving force for management activity?

(b) Think of five practices or schemes you have introduced. In each case to what extent do you think the practice you introduced was to do with legitimacy, or a rational response to the situation?

Deconstruction

Deconstruction was an approach originated by the French philosopher Derrida as a means of exposing the values implicit in our plans and actions. For example much Anglo-Saxon thought is framed in terms of binary oppositions such as good and bad or order and disorder. By implicitly valuing order, light and high culture we implicitly devalue chaos, dark and low culture, as the preference for one term always works at the expense of another (Sim, 1998).

Management is full of these kind of polarities – management and workers, office and shop floor, efficient and wasteful, committed and uncommitted, qualified and unqualified. Attending to the less prestigious side of these couples can be revealing (Burrell, 1996).

Activity 3.12

Management tends to privilege terms like order, plan, strategy, control. This book has privileged terms like creativity, innovation and change. What are we neglecting by drawing attention to these terms? Hint: Is it more important to be a creative organization or a survivor?

This book espouses a participative, emergent and constructivist approach to management. But it could be argued that these values are rooted in Western culture. It is no accident that the notions of creativity and innovation arose in an individualistic nation. Perhaps by concentrating on these approaches we omit giving sufficient attention to other routes to entrepreneurship, for example the interdependent family networks found in Chinese cultures. The idea of problem solving may be similarly culture-bound, as it is based on the rational idea of planning before we act.

This section has alerted us to the need to attend to what we are neglecting when espousing particular doctrines. By espousing creative management, innovation, climate and change we are privileging these terms and neglecting their counterparts. Perhaps highlighting these concepts acts as a corrective against the traditional management focus on strategy, order and control. It also suggests new ways of organizing and co-ordinating activity that appear to be appropriate for a globalized and fast-changing environment. However, time will tell if this book is espousing practices that are part of a paradigm shift in approaches to management of universal interest, or whether it is promulgating an essentially Western route to change that is as bounded by time and culture as mass manufacturing.

3.5 REVIEW

Studies of management thinking show that, though not much talked about, intuitive thinking is central to the manager's job. Recent work in cognitive psychology supports this by demonstrating that the unconscious mind has impressive information-processing powers which the conscious mind often fails to match, particularly where information is incomplete.

Tacit knowledge, unconscious information processing and intuitive forms of knowing play a key role in dealing with uncertain and ambiguous situations: that is, just the type of situation managers face every day. This chapter has illustrated why intuitive thinking is often superior in situations such as these. It described the large extent to which managers rely on intuitive judgement, and drew attention to the judgement biases which we are all subject to. It went on to explain how mind-sets constrain the possibilities individuals, groups and organizations can envisage, and to advocate reframing and deconstruction as routes to help get round this kind of perceptual limitation.

Further reading

G. Kaufmann, 'Problem solving and creativity', in Henry (2001).

4 METAPHORS

An iron curtain has descended across the Continent.

(Winston Churchill)

Over a period of time mind-sets can become so automatic that we only think of phenomena in their terms. Something like this can apply to how we conceive of organizations. In this chapter we examine the different metaphors that have underpinned thinking about management and organizations. We look at mechanistic, ecological, social, cognitive and systemic metaphors. You are asked to experiment with employing different metaphors for management, and the chapter concludes by considering whether management is undergoing a paradigm shift.

A metaphor represents an object in terms of something it resembles, as when you call a ferocious person a tiger or a meek person a lamb. Metaphors offer a way of making the strange familiar, summarizing insights, and representing related ideas; and they tend to entail a central image. Indeed, a good deal of our understanding and reasoning is based round the use of analogy and metaphor.

Though metaphors provide valuable tools for analogous reasoning, they can become so entrenched that we cease to realize they are just metaphors and not reality. Talk of the 'top' and 'bottom' of the organization is a case in point. At the same time, since metaphors necessarily draw attention to one aspect of a situation and not others, they tend to limit the ways in which we conceptualize and choose to act. Thus, whether we see the organization as a machine or garden, and the manager as a conductor or captain, will affect the strategies we entertain and how we behave. The metaphors we choose are in turn affected by our values and beliefs, including many implicit unacknowledged assumptions about how things work.

4.1 ORGANIZATIONAL METAPHORS

Practitioners and academics alike have not been shy in using metaphors to capture aspects of organizational life. Organizations have been likened to machines, organisms, the theatre, a brain, an iceberg, a network, prison, and a dustbin.

Morgan (1986, 1997) uses eight organizational metaphors with which to organize the entire output of management thinking to date, in his excellent book, *The Images of Organization*. These are:

Machine	Political system
Organism	Psychic prison
Brain	Flux and transformation
Culture	Instrument of domination.

Activity 4.1

Before reading on, pick three metaphors for organizations, for instance the organization as machine, organism or political system.

List the characteristics you associate with each.

Try and relate each characteristic to a feature in an organization that you know.

What sorts of feature of organizations do these characteristics highlight, and what do they conceal?

Machine metaphors

Organization as machine

Two classic metaphors for organizations are the organization as machine and the organization as organism (Burns and Stalker, 1961). Traditionally organizations have been envisaged and structured as if they were machines. The machine metaphor conjures up the image of an organization that aims to run like clockwork, and is

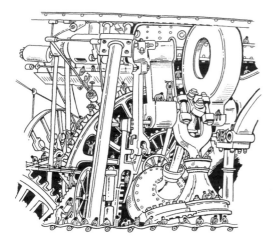

epitomized in the classic picture of the bureaucracy. In such organizations, structure, rules, procedures and tasks dominate. Employees are pictured as unintelligent cogs in a technological mechanism, who are required to conform rather than create.

This metaphor embodies the idea of an unfeeling rationality. Bureaucracies encourage efficiency within a predetermined system, but discourage thinking about fundamentals by those operating the system and in contact with the customer, since decisions are taken at the top. They are inflexible and slow to adapt. We can see the extensive heritage of viewing organizations this way in Taylor's work on scientific management, time and motion studies, Ford's assembly line, management by objectives, the preference for quantitative measures and the idea of strategy as predetermined plans.

Biological metaphors

Since the 1960s, biological metaphors for organizations have come to the fore. The original was 'organization as organism'. Biological metaphors recognize that the inhabitants of organizations are alive and have needs of their own, instead of viewing them as parts to be ordered around as the designer chooses. They also suggest an image of interdependent parts, acting together to respond to the **Organization as organism** changes in an unstable environment, to meet its needs. This type of metaphor has been applied to organizations involved in complex businesses in changing environments such as electronics and plastics. These organizations co-evolve with the environment, collaborating as much as competing with each other.

Biological metaphors also direct attention to the individual organisms (people) in the organization and their needs. Indeed, they have become associated with the human relations approach to organizations epitomized by the likes of Hawthorne, McGregor and Argyris. The evolutionary analogy also draws attention to differences between species, with the implication that, for example, innovative companies might have different needs from mature industries, and to the different ways organizations fit in the environment. Systems theory is one approach that has explored the latter issue.

Appealing though the organism metaphor may be, it tends to over-emphasize unity within the organism: the parts of a biological organism are subservient to the whole in a more extreme way than is normally found in a social system. The biological metaphor also neglects the role of culture or mind in constructing images and ideas.

Table 4.1 draws together some of the differences between the metaphors of the organization as machine and as organism.

Table 4.1	Organizational metaphors	
	Machine	**Organism**
Character	Authoritarian	Participative
Flair	Administrative	Entrepreneurial
Structure	Hierarchical	Relatively flat
	Parts	Processes
	Centralized	Decentralized
Climate	Closed	Open
Style	Uniform	Varied
Authority	Position	Expertise
Form	Formal	Informal
Control	Tight	Loose
	Control	Collaborative
Decisions	Authoritarian	Consensus
	Top-down	Bottom-up
Strategy	Reactive	Proactive
Adaptability	Slow	Fast
Orientation	Past	Future
Approach	Fixed	Flexible
	Low redundancy	High redundancy
Procedure	Follow rules	Responsive
Attitude	Critical	Caring
	Compliance	Commitment

Activity 4.2

Imagine that each of the paired items in Table 4.1 lies at one end of a bipolar scale, where an extreme case of the items under 'Machine' represents 1 and an extreme case of those under 'Organism' represents 10. In each case, where would you place:

(a) your own organization

(b) yourself?

There are no prizes for guessing that creative and innovative organizations generally have more in common with the characteristics associated with the organism metaphor. Interestingly, most people place themselves near the organism end of the scale. Would their friends be as kind? Westerners are also usually kinder to themselves in this respect than they are to their organization, as the average score for individuals is usually much nearer the organism pole than the machine pole, compared to the average score for organizations. It may be objected that the values advocated are apparent in the way that the list has been phrased. As a colleague pointed out, when did a machine ever start a war? (Though this could happen inadvertently through a computer fault.)

Ecological metaphors

An ecological metaphor provides another biological metaphor that draws attention to the need to find niches (for products and services) in suitable environments, to nurture staff to develop their potential, as well as to the need for sufficient space and balance within and across organizations in a region. The ecological metaphor seems apposite for the twenty-first century with its emphasis on the nurturing and facilitative aspects of management, but it may under-emphasize the ability of people to fight back. Plants may compete with each other but not with the gardener (see Box 4.1).

BOX 4.1 THE KARMOY GARDEN METAPHOR

The CEO of Karmoy, the largest aluminium plant in Europe, used a visual metaphor of a garden to explain his vision of the company to workers. The pictures below show how the different divisions were portrayed as different plants, products as flowers and fruit, R and D as birds, new business as roots, the soil as knowledge, and management as the water sustaining the business (Henry, 1992). The three garden pictures portrayed the company as it had been, as it was and as they intended it to be. The first picture was dominated by a large flower – one particular division – taking sunlight from the other divisions. The second picture showed a more balanced garden – with the other divisions beginning to grow and develop. The last has more customers and the rudiments of new business units. Since most people (in Norway) garden,[18] this metaphor was easy to relate to, though a few staff found the picture a bit too rosy.

As had been

As was

---

[18] Scandinavians also tend to have a more developed concept of nature than their Anglo-Saxon counterparts which may make this metaphor even more obvious to them.

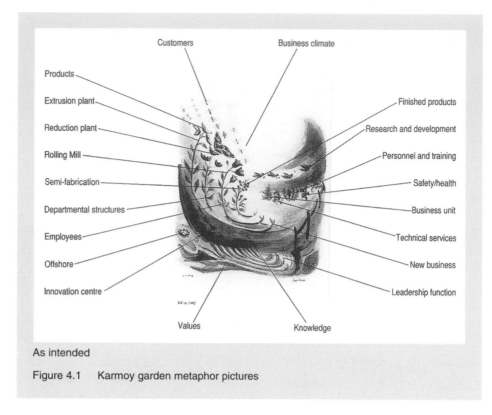

As intended

Figure 4.1   Karmoy garden metaphor pictures

There are of course many other metaphors that could be used to describe organizations. Three that have come into prominence lately include social metaphors, such as organizations as culture, cognitive metaphors, such as the organization as brain, and systemic metaphors, such as the organization as network.

Social metaphors

Social metaphors focus on the relationships and communication patterns in an organization.

In the 1990s, many organizations around the world woke up to the fact that *organizational culture* was a key determinant of performance. The idea of

culture switches attention to the people who work within the organization, their needs and their shared meanings; also to the rhetoric, myths and rituals through which people act out their ideas and around which organizational life is performed. One aspect of this is the power games often played by those who want influence. Many management writers have focused on the different subcultures in different organizations and the implications of cross-cultural differences (Deal and Kennedy, 1982; Schein, 1985; Ouchi, 1981). Other writers have focused more on the power relations between organizational members (Foucault, 1980).

The idea of organization as *theatre* and management as performance provides a metaphor that takes account of the social context of work. This metaphor is also present in everyday speech: we perform tasks, enact roles, play our part, act on cue unrehearsed, and prompt others. At one level it directs attention to the fact that people in organizations have to perform well and play out the roles expected of them, and that departing from the script can be penalized. It also draws attention to the showman aspect of leadership, the extent to which leaders and managers have to entertain and impress their staff with their brilliant or apt performance and the lines associated with that role. It reminds us of the significance of organizational ceremonies and rhetoric we might otherwise take for granted.

Organization as theatre of enactment

Another reading of this metaphor focuses more on the idea of *enactment* – the way in which organizational life is co-created by the performers in collaboration with the audience (Weick, 1979). The metaphor of enactment perhaps captures the idea that knowledge is emergent and tied closely to the field from which it emerges.

Activity 4.3

What metaphors would you use to describe the culture or climate in your organization or part of it?

Morgan (1989) suggests four possible metaphors for organizational culture – sticky glue, an iceberg, an onion and an umbrella. *Glue* directs attention to the invisible and unspoken norms and routines of corporate culture. The *iceberg* suggests the hidden values and beliefs below the surface that may need to be addressed if the culture is to be changed. The *onion* is similar, highlighting the many layers there are to go through before reaching the core. The *umbrella* offers a more integrated image, pointing to the need to unite the different interest groups.

Metaphors for an organization's culture can easily become so entrenched they make it difficult for the organization to move on; for example the family firm, the whiz-kid outfit, or the craft-based organization. Open University Business School MBA students studying the *Creative Management* and *Creativity, Innovation and Change* courses (Henry and Martin, 1991; Henry et al., 1999) have come up with numerous other metaphors. One manager saw his organization as a supertanker, big, modern, strong but (with a supertanker's stopping distance of 27 miles) perhaps being slower to change than it might be!

Cognitive metaphors

Learning organization
Creative network
Knowledge management

Recently our talk about the nature of organizations has come to be dominated by a series of metaphors with a distinctly cognitive edge. We now speak of the learning organization and knowledge management, and we compare the organization to a brain or computer. These new metaphors seem entirely fitting for the information age (Senge, 1991; Nonaka, 1995).

These metaphors emphasize the role of intellectual rather than economic capital, and intangible assets rather than the tangible ones emphasized in the machine metaphor. They focus on the importance of developing individuals within organizations so they are better placed to learn and create. In the UK this is now embedded in policies and schemes like Investors in People. (It is no longer just the product that gets the quality mark, but the organization's system of development – its brain, if you like.)

Learning

The idea of *learning* as a metaphor for organizations has been criticized on various grounds, one of which is that it is individuals in organizations, not the organization as a whole, who learn. The idea of organizations as *centres of knowledge* can be criticized for conceiving of knowledge as a static entity that can be represented, captured and transferred. The previous chapter suggested that much knowledge was implicit, too complex to be mapped out in words, and situated rather than transferable.

Brain

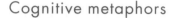

Another cognitive metaphor is the idea of organization as *brain*. This metaphor draws attention to the channels of communication, including serendipitous informal conversations, through which ideas emerge and develop. Modern brain research presents an image of distributed knowledge. Thus the metaphor draws attention to the distributed nature of many organizational functions and the horizontal connections between them. It highlights the idea of interconnected networks and the concept of learning. We can think of the personal computers on the desktops of managers as links in the organizational net, offering access to information about the organization's activities. The brain metaphor is implicit in the cognitive approach to organizations which concentrates on communication and decision-making processes (Simon, 1960).

The metaphors of brain, learning, and knowledge are all associated with conscious thought; and in the West, at least until recently, thinking has been associated with the development of rational and explicit ideas. Yet in organizational life, as much as in personal life, much of what goes on is hidden. The organizational underbelly, or the organization as iceberg or onion, draw attention to these hidden aspects of organizational life. The *positive* aspect of this hidden world is the *tacit* knowledge locked away inside employees' heads, as recognized by Polyani (1958) and popularized by Nonaka (1995).

But hidden knowledge also has a *shadow* side. Secrets are closely guarded: people are afraid things will fall apart, and they go to great lengths to pretend that this is not the case and that all is well, so they appear to be in control. The effect of their repressed feelings leads to unacknowledged defence mechanisms. Bion and Argyris argue that such unconscious processes play a large, and chiefly unacknowledged, part in organizational life at the individual and group levels (Bion, 1968; Argyris, 1994). Several writers have suggested that the neglect of these aspects leads to an essentially defensive orientation among managers, who need to feel in control to feel safe. (Gabriel expands on the psychodynamics of organizations in his chapter in Henry (2001).)

Some have gone so far as to suggest that organizational man appears to have an anal-compulsive character that leads to a need to control, and to a resultant tendency to treat staff as children who need to be told what to do and punished if they do wrong (Semler, 1991). Even if this narrative is not accepted, many people would acknowledge that organizations are typically experienced as confining, which makes it likely people will react by putting up defences against perceived threats. (These tendencies may be exacerbated by the real threat of potential lay-offs and the increasing use of short-term contracts.)

The organizational unconscious
Working with mental models starts with turning the mirror inward.
(Senge, 1991, p. 8)

Reactions to uncertainty

Stacy (1996) has suggested that increasing uncertainty in the environment makes managers feel uncomfortable and that, as a consequence, their anxiety increases, which leads to a vicious circle. In order to reduce their anxiety, they redouble their efforts to keep control, clinging to procedures, pre-specifying objectives and, if need be, rearranging divisions in a vain attempt to increase order and certainty. If these strategies fail, managers may then flee to the latest restructuring technique in the hope of finding a magical recipe that will provide the stability they crave and have been led to expect. Stacy suggests that denying uncertainty in this way sustains the myth of being in control but, since it is an essentially defensive response, it cannot last. He points out that the widespread faith in gurus is essentially a dependent stance. Why do managers believe there is some saviour who can fix their problems?

Systemic metaphors

Network

Recently, the idea of the organization as a *network* (instead of a hierarchy) has been gaining currency. Morgan (1993) used the metaphor of a spider plant to convey the idea of a network. Other writers have drawn on metaphors that evoke the dissipative nature of the modern organization, as in Handy's (1989) use of the shamrock (Irish clover) to represent the federal nature of many organizations.

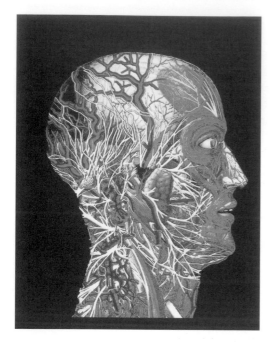

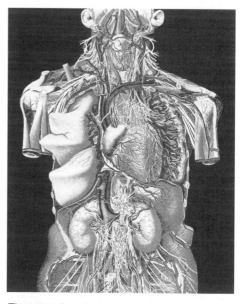

The network metaphor – the idea of
organization as a complicated web of
interconnections

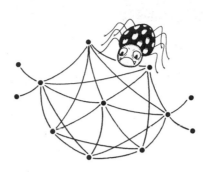

The organization as network

The organization as network draws attention to the communication between actors in and outside the organization over time, and conjures up the idea of a pattern of relationships, while presenting a different image of the structure of organizations. It focuses attention on the channels of communication across departmental and organizational boundaries.

It also highlights the role of informal communication, something mechanistic metaphors tend to neglect entirely. Like the brain metaphor, a network stresses the *distributed* nature of much organizational activity. We now give much greater attention to the bigger picture within which organizations are embedded, and to the networks of communication across the whole supply chain. We look not just at how to improve our bounded organizations but at the niches they occupy across sectors. In short, we are beginning to remember the space in between organizations and look at the patterns of relationship between them, rather than just trying to analyse the elements of which organizations are composed. This in turn is changing the framework within which we conceive of organizations.

Complexity

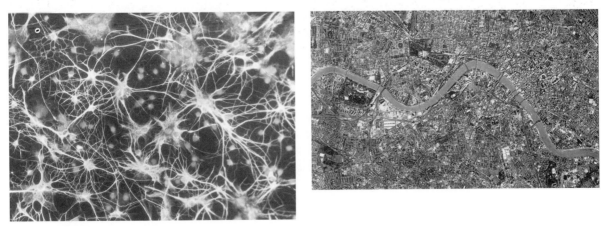

Complex adaptive systems: (left) Brain cells; (right) City

Complexity theory suggests a new metaphor that gives a very different perspective on organizations. The metaphor draws on work on chaos, complexity and non-linear dynamics in maths, physics, chemistry and biology now being applied to sciences like economics and management. Complexity focuses on the patterns of transformation that emerge spontaneously in complex adaptive systems. The non-linear patterns of transformation identified in complex adaptive systems have led to a new way of looking at the dynamics (changing patterns) of complex organization, one that highlights the importance of self-organization.

Complexity examines how systems are constantly transformed by the agents that make up the system (whether these be ants, people or neurones) simply doing what comes naturally to them. The focus is on the dynamic patterns that emerge from the collective activity of the agents in the system over time. A key characteristic of these systems is that surprisingly simple patterns can easily generate coherent and complex behaviour, the agents spontaneously self-organize and coherent adaptive behaviour emerges. However, another feature of these systems is that the outcome in any individual case is unpredictable. In addition, very small changes in the initial conditions can have major effects on the outcome (as epitomized by the proverbial butterfly flapping its wings on one side of the world affecting weather on the other side). Box 4.2 gives two further examples that illustrate the principles of complexity.

Chaos theory

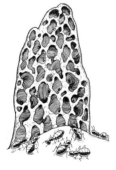

BOX 4.2 COMPLEX ADAPTIVE SYSTEMS

Work on complex adaptive systems suggests that, if you allow independent agents following a few simple rules to interact, good solutions will evolve naturally (as they have done in markets and with animal behaviour) without the intervention of someone trying to manage the process.

A termite mound is a case in point. Each termite drops its ball of mud anywhere, but adds a chemical attractor. Initially there is no pattern in the droppings; however, termites are more inclined to drop their bundles on earth where the smell is stronger, so the larger, stronger-smelling piles get larger, and rise into columns. When columns are close the chemical attractor inclines the termite to drop the ball on the side of the column nearest its neighbour. Eventually these extensions form an arch. Over time columns link to form a series of cells and chambers, in extraordinary multi-storey structures of four or five metres. No termite leader, design, plan or co-ordination is needed for this structure to emerge naturally from collective action.

Flock movements provide another example. The precision movements of flocks of birds and shoals of fish seem hard to explain. But a flocking program in which birds obey four simple rules seems to simulate the behaviour perfectly. The rules are: steer to maintain a certain distance from other birds, steer for home, fly at a constant speed, and avoid collisions. The rules, not the programmer, determine the nature of the flock's movements. Presenting this simulation at a conference the programmer was surprised that the managers in the audience were impressed and asked why. She received these replies. 'Maybe because *they see behaviour without anyone telling them what to do*'. 'They don't realize that means there's nothing for managers to do.'

An aggregate of independent actors can behave as if they were a single unit responding to the environment. Markets do this in response to economic changes, and brain cells in response to electrical stimulation from the senses; and the assertion is that people in organizations do too.

An aeroplane simulation illustrates the idea. The task is to steer the aeroplane over mountains, through clouds and down valleys. The audience watches intensely as the plane flies perfectly across the landscape, for it is the whole audience, not one pilot, who collectively control the flight. A quarter control movements to the left, another quarter movements to the right, a further quarter can affect upward movements and the remainder downward movements. The plane follows the majority vote, which cancels out oddball, incompetent, inattentive or would-be plane-crashing individuals, without the intervention of a manager or controller.

(Adapted from Berreby, 1998, p. 45 and Clark 1997, p. 75)

The complexity metaphor is generating interest in business because it presents a very different picture of the nature of organization and transformation than that normally taken for granted, and because it seems to offer a better metaphor for important but hitherto neglected aspects of organizational life (Stacy, 1996; Wheatley, 1994). Most management works within a functional perspective that implicitly assumes that the way forward is to agree goals, design a plan to achieve the goals and then work towards realizing these prior intentions. Much management comprises an attempt to control this process, assuming there are objective methods of determining better ways of doing so. **Self-organization**

In contrast, complexity offers a metaphor of emergence, self-organization, informality, and unpredictability which finds little room for management or the manager. Instead of focusing on the task and structure, it views the world not as a rational place where experts can analyse what is going on to produce better plans for controlling events, but as comprising loosely coupled networks of self-organizing actors, where local action emerges from intersubjective conversation – a network with decentred agency, rather than a hierarchy with a central control centre. It highlights the role of spontaneous self-organization, which is perhaps appropriate in the new flatter type of organization with empowered employees. The implication is that people do not need to be told what to do: they are intelligent agents continuously learning and modifying their behaviour on the basis of feedback. So the metaphor is more concerned with evoking creative potential than policing the present. It seems to provide a modern metaphor for emergent creativity and the role of informal intersubjective interactions that has hitherto been neglected.

While much of management activity has concerned keeping or anticipating ways to maintain stability, the science of complexity focuses on instability. In so doing it highlights the inherent unpredictability of most complex adaptive systems, from the way your water goes down the plughole to the weather, and including, by implication, much human, managerial and creative endeavour, such as the time needed to develop, and the likely success of, innovations. The **Unpredictability**

83

traditional management response to dealing with complexity is to build ever more elaborate systems and maps in an attempt to predict outcomes: the complexity metaphor invites you to let go of the illusion that you can control and predict the outcomes of creative endeavour. This also means letting go of many other management concepts: for example, the idea of optimizing becomes suspect, because ever-changing conditions mean today's optimum is not necessarily tomorrow's. This is not to say there is no order, rather that it is emergent.

Complexity also has plenty to say about evolutionary strategies. One implication of the work in this area is that redundancy aids long-term survival and the ability to be creative. Highly focused survival plans or strategies can be very efficient in the short term but rarely prove optimal in the long run, whereas an element of mess, and random detours, offer the possibility of important and expected adaptions (Stacy, 1996).

For one proponent, the metaphor of complexity has suggested a whole new way of working:

> Now I look carefully at how a workplace organizes its relationships, not only its tasks, functions and hierarchies, but the patterns of relationships and the capacities available to form them.... First I try hard to discipline myself to remain aware of the whole and to resist my well-trained desire to analyse the parts to death. I look now for patterns of movement over time and focus on qualities like rhythm, flow, direction and shape. Second, I know I am wasting time whenever I draw a straight line between two variables in a cause and effect diagram, or position things as polarities, or create elaborate time lines. Third, I no longer argue with anyone about what is real. Fourth, the time I formerly spent on detailed planning and analysis I now use to look at the structures that might facilitate relationships. I have come to expect that something useful occurs if I link up people, units, or tasks even though I cannot determine the precise outcomes. At last I realize more and more that the universe will not co-operate with my desire for determinism.

> *(Wheatley, 1994, pp. 43–4)*

This type of generative metaphor may apply better to companies that are investing in new knowledge than those aiming at a lower cost base for essentially the same product or service.[19]

Implications of organizational metaphors

The machine metaphor places a clear boundary round an organization and directs attention within. The organism metaphor directs attention out to the environment and other organisms competing in that environment. The theatrical metaphor emphasizes the place of performance and enactment in managerial life. Cognitive metaphors focus on the role of learning and knowledge in organizations. The notion of network offers a metaphor that looks at relationships across organizations and through the supply chain. (Note also the metaphor of chain – embedded within that image is the idea that the supplier,

When travellers coming to medieval Europe wanted to describe a rhinoceros they said it was like a dragon and a unicorn. Neither exist but they helped people envision something that does.

(Adapted from Berreby, 1998, p. 49)

---

[19] In 'Complexity and the unconscious', *Creativity, Innovation and Change* Audio 2, Brian Goodwin, Ralph Stacy and Richard Pascale debate the importance of complexity as a new metaphor for management.

manufacturer and customer are indeed interlinked.) Complexity highlights the importance of self-organization and directs our attention back to informal patterns of emergence in a largely unpredictable world.

I must add that the metaphors chosen also tend to reflect the chooser's values. In the discussion above, I have made little of political metaphors. I could have painted a picture of organizations dominated by self-seeking fat cats out to exploit workers, and inadvertently destroying the environment in the process. Handy (1997) in Henry (2001) elaborates on the implications of a less pejorative political metaphor for organizations: the citizen company, where organizations are seen as communities of citizens.

The point is not that any particular metaphor is right, rather that metaphors offer different ways of perceiving organizations. Taking the trouble to view a situation from different angles is likely to lead to greater understanding, and avoid the danger of missing important insights by being limited to a particular perspective. Much like Nasrudin's Sufi story of the blind men and the elephant – where one blind man feels the trunk, another the tail, and another a leg or ear, each coming away with a different impression – so each metaphor alerts us to a different piece of organizational life. The various metaphors do not provide a different way of expressing some central understanding about organizations, but draw attention to different aspects of the organization.

There is a strong relationship between the way we think and imagine and the actions we subsequently perform, and metaphors play a major role in mediating between the two. Images and metaphors are not only interpretative constructs or ways of seeing; they also provide frameworks for action. Their use creates insights that often allow us to act in ways that we may not have thought possible before. The use of different metaphors can lead to different ways of organizing and managing.

> The word organization derives from the Greek 'organon', meaning tool or instrument. It is thus hardly surprising that the concept of the organization is usually loaded with mechanical or instrumental significance. My intention is to break free of this mechanical meaning by symbolizing the close link between ideas and images; we organize as we imaginize; and it is always possible to imaginize in different ways.

> When we think about organization in this manner we are provided with a constant reminder that we are involved in a creative process where new images and ideas can create new actions. In the field of architecture new kinds of building have arisen from major revision in the concepts underlying the building process. For example [as shown in Figure 4.2 overleaf], the assumption that sturdy buildings depend on a satisfactory pattern of stress compression confines the architect to producing traditional structures. The idea that buildings can be held in place through appropriate patterns of tension gives rise to freer-flowing forms held in place by wires and buttresses. I believe that we can create similar revolutions in the way we organize by being aware that we are always engaged in imaginization.

> Rather than just interpreting the way organizations are, I seek to show how we can change the way they are. In recognizing the close links between thought and action in organizational life, we recognize that the way we 'read' organizations influences how we produce them. Images and metaphors are not

just interpretative constructs used in the task of analysis. They are central to the process of imaginization through which people enact or 'write' the character of organizational life.

(Morgan, 1986, pp. 333–4)

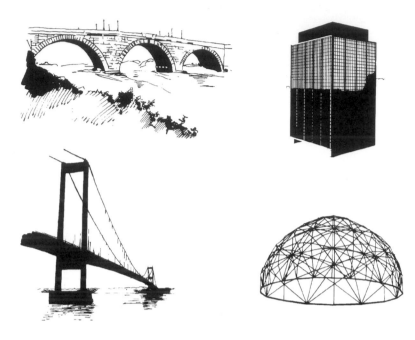

Figure 4.2   Different assumptions and organizing principles generate different designs. Top left and right: examples of architecture based on the principle of compression; bottom left and right: examples of architecture based on the principle of tension

The critical insight here is that objective-setting, strategy and other management processes are embodied within the dominant organizational metaphors. However, when you are inside an organization, deeply embedded in its dominant metaphors, the assumptions built into them can easily seem to be 'facts of life'. As you become aware of the metaphors, you have more freedom to assess the assumptions, which may turn out not to be as necessary as they seemed.

Activity 4.4

(a) What metaphor would you use to characterize your own organization?

(b) Ask several others from your organization to suggest a metaphor for the organization.

(c) Compare the qualities highlighted in each case.

4.2   MANAGEMENT METAPHORS

We also use metaphors to describe the processes of management and the managers and consultants who work in organizations.

Management

Activity 4.5 _____

Write down some metaphors that you think are appropriate to describe the process of management as you experience it. Try to decide on five different metaphors before reading on.

Did you see management in terms of keeping your head down, of getting a fresh view on the situation, of battling through the waves, of keeping people happy or of holding them off? A person who perceives management as a business will probably behave rather differently from someone who sees it as an art. Similarly, people who believe that the skill of managing lies in bringing out the best in others will probably adopt a style at variance with people thinking in terms of fighting their corner.

Metaphors of war and hostility have traditionally been the order of the day with managers trying to get a competitive edge, but recently more collaborative metaphors, usually based around team sports, have become more popular. The language of management has even borrowed from spiritual sources: many organizations now have visions and mission statements, and they seek to inspire and gain commitment from their employees rather than trying to coerce and control them. Some examples follow:

- *Warlike metaphors*: beat the opponent into the ground, be right on target, get an extra shot or two, charge forward, attack on all fronts, break into a new market, demolish an argument, hunt for opportunities.

- *Sporting metaphors*: keep your eye on the ball, watch the competition closely, team up with one another, get them when they are off-balance, he's a good coach.

- *Spiritual metaphors*: develop the vision, explain the mission, inspire staff, believe in the product, partnership through people.

Weick (1998) suggests that *improvisation* offers a good metaphor for management, capturing as it does the idea of reflection in action: 'a mutually satisfactory response that embellishes on known approaches in a way that meshes with whatever else is happening in the moment'. Other metaphors include disentangling, scanning, mapping, adjusting the levers, listening for noises in the woodwork, sensing the climate, seeing where the current issue is taking you, keeping the peace, going with the flow, connecting, learning a new role or drawing out a good performance.

Managers

Activity 4.6

Think of a metaphor which describes your management style.

Managers as coaches.

Common metaphors for the role of manager have changed over time. Traditionally, the manager was likened to a *captain* who is clearly in charge and led from the front, making decisions for others, deciding on the best route himself, and directing proceedings to ensure everyone plays their part. Recently the idea of the manager as *coach* has become commonplace in the West. This presents a very different picture of the manager's tasks, one that places much greater emphasis on facilitating and nurturing staff to bring out the best in them rather than on making decisions for them.

Shotter (1993) uses the metaphor of *author* to describe the manager's task as less a matter of choosing than generating 'a clear and adequate problem formulation from incoherent and disorderly events and doing this in continual conversation with others who are involved ... to be justified in their authoring, a good manager gives a shareable linguistic formulation to already shared feelings, arising out of shared circumstances – that is perhaps best done through the use of metaphor'. This image of managers highlights their role in making sense of and providing meaning for their team.

Weick (1998) disputes the idea that a manager is like the architect who has to plan in advance and then carry out their plan though building, but suggests instead that the manager is more like a *jazz musician* who acts on the hoof, and makes sense of what he or she does in retrospect. This seems to tie in with the short-term time frames Mintzberg and Isenberg suggest managers are faced with.

Mintzberg (1987) has promoted the idea of the manager as *potter*, as this captures the trial-and-error, hands-on way in which a manager works, with experience built on years of knowledge, much of which is felt rather than spoken.

Isenberg (1987) quotes two senior managers who saw themselves as:

> ... a beachcomber, examining the spoils of high tide and deciding whether to pick up the flotsam, leave it or throw it back – perhaps to study it later, when it washes up at a different place and time. ...

> ... a frog on a lily pad waiting for flies to buzz by. He chooses his vantage point carefully so as to attract the fattest and slowest flies.

Both these metaphors draw attention to the need to wait until the time is right before acting in the environment, rather than attempting to impose the manager's will. They describe a process in which the manager collects ideas somewhat haphazardly: a continuous background activity which comes to the fore only when appropriate.

Leaders as conductors.

Thayer (1988) believes that a leader's role is very much bound up with providing a vision people can identify with, 'one who alters the way in which their followers mind the world by giving it a compelling face ... a leader does not tell it as it is but as it might be.'

A modern metaphor for the *leader* is that of conductor, whose role is both to inspire and bring out the best from his or her orchestra. This metaphor entails an element of the showman as well as coach. It also captures the element of performance in management and organizations well.

Consultants too can be described in metaphors. What is your image? Do you see them as the expert doctor who will diagnose what is wrong and prescribe a cure, the detective who will seek out the cause of your troubles, the therapist to comfort, challenge, and support you through hard times or the shaman to perform an exciting, unexpected, magical ritual that might do the trick in some unexplained and perhaps colourful way?

Consultants as shamans.

Of course the way any particular metaphor is interpreted can be affected by the culture of the recipient. Chikudate (1991) reports that the Japanese tend to see supervisors as company friends, whereas Americans tend to view them as authority figures: thus the idea of manager as supervisor may have quite different connotations in the two countries.

The metaphors we use also reveal our values and beliefs.

Activity 4.7

Check through some reports you have written, or take note of what you say over the next week. Do any classes of analogy and metaphor tend to recur?

Listen to one or two senior colleagues and notice what metaphors they are fond of.

It has been suggested that people are more likely to respond to ideas positively if they are phrased in metaphors the recipient is sympathetic to. So, if your metaphors are at odds with those of colleagues, and you want to persuade them of your view, you might consider altering your metaphors.

Activity 4.8

Choose a problem that you are currently working on and try and formulate a metaphor that captures your approach. Then select another metaphor that is as far removed from the original as possible.

Compare the two angles on your issue and identify the different aspects that each highlights and conceals.

Any metaphor emphasizes some aspects of the story at the expense of others. The point of metaphors is their power to alert us to new and useful ways of viewing a situation, highlighting aspects that had previously been taken for granted.

4.3 PARADIGMS

Over time a school of thought can harden into a fixed *world view* or *paradigm*, which contains assumptions that we never even think to question. The process is most obvious in science. For many centuries common sense (and the prevailing theological assumptions) led people to conclude that the sun moved round the earth, the world was flat and time progressed forward at a uniform rate. Thanks to Copernicus and Einstein, we now know that none of these assumptions is true.

Newton transformed the scientific paradigm regarding the movement of heavenly bodies. To do so, he had to step outside the tacit assumptions of the medieval mind that saw the celestial and earthly worlds as different sorts of matter, and realize that the moon, like an apple, had a tendency to fall to earth. His theory transformed the implicit picture of the universe into one of discrete long-lived, essentially dead, entities working like clockwork or a giant machine. These images made it natural for people to accept the idea of a fixed objective world out there. But the Newtonian world view of a mechanistic universe that ran like clockwork, according to principles designed by the creator, was destroyed at the turn of the twentieth century. Einstein and Bohr began to develop a very different picture of the universe, one made up of an infinite number of unstable energies which are intimately interconnected with each other. This view has made it easier to begin to doubt human senses' version of reality, and to accept the existence of the unconscious.

Organizational paradigms

Organizational thinking also goes through fashions, which rest on assumptions that tend not to be questioned until a new paradigm comes along.

Morgan (1991a) suggests that the machine, organism, culture and political metaphors for organizations (cited earlier in this chapter) share functionalist assumptions that dominate much of the thinking about organizations. The *functionalist* paradigm views the world as having an objective reality and a manager's task as understanding the world in order to be in a position to regulate it better. The manager is thus seen as being in the position of an outsider looking on and organizations as being goal-oriented. The mechanical, organic and cybernetic metaphors draw on the natural sciences and view organizations as adaptive systems, whereas the cultural and political metaphors stem from the social sciences and humanities and draw attention to the social dimensions of organizations.

Morgan argues that organizational science, like many other academic disciplines, has been constrained by functionalist assumptions. He offers interpretative and radical perspectives as alternative world views. The *interpretative* paradigm views the world of social relationships as the product of social constructions, and hence presents a more precarious and transitory image than the functional picture. Organizations are seen as symbolic structures in which participants act out the agreed management games. More *radical* paradigms present organizational life as a process of social domination, which is best understood by viewing organizations as part of a wider social order.

Kolb (1984) draws on Pepper (1942) to present four fundamental ways of thinking about the world (mechanistic, realist, organicist and pragmatic) which parallel his four thinking styles (assimilator, converger, diverger and accommodator). He aligns the mechanistic approach with an assimilator style (tendency to theorize), the realist approach with a convergent thinking style (a preference for planning and going by the rules), and organicism with a divergent thinking style (many ideas). He associates his fourth position, contextual pragmatism, with accommodation (spontaneous people who can think and act on their feet).

Other attempts to draw together management thinking into a few fundamental perspectives includes Whittington's (1993) discussion of four approaches to strategy: classical (rational planning), evolutionary (processes in an unpredictable environment), processual pragmatists, and systemic (recognizing the socially embedded nature of knowledge).

Table 4.2 relates these paradigms to some of the metaphors we discussed earlier. Note that most management discourse occurs around the top end of the diagram. Until recently the perspectives at the bottom have been neglected.

Table 4.2	Organizational metaphors and paradigms					
	Metaphor				**Paradigm**	
	School	**Process emphasized**	**Exponent**	**Morgan**	**Pepper**	**Whittington**
Machine	Traditional	Plan	Taylor	Functionalism	Mechanism/realism	Classical
Organism	Evolutionary	Adapt	McGregor		Organicism	Evolutionary
Cognitive	Pragmatic	Learn	Simon		Contextualism	Processual
Network	Systemic	Embedded	Pascale			Systemic
Drama	Interpretative	Enact	Weick	Interpretative		
System	Participatory	Co-create	Stacy			
Prison	Critical	Resistance	Marx	Radical		
Chaos	Postmodern	Play	Burrell			

(Source: Henry, 1998)

Note that realism is used to replace Pepper's original term formism.

Activity 4.9

What metaphor would you offer for management in the twenty-first century?

A paradigm shift in management thinking

The Western tendency to favour abstract thinking has underpinned the mechanistic paradigm that favours rational analysis and neglects intuitive apprehension. The mechanistic world view derives from the hard sciences, especially classical physics. Its 'atomic' roots, following Newtonian physics, lead to reductionist attempts to understand through an analysis of what are perceived as separate parts, with a view to predicting and controlling them better. In such an impersonal approach, the focus is on the task, not the people, and attention is given to hard data with little room for soft data like feelings, impressions and images. For a long time the archetypically mechanistic classical management theory and management science has dominated thinking about organizations. From Taylor on, quantitative methods that offer rational measures were favoured as means of solving management problems, in time and motion studies, forecasts, plans and budgets. Such an approach is entirely in keeping with the machine metaphor. This approach has also been associated with polarized thinking, generally linked back to Cartesian dualism, where the world is split into right and wrong, black and white. Naturally, it sees the world as a place where one has to compete to survive, an idea philosophers say derives from Darwin's theories of evolution.

More recently, behavioural science and psychological understanding have entered the picture (a trend that perhaps began with the Hawthorne studies). The human relations school, systems thinking and contingency theory have become fashionable. Morgan (1991a) associates these with the 'organization as organism' metaphor, not least because of their greater stress on the relationship between organizations and the environment, and the emphasis on the needs of organization and the people within them.

In contrast to the long-range planning methods that became popular as a means of forecasting the future and planning strategic responses in the 1970s and early 1980s, a number of eminent writers of the later 1980s and 1990s (e.g. Drucker, 1985; Peters, 1988; Naisbitt and Aburdene, 1990; Kanter, 1988) began to advocate more creative and innovative management techniques. Such approaches offered the hope of original solutions for complex problems, where decisions are required too quickly and information is too sparse for conventional means of analysis. These more entrepreneurial forms of management require a different kind of thinking, one that enhances powers of perception rather than analysis. Such changes in management practice have moved managers away from a concern with fixed analysis and control to a more fluid perception, emphasizing partnership and co-operation rather than competition. People also focus increasingly on relationships rather than tasks, talk of 'possible scenarios' rather than 'fixed plans' and make sure to consult the focus groups, not just the next quarter's figures.

Stacy (1996) argues that many of the newer perspectives are not really so different. Although we may not be running things according to comprehensive plans, we still seek to realize visions and improve incrementally: in other words, we are still trying to predict and control the future.

Traditionally most businesses were run on principles in line with the mechanistic paradigm. They were structured hierarchically and aimed to compete with (not to partner) others operating in the same field. Large firms adopted a fragmented form of production – the assembly line – and command structures that kept tight control of the cogs (employees) in the production machine.

However, many businesses nowadays do seem to be operating on very different principles, and most employees have seen many changes in how their companies organize themselves. Many firms have decentralized and divisionalized; they form cells and base production round multidisciplinary teams. Hopefully workers are treated less like factory fodder and more like people, as managers strive to nurture the development of their empowered staff. Portfolio careers mean managers have less control over employees.

The boundaries between job descriptions, departments and the company are less distinct as portfolio workers are split across many organizations. Attention has shifted from reductive analysis (like time and motion studies) and predetermined plans (like management by objectives) to holistic analyses, not of the individual worker but of the whole system – the supply chain from supplier to customer. Similarly, after decades of short-term thinking in which managers were driven by the next quarter's figures, they are now enjoined to think longer term. Governments are introducing 'polluter pays' policies to help the environment. Management rhetoric which was hitherto almost entirely rational – plans, objectives, forecasts, quantitative measures – now finds a place for more impressionistic, soft, qualitative data – vision, mission statements, scenarios and focus groups.

These changes in perspective lead some to argue that management is undergoing a *paradigm shift* that is fundamentally changing the way managers see the world, how they think and what they value. Table 4.3 overleaf contrasts the values associated with the old modernist paradigm and the new paradigm respectively. Similar changes can be seen across many disciplines, not just in business, so it can be argued that there is a paradigm shift in Western thought.[20] There are many aspects to this shift, but it could be summed up as moving from a concern with rationally analysing elements in a predictable world to intuitively perceiving relationships in an unpredictable world.

[20] Another way of looking at this is in terms of the shift from modernist to postmodernist thought.

Table 4.3	The paradigm shift: from analysis to perception
Old paradigm	**New paradigm**
Mechanistic	Organistic
Reductionist	Holistic
Elements	Ecology
Rational	Intuitive
Materialistic	Sustainable
Fragmented	Systemic
Control	Commitment
Short term	Long term
Hierarchy	Network
Structures	Relations
Generalized knowledge	Situated knowledge
Explanation	Construction
Competition	Co-operation
Individualism	Interdependence

(Source: Henry, 1997)

4.4 REVIEW

In this chapter we have looked at the various mechanical, biological, social, cognitive and systemic metaphors that underpin management thought. We have introduced the metaphor of complexity as one organizational metaphor which highlights the unpredictable nature of much organizational enterprise; and the role of emergent, bottom-up self-organized, informal, intersubjective action. We have also looked at metaphors for management such as crafting, improvization and authoring which again draw attention to the intersubjective and emergent nature of managers' action.

The changed metaphors now being used to discuss organizations may indicate a paradigm shift in management thinking. This shift changes the emphasis from analysing parts to perceiving relationships, from a concern with individualism to interdependence, and from a focus on competition to recognition of the part that co-operation plays (Harman, 1988).

The traditional management focus on prediction, planning and conscious knowledge is finally beginning to give way to greater concern with possibility, perception and unconscious know-how, a shift that challenges the fundamentals of management.

Further reading

G. Morgan, 'The theory behind the practice', in Henry (2001).

G. Boekstra, 'Metaphor and the evolution of the living organization', in Henry (2001).

G. Morgan, 'Paradigms, metaphors and puzzle-solving in organizations', Chapter 9 in Henry (1991).

G. Morgan, *Images of Organization* (London: Sage, 1986, 2nd edn, 1997).

PART 3
STYLE

This part looks at the impact of personal style on creativity, problem solving, decision making and communication. It goes on to examine the various roles involved in innovation.

5 STYLE

This chapter deals with the issue of cognitive style. Cognitive style refers to our preference for working and behaving in particular ways. Style has a significant effect on the way people set about communicating, solving problems and relating to each other.

There are three obvious ways to determine cognitive style: to *observe* how we set about tasks, to *ask others* how they perceive our style, and to fill in one or more psychological *inventories* that aim to assess our style. Psychological inventories are widely used in organizations to assess differences in the way people are likely to approach tasks and tackle problems.

There are three broad kinds of psychological test and inventory: tests of *ability*, *personality* inventories and *projective* tests. Tests of ability, like IQ or intelligence tests, aim to measure how good or bad a person is at the variable being measured. Personality inventories aim to measure where a person's preferences fall on a range of characteristics. Projective tests, like the Rorschach inkblot test, aim to assess the unique pattern of anxieties, conflicts and concerns held by the individual being tested. Tests of ability are used primarily in educational settings but also in occupational ones; personality tests are used in organizations for personal development, team building and as an aid to selection. Projective tests are commonly used in clinical settings.

There are numerous personality inventories. Ones commonly used include the 16PF, the California Psychological Inventory, Firo-B, MBTI, MMPI, Belbin and Team Management Index.

This chapter introduces several well-known personality inventories and measures of cognitive style, and a team role inventory, and discusses the relationship between inventories.

5.1   PERSONALITY INVENTORIES

In this chapter we are concentrating on personality inventories with implications for cognitive style. We refer to the following inventories:

NEO personality traits

MBTI psychological types

KAI creative style

LSI learning style

Belbin team roles.[21]

---

[21] This is described more fully in the next chapter.

One of the reasons why we have selected these inventories is because they are widely used, have been extensively studied and concern cognitive style. They are also related. (Other measures of style not covered here include a preference for holist or serialist learning, and field independence or dependence, for example.)

Note that the MBTI, KAI, LSI and Belbin inventories are all measures of psychological preference, not skill or ability. Therefore there is no 'good' or 'bad' answer, as each preference has strengths and weaknesses. A good analogy is handedness: some people prefer to use their left hand and others their right hand, but this preference is unrelated to how dextrous any given individual is, though there are occasions when a left-handed player has the advantage and others where the right-handed player has the advantage.

Reliability and validity

Any good inventory needs three key qualities:

*   *validity*, i.e. measuring what it is supposed to measure
*   *reliability*, i.e. people answer similarly over time
*   *freedom from social desirability bias*, i.e. not easy to cheat.

Inventories vary enormously in terms of reliability and validity. Most of the questionnaires you see in popular magazines, for example, are utterly lacking in these qualities. A number of inventories commonly used in business, e.g. Kolb's early Learning Styles Inventory or Belbin's team role inventory, have face validity in that they appear to measure stylistic preferences that are very relevant to business, but a deeper analysis reveals that the questions that are supposed to measure a particular style do not cluster very reliably, making the measure suspect. Of course, it takes a lot of money to develop and test an inventory that is valid, reliable and reasonably immune to the more obvious social desirability biases.

The British Psychological Society rates the NEO, MBTI, KAI and TMI (team role) inventories as follows (Bartram, 1995):

	Validity	Reliability
NEO	Reasonable	Good
MBTI	Reasonable	Reasonable
KAI	Adequate	Excellent
TMI	Adequate	Reasonable

Ratings are excellent, good, reasonable, adequate, poor. In terms of reliability, excellent is r >.85, good >.8, reasonable >.7, adequate .6 and poor <.6.

In considering which inventory should be used for a particular purpose you could consider the following criteria: technical soundness (e.g. reliability, validity), acceptability, administrative convenience and cost.

However, even well-constructed inventories rely on a form of *self-report,* in that it is the person who is being assessed who completes the assessment instrument. To what extent people's self-reports, in inventories or elsewhere, match their behaviour is a more open question. Certainly the match is far from perfect. Despite this shortcoming, most people find the results of inventories illuminating, offering insights into their own and others' behaviour, illustrating how very differently brains work and how best to deal with people of a different type from oneself.

One further word of warning: no inventory is perfect. If, after completing an inventory, you feel the type it suggests you are does not seem appropriate, don't worry. We suggest that you read the descriptions of the types and see which one you think is closest to your style.

Activity 5.1

After completing (but not scoring) a personality inventory, such as the MBTI, look at the range of types it describes. Which do you think matches your personal style most closely? Score the inventory. Does the result agree with your subjective assessment?

If the scored type disagrees with your subjective rating, you might like to ask a few friends or colleagues which type they consider you to be. Note areas in which their appraisal of you agrees with or differs from your self-appraisal.

Only about 80% of people completing the MBTI agree with the type indicated by the score. If your friends and colleagues agree with your self-appraisal, congratulations! – it seems you know yourself well. If they differ, you might wish to consider why this is and whether your self-assessment or public presentation needs a reframe.

5.2 THE 'BIG FIVE'

Until the 1960s there was a tremendous amount of work on personality traits. This then went out of fashion, and in the next twenty years more attention was paid to situational factors – nurture rather than nature. However, longitudinal twin and adoption studies have renewed interest in the idea that a tendency to certain personality traits may have a genetic component. In addition, the large body of work that has analysed common factors in people's responses to numerous inventories and personality tests has led to increasing consensus that the various personality traits can be subsumed under five overarching traits, referred to as the 'big five' (Goldberg, 1993). Table 5.1 summarizes these five traits.

	Trait	
Domain	**Desirable**	**Undesirable**
Extraversion	outgoing, sociable, assertive	introverted, reserved, passive
Agreeableness	kind, trusting, warm	hostile, selfish, cold
Conscientiousness	organized, thorough, tidy	careless, unreliable, sloppy
Emotional stability	calm, even-tempered, imperturbable	moody, temperamental, nervous
Intellect or openness	imaginative, intelligent, creative	shallow, unsophisticated, imperceptive

Table 5.1 Big five personality domains and representative traits

(Source: Hampson, 1999, p. 285)

A feature of these trait descriptions is that they have an undesirable and desirable pole for each dimension (perhaps because, so far, they tend to be thought of as traits rather than style preferences, a point we return to below). The 'big five' flatters those who score to the left-hand side, i.e. the extraverted, agreeable, conscientious, emotionally stable and open style, and appears critical of those who score low, i.e. the introverted, logical, spontaneous, less emotionally stable and adaptive.

Many other personality inventories, including all those discussed elsewhere in this chapter, are based on a quite different premise, i.e. that differences on each dimension of personal style that they measure have both an upside and a downside. (The trait and type measures are correlated so they are referring to the same underlying characteristics and just describing them differently.) Four of the 'big five' dimensions are related to the MBTI constructs which, as we shall see, make a much better job of describing the strengths and weaknesses of having either a low or high preference on each style. (Bayne (1994) in Henry (2001) elaborates on the similarities and differences between the 'big five' and the related MBTI.)

The suggestion is that the 'big five' traits or preferences appear to be *innate*, and based on a genetic tendency. If we are born with a tendency towards certain traits then there will be a limit to the extent to which we can change our natural style, and we are unlikely to change much over the course of a lifetime. Though as we get older we learn *coping* skills that aid us in dealing with skills that are not natural to our style – shy people develop more confidence and learn to speak in public, for example. However, this only works to a degree: for example, certain people (including those low in conscientiousness on 'big five' measures and high on perceiving on the MBTI) may always have more problems with time management and tidiness than the more orderly judging types. Extraverts are always likely to be more at ease with small talk than introverts, and intuitives are likely to continue finding it very hard to attend to details. One solution is to recognize and make allowances for our style differences: for example, when big picture people opt to work with completer finishers who are better with detail than they are. (The ensuing discussion describes the types referred to above.)

NEO Personality Inventory

The 'big five' scheme is relatively new, so measures of these traits are still being developed. They are likely to come into increasing prominence in the years to come.

One fairly sound measure is the NEO-PI-R personality inventory which attempts to measure six facets underlying each of the 'big five' factors. These are shown in Table 5.2.

Table 5.2   NEO Personality Dimensions

Extraversion	Agreeableness	Conscientiousness	Openness	Neuroticism
Warmth	Trust	Competence	Fantasy	Anxiety
Gregariousness	Straightforwardness	Order	Aesthetics	Angry hostility
Assertiveness	Altruism	Dutifulness	Feelings	Depression
Activity	Compliance	Achievement-striving	Actions	Self-consciousness
Excitement seeking	Modesty	Self-discipline	Ideas	Impulsiveness
Positive emotions	Tender-mindedness	Deliberation	Values	Vulnerability

The NEO-FFI is a shorter related inventory, measuring the five underlying dimensions. An indication of the personality type associated with high, medium and low scores on each of the five main dimensions on either measure is given in Table 5.3.

Table 5.3   NEO Personality Characteristics

Dimension	High	Medium	Low
Extraversion	Extraverted, outgoing, active, high-spirited. Mainly prefer to be round people	Moderate activity and enthusiasm. Enjoy others' company and value privacy	Introverted, reserved, serious. Prefer to be alone or with a few close friends
Agreeableness	Compassionate, good-natured, eager to co-operate and avoid conflict	Generally warm, trusting, agreeable, but sometimes stubborn and competitive	Hardheaded, sceptical, proud and competitive. Expresses anger directly
Conscientiousness	Conscientious, well organized. High standards, strives to achieve goals	Dependable, moderately well organized. Clear goals but can set work aside	Easy-going, not very well organized, sometimes careless. Prefers not to make plans
Openness	Open to new experiences. Broad interests and very imaginative	Practical, willing to consider new ways of doing things. Balance between old and new.	Down to earth, practical, traditional, set in ways
Neuroticism	Sensitive, emotional, prone to experience upsetting feelings	Calm, able to deal with stress, sometimes experience guilt, anger or sadness	Secure, hardy and relaxed even under stressful conditions

Source: adapted from NEO Summary, 1991, Psychological Assessment Resources

Further reading

R. Bayne, 'The "big five" versus the Myers Briggs', in Henry (2001).

S. Hampson (1999) 'Personality', *Psychologist*, 12, 6, pp. 284–8; also in Henry (2001).

5.3 MBTI TYPES

The Myers Briggs Type Indicator (MBTI) is the most commonly used occupational inventory. It draws on Jung's theory of personality types, addressing how people set priorities, acquire information, relate to others, and make decisions.[22]

The MBTI claims to measure four bipolar preferences:

extraversion (E) –	introversion (I)	How you relate to others and the world
sensing (S)	– intuition (N)	The way you gather information
thinking (T)	– feeling (F)	The way you make decisions
judging (J)	– perceiving (P)	The way you choose priorities

These in turn combine to describe four temperaments and sixteen personality types. A central feature of the MBTI is mutual respect for and the usefulness of the different types.

Preference

Extraversion (E) refers to a preference for directing attention to the outer world of action, and introversion (I) to directing attention to the inner world of ideas. The sensing/intuition (S–N) dimension concerns where people place their attention. Sensing types prefer to find out about things by working with facts according to tried and tested procedures, and are practical. Intuitives are usually less concerned with detail and like to use their imagination. The thinking/ feeling (T–F) dimension refers to the way people make decisions. Thinkers are

---

[22] Jungian theory talks of the extraversion/introversion, sensing/intuiting and thinking/feeling dimensions. Myers and Briggs, the MBTI orginators, added the perceiving/judging dimension. Unusually for a personality inventory, MBTI type theory predicts that there are a set number of personality types rather than a series of traits which can be scored on a continuum. As a consequence the MBTI was not designed to produce a normal distribution of scores, as would normally be the case.

good analysers who decide logically. Feeling (or Valuing) types pay more attention to values and take account of their own and others' preferences. Judging (J) refers to the type of person who leads life in a planned and organized way and likes control. This contrasts with perceivers (P) who prefer a more spontaneous and flexible approach, which keeps options open and allows for adaptation. Table 5.4 summarizes some of these characteristics. At different times most people use a variety of behaviours associated with the preferences on each of the four bipolar scales, but not usually with equal comfort.

Table 5.4 MBTI preferences	
Extraversion	external, outside, people, do
Introversion	internal, depth, ideas, think
Sensing	realist, practical, step by step
Intuition	possibilities, theoretical, insights, leap around
Thinking	head, logical, reason, firm
Feeling	heart, subjective, compliment, compassionate
Judging	planned, set goals, decisive, organized
Perceiving	spontaneous, gather information, open, flexible

Activity 5.2

What do you think the relationship is between the MBTI factors and the 'big five' traits? Which factors seem related?

Four of the MBTI factors relate to the 'big five' traits: the dimension of extraversion/introversion is common to both schemes; while the MBTI feeling/thinking dimension relates to agreeableness on the 'big five', perceiving/judging to conscientiousness and intuiting/sensing to openness. The MBTI seems to have made a much better job of identifying the positive aspects of introversion – thinking, perceiving and sensing – and the weaknesses of extraversion – feeling, judging and intuiting – than their 'big five' equivalents. Bayne (1994) elaborates on the similarities and differences between the MBTI and the 'big five'.

It is estimated that approximately 55% of the UK population have a preference for extraversion and 45% for introversion. Similarly, approximately 55% have a preference for sensing and 45% for intuition; approximately 50% favour the judging style and 50% the perceiving style. The thinking and feeling preference shows a marked sex difference, with approximately 60% of males having a thinking preference compared to 40% of females and vice versa for a feeling preference (figures given by Oxford Psychologists, 1990).

Work preference

Each type may adopt different styles at work. Extraverts often prefer to communicate verbally as opposed to in writing, a preference that is common in managers. They like to think out loud and take action. Introverts prefer to spend more time alone and to work quietly without interruptions. It seems that perceivers often do things at the last minute and start more things than they finish, whereas judging types usually prepare ahead of time. Different types may also react differently to different situations. The manager with a feeling preference may find it harder to be tough than the manager with a thinking preference, but may be better in face-to-face situations. The employee with a feeling preference may appreciate praise, whereas the employee with a thinking preference may find a 'touchy feely' approach distasteful. Table 5.5 summarizes these tendencies. The bracketed comments indicate possible weaknesses of that style.

Table 5.5	MBTI work preferences
Extraverts	like action, don't mind interruptions, like people around (impatient, act before they think)
Introverts	like quiet, can concentrate, interested in ideas, like to work alone (think before they act, dislike interruptions)
Sensors	like applying what they know, correct facts, practical, details first (prefer continuation of status quo, step-by-step approach)
Intuitives	like new problems, innovative, overview first, work in bursts (possible errors of fact)
Thinkers	decide impersonally, can be tough, do job well, can criticize (insufficient attention to people)
Feelers	use values, tender-minded, prefer harmony, meet people's needs (decisions influenced by own and others' likes and dislikes, avoid telling others unpleasant things)
Judgers	work best following plan, task-oriented, stick to schedule, decisive (may not notice new things that need doing)
Perceivers	adaptable, curious, enjoy flexibility (may postpone unpleasant tasks and decisions, last-minute)

Perhaps the main value of an inventory like this is to remind us of the difference in style between ourselves and others, and to encourage us to take account of this in our dealings with others. Sensors, for example, appreciate facts and prefer a systematic approach and not too much risk. In contrast, intuitives are more interested in looking at a subject from a wider angle. Thinkers like a logical approach, stressing costs and benefits, whereas feeling types prefer a friendly approach that explains the value of an exercise and pays attention to the people involved.

Communication

The type preferences also lead to different styles of communication and this is usually evident in meetings, as shown in Table 5.6. You probably stand a better chance of persuading a colleague if you bear in mind the style of the person you are talking to and adapt your own style accordingly. Because each type concentrates on different aspects of a case, a different form of presentation may be appropriate for each type.

Table 5.6 MBTI communication and meeting preferences

Communication preferences

Extraverts	energetic, quick, focus on people and things, prefer face-to-face communication, like groups (need to moderate expression)
Introverts	think before responding, focus on ideas, prefer written or one-to-one communication (need to be drawn out)
Sensing	like evidence (facts and details) first, like practical and realistic applications
Intuitive	like overview of possibilities and alternatives, want future challenges discussed, roundabout presentations
Thinking	brief, concise, consider consequences, convinced by reason
Feeling	prefer to be friendly, want to know how it will affect people
Judging	task-focused, schedule-oriented, dislike surprises, expect others to follow through, state position early
Perceiving	enjoy surprises, dislike tight deadlines, expect others to adapt, present tentative views

Behaviour in meetings

Extraverts	talk out loud before coming to conclusions
Introverts	express already well thought out conclusions
Sensing	follow the agenda
Intuitives	use the agenda as a starting point
Thinking	seek involvement with tasks
Feeling	seek involvement with people
Judging	focus on the task at hand
Perceiving	focus on the process to be used

(Source: based on information in Hirsch et al., 1994, p. 24)

Each type can irritate the opposing type if people forget that their differing concerns derive from a difference in working style. Where such differences are accommodated, each type usually benefits from working with people with opposing preferences, as each type will attend to areas that the opposing type is inclined to forget. Table 5.7 outlines both characteristics that can lead to conflict and the benefits of working with an opposing type. (Each type is represented by its initial letter, except that N is intuitive.)

Table 5.7 Type conflicts and complementarities

Conflict	Complementarity
S finds N: impractical, difficult to follow	S needs N: to prepare for the future, offer radical ideas
N finds S: materialistic and pessimistic	N needs S: to remind them of facts, be realistic, have patience
T finds F: illogical, over-emotional	T needs F: to be in touch with feelings, persuade and reconcile
F finds T: critical, insensitive	F needs T: to be tough and weigh costs and benefits
E finds I: withdrawn, cool	E needs I: for reflection and depth of understanding
I finds E: superficial, intrusive	I needs E: to make contacts and take action
J finds P: disorganized, irresponsible	J needs P: for adaptability and information gathering
P finds J: rigid, inflexible	P needs J: for organization and for completion

(Source: adapted from Oxford Psychologists' training material, 1990)

Activity 5.3

(a) Think of three colleagues who are, respectively: your superior, your peer, your junior.

(b) In each case estimate whether you think that the person would be classified as E or I, S or N, T or F and P or J.

(c) Do your reactions to these colleagues match those suggested for your type in Table 5.7?

(d) Repeat the exercise for one or more colleagues to whom you find it difficult to relate.

Problem solving

Each type also has a problem-solving preference. The sensor likes to be involved and will look after the details, taking a 'hands-on' approach, whereas the intuitive is more comfortable making connections in the overall picture. It is the thinker who is likely to be concerned with the end product, leaving the feeler to look after the process of getting there. The cautious judge provides order, wanting to regulate proceedings, whereas the perceiver will remain flexible and adaptable. Hirsch (1985) outlined the role each MBTI type inclines to when problem solving:

E – communicates, acts and carries it out.

I – dreams up ideas, reflects in advance and uses concepts.

S – creates order, practises, forms habits and applies experience. Gets things into use.

N – develops theories, gets things designed, uses hunches and intuition. Applies ingenuity.

T – logical, organized, reforming. Creative with impersonal data.

F – stresses values and supplies meaning. Arouses enthusiasm for change. Is creative with personal data.

J – methodological, cautious, plans, seeks closure. Has few inputs.

P – fearless adventurer, seeks more data. Has many inputs.

Type and time

Hurst *et al.* (1991) suggests that there is a link between cognitive preference and time, i.e. that intuitives are oriented to the future, sensors to the present, thinkers to the near future and near past, and feelers to the past. They relate these cognitive preferences and time orientations to Miles and Snow's (1978) strategic archetypes – prospector, analyser, defender and preserver, reactor or reflexor – and add a fifth strategic orientation – renewal (see Table 5.8 below).

Hurst *et al.* assert that different types and strategies are appropriate at different stages of development. For example, the intuitive mode might be useful in the early stages of an innovation. Feeling might then be needed to gather support for shared values. Subsequently, thinkers and sensors would come to the fore, planning and acting on the necessary changes. Since these preferences appear to be relatively stable, no one leader is likely to be adept at all these roles. Hurst *et al.* argue, with Belbin (1988), that a team is best made up of a combination of types. This particularly applies to a creative team working on a novel problem. The implication for leadership is that those best suited to the stage reached come forward at that time and retire when the subsequent stage calls for different skills.

Table 5.8	Relationship between cognitive style, time and strategic orientation	
Dominant cognitive style	**Time orientation**	**Strategic orientation**
Intuitives	Future	Prospecting
Thinkers	Near future and near past	Analysing
Sensors	Present	Reflexing
Feelers	Past	Preserving
Combination of types	Future –> past	Renewing

Hurst *et al.* (1991) argue that 'the innovative and creative processes which allow organizations to enact fundamental change to renew themselves' require new activities 'which lie outside the structure of the managers' current understanding of their existing business'. These activities involve perceptual abilities of envisioning, recognition and framing. Hurst *et al.* argue that intuition and feeling styles are necessary for this type of creative management, and that they have been neglected in traditional management literature. Hurst *et al.* suggest that the founders of organizations are more likely to be intuitive feelers, while sensation and thinking come into their own in more mature organizations.

Temperament

There is no particular merit in any specific preferences or combination of them. Each type has strengths in certain areas. For instance, STs (sensor/thinkers) are usually analytical and good with facts, while NFs (intuitive/feelers) are more at home with people and envisaging possibilities. Rather than conferring particular strengths, the tendency to emphasize and focus on one aspect of life necessarily means that another aspect receives less attention, which in turn leads to certain weaknesses. An NT may react against routine by rebelling in some way. NFs usually hate conflict and may sacrifice their desires to avoid it.

Table 5.9 Temperament	
ST (Sensation–Thinking)	**NT (Intuition–Thinking)**
Facts, order, control, certainty	Patterns and possibilities
Low risk, step by step	High risk
Short term, everyday technical knowledge	Longer range, developing theory
SF (Sensation–Feeling)	**NF (Intuition–Feeling)**
People	Broad themes
Practical use of own instincts	Prefers ambiguity, creating
Short term	Long term

Activity 5.4

Given the information in Table 5.9 on ST, SF, NT and NF orientations, which of these, if any, would you expect to predominate in people working in accountancy, banking, creative writing, sales and scientific research?

Different types predominate in the various occupational groupings. Some two-thirds of accountants are STs compared with nearly half of bank employees. Some four-fifths of those in sales are SFs, two-thirds of creative writers NFs and over three-quarters of research scientists NTs (Briggs Myers and Myers, 1989).

Cognitive bias and MBTI type

Haley and Stumpf (1987) argue that not only have each of the four temperaments, ST, NT, SF and NF, different ways of approaching problems, but that these differences are likely to lead to different cognitive biases for each type. Their hypotheses about type and cognitive bias are summarized in Table 5.10. They point out these biases could affect the type of decision and strategy that a manager adopts, and suggest that this subjective influence is likely to be particularly strong in situations of stress and/or ambiguity.

Table 5.10 Cognitive bias associated with four MBTI cognitive preferences	
STs	**NTs**
Ignore qualitative data	Ignore disconfirming and contradictory information
Ignore new data and procedures	Over-emphasize positive confirming information
Over-rely on standard procedures	Succumb to representativeness bias
SFs	**NFs**
Over-emphasize value-laden and emotional information	Over-emphasize successful outcomes
Enact majority view rather than own view	Incline to over-simplification
Over-emphasize person as against situation in judgement	Jump to conclusion based on inadequate data

Haley and Stumpf offer some preliminary evidence in support of their hypotheses, based on the performance of junior, middle and senior bank managers in a simulation. Four-fifths of the SFs showed an availability bias – over-emphasizing value-laden and emotional information – compared with less than one-fifth of each of the other three types. Nearly three-fifths of the NFs exhibited a vividness bias – over-emphasizing idiosyncratic, memorable information – compared with approximately one-third of STs, one-quarter of NTs and two-fifths of SFs.[23]

These cognitive biases may be exacerbated by the unequal distribution of types in any given occupational grouping. For instance, in a sample of over 1,000 American managers, Campbell and Velsor (1978) found that 46% were ST and 37% were NT. Haley and Stumpf suggest that this fact may partially account for organizational difficulty in adapting to environmental change.

Leadership

Different combinations of the E–I and S–N dimensions lead to different leadership styles, with the Es being more action-oriented, the Is more thoughtful, the Ss more realistic and the Ns more innovative.

Different combinations of S–N, T–F and J–P dimensions suggest a preference for the work roles shown in Table 5.11.

Table 5.11	Work role
SJ	Traditionalist, stabilizer, consolidator
	Loyal, step by step, timely
SP	Trouble-shooter, negotiator, fire-fighter
	Active involvement, handles the unexpected well
NF	Catalyst, spokesperson, energizer
	Interacts with people, personalized learning, offers vision of possibilities
NT	Visionary, architect, builder
	Analytical, impersonal, strategies

Innovation style

In terms of innovation style, Miller (1987–88) distinguishes between modifiers, explorers, visioners and experimenters, using a scheme related to the SN and JP dimensions. Miller calls these dimensions facts and insights, and decision-making and perceiving.

Miller suggests that modifiers (SJ) build on what is known. He uses the development of the Sony Walkman as an illustration. This derived from combining a miniaturized tape-player (which had failed because it lacked a

---

[23] It may be objected that a simulation is not an adequate test of management bias in real-life decisions. Furnham (1995, pp. 66–70) summarizes some of the managerial behaviour that has been shown to correlate with the MBTI, including problem-solving, decision-making, risk-taking, and scholastic aptitude.

recording facility) with a traditional product – headphones. Visionaries (NJ) trust
their instincts. For instance, Steve Jobs's apparently crazy vision of a low-cost
personal computer that was easy to use inspired his team to produce the
Macintosh computer in two years. Experimenters (SP) emphasize information
gathering. Miller cites as an example the information-sharing in Veraldi's
multidisciplinary team, which developed the acclaimed American Ford Taurus.
Explorers (NP) use their instincts as a guide to new avenues. For instance, Art
Fry felt that there must be some use for a failed glue that did not stick very well.
His repeated attempts to find a use eventually generated the billion-dollar
business of Post-it™ pads.

Traditionally, creativity has been associated with the characteristics that Kirton
ascribes to the innovator, captured by the MBTI in the intuitive perceiver, which
Kolb terms the diverger and Miller the explorer. However, both Kirton and
Miller emphasize that there are *many ways of being creative*. Greater
recognition of the part played by the constant improvements of the adaptor and
the modifier may account for the successful incremental creativity seen in Japan
and the Pacific Rim, in contrast with the dramatic efforts of the Western
'inventor hero'.

Miller suggests that people with different cognitive styles may favour different problem-solving techniques. According to Miller, experimenters and modifiers are likely to favour techniques such as attribute listing and force-field analysis, which start with concrete facts, whereas people with a more visionary and exploratory disposition may prefer more intuitive techniques, such as imaging. He further proposes that essentially convergent techniques, which ask a single question and expect a response, may appeal more to those associated with a judging preference, whereas those with a perceiving preference may find techniques that consider many options, and in which one question leads to others, more appealing (Miller, 1988).

Type

The eight MBTI preferences combine to give 16 personality types. For example, introverted, intuitive, feeling, perceiving types (INFPs) are expected to take a

Table 5.12	MBTI types
ISTJ	immediate needs, steady pace (can overlook long-range implications)
ISTP	gets things done in spite of rules, calm during crises, minimal supervision, takes shortcuts, action- and project-oriented (may need to set goals)
ESTP	results-oriented, persuasive, expedient (may overlook others' feelings)
ESTJ	organizes well and follows through, direct, traditional leader, task-oriented (can overlook need for change and niceties)
ISFJ	practical, detailed (needs to remember there are alternative approaches, be more assertive)
ISFP	co-operative, flexible (easily hurt, may need to learn to be more sceptical and assertive)
ESFP	good teamwork, lively (may need to work on time management)
ESFJ	good relationships, hard-working (may need to remember own priorities)
INFJ	other-oriented, wins co-operation, quietly persistent (may need to learn to be more forthright)
INFP	facilitative, works independently, perfectionist, unbureaucratic (needs to learn to say no and be less perfectionist)
ENFP	insightful, enthusiastic (needs to learn time management)
ENFJ	good facilitator, inspires loyalty (may need to attend to detail)
INTJ	driven, decisive (can find it hard to give up impractical ideas)
INTP	designs logical complex systems (may be too abstract, needs to state things more simply)
ENTP	offers conceptual schemes, logical systems (maybe overextended)
ENTJ	good planner, takes charge (may neglect practical and personal)

very personal approach to life and may appear quiet and reserved, but are open-minded and adaptable. They may be burdened by a sense of inadequacy if their accomplishments do not meet their ideals, whereas extraverted, sensing, thinking, judging types (ESTJs) are likely to be naturally decisive and may need to work at listening to other people's viewpoints and developing the art of appreciation. Table 5.12 gives an overview, with the potential weaknesses of each type bracketed. The preferences and types are described in more detail on the MBTI report form. For a fuller account, see Briggs Myers and Myers (1989).

Table 5.13 shows the MBTI results for a population of UK managers. Note the high percentage of thinking, judging types among the UK managers. Japanese and Hong Kong managers do not show this pattern and are more evenly distributed among the 16 types.

Table 5.13	Percentage of MBTI types among UK managers						
ISTJ	22	ISFJ	8	INFJ	2	INTJ	7
ISTP	5	ISFP	2	INFP	4	INTP	2
ESTP	5	ESFP	1	ENFP	3	ENTP	6
ESTJ	18	ESFJ	7	ENFJ	2	ENTJ	8

(Source: based on data collected from 1,000 managers by Lewis at Cranfield University; figures given by Oxford Psychologists, 1990)

Further reading

S. K. Hirsch and J. M. Kummerow (1994) *Introduction to Type in Organizations*, Oxford: Oxford Psychologists Press.

5.4   ADAPTORS AND INNOVATORS

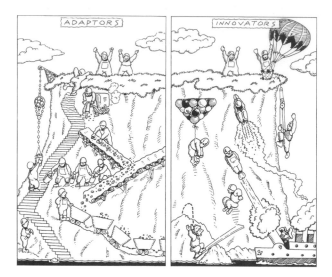

Traditionally, creativity has been presumed to be the prerogative of the gifted few and, in the West at least, it has been associated with new and radically innovative ideas. This led to us thinking of creativity as an ability, but Kirton (1984) has drawn attention to different creative styles, in particular the neglected adaptive approach to creativity that tries to improve on existing ways of doing things. Kirton's Adaption–Innovation Theory and the associated KAI Inventory refer to preferred thinking styles in respect of problem solving, creativity and decision making. Kirton posits that everyone can be located on a continuum from the highly adaptive to the highly innovative. (He developed his theory after observing the different ways in which managers set about change.)

Characteristics

Kirton characterizes adaption as a preference for improving existing practice, i.e. to do things better. He contrasts this with innovation, which, he argues, represents a preference for reframing problems and offering solutions that may challenge accepted practice, i.e. doing things differently. Table 5.14 summarizes some of the behavioural differences between people with a clear preference for adaption or innovation. These differences in approach can affect the way people communicate, tackle problems, and make decisions.

Table 5.14   Adaptors and innovators: style differences

Adaptors	Innovators
Do it better	Do it differently
Work within existing frame	Challenges, reframes
Fewer, more acceptable solutions	Many solutions
Prefer well-established situations	Set new policy, structure
Essential for ongoing functions	Essential in times of change

Three factors appear to make up this adaption-innovation dimension: *SO* for sufficiency versus proliferation of originality (number of *ideas*), *E* for *efficiency* (level of attention to detail) and *R* for *rule and group conformity* style (working with versus challenging the status quo). Kirton reports these three subscales are correlated.[24] As regards sufficiency of originality, more adaptive types will tend to produce a few relevant and manageable ideas while more innovative types are likely to produce many ideas whether they are needed or not, knowing some will be discarded. The efficiency factor refers to more adaptive types' preference to attend to detail, and more innovative types' preference for working in several areas at once, shedding attention to detail in favour of a wider overview. On the role conformity factor, the adaptive end of the continuum suggests a preference for working within existing practices, using rules and working with groups, and the innovation end suggests the non-conformity that is the hallmark of the innovator – bending the rules and challenging the status quo.

Problem solving

Those with a clear adaptive or innovative preference tend to adopt very different problem-solving styles. The more adaptive will probably search thoroughly in a limited area, whereas the more innovative have more permeable search boundaries, scattering effort and gathering ideas from every direction. As a consequence, the more adaptive approach is likely to offer a fuller and deeper search of one or a few ideas, whereas the more innovative will present many, less formulated possibilities. Adaptive ideas are likely to be more readily accepted than innovative ones.

The adaptors' attention to detail means that it is probably they who will ask for clarification – the innovator rarely will – and it is the adaptor who will bother to read instructions or explain detail. The innovator typically does many things at once, and may be difficult to get on with. At heart, innovators are risk-takers who are ready to challenge the system, whereas adaptors prefer to work within it. These preferences may have very tangible effects on decisions taken. There is some evidence to suggest that adaptors and innovators actually perceive the same environment differently: innovators see the organizational climate as more turbulent than adaptors, who see it as more placid.

These differences in style result in adaptors and innovators being perceived differently as shown in Table 5.15. A weakness of the adaptive style may be a tendency to resolve a problem prematurely, whereas weaknesses of the innovative style may be not thinking through the consequences of action and lack of attention to detail.

[24] Kirton treats KAI as if it is a unidimensional construct, but Payne (1987) points out that the correlations between the three subscales are modest. Taylor (1989) has argued on empirical grounds that the SO scale is better split into two – idea generation, and a preference for stability versus change – to give four underlying factors.

Beware generalization
– it takes all types to
make a world.

A hallmark of the
successful person is
supposedly a capacity
to thrive on little sleep.
For example, Margaret
Thatcher was said to
require only four hours'
sleep a night. Einstein,
heavy sleepers may
be pleased to know,
liked to have 10 hours'
sleep a night.

Table 5.15 Perceptions of adaptors and innovators	
Adaptor seen as someone who:	**Innovator seen as someone who:**
Is reliable	Is undisciplined
Uses standard approaches	Challenges assumptions
Improves	Reframes
Acts in a cohesive way	Is abrasive
Is cautious	Takes risks
Is practical	Is idealistic

Relations between opposing types

Table 5.16 lists the strengths that adaptors and innovators attribute to
themselves. An intriguing piece of research by Gryskiewicz suggests that, while
innovators are unaware of their faults, adaptors may not be (Kirton, 1987).

Table 5.16 Strengths adaptors and innovators attribute to their own style	
Adaptors	**Innovators**
Supportive	Full of ideas
Practical	Energetic
Stable	Challenging assumptions
Consistent	Accepting change
Methodical	Intuitive
Co-operative	Unconstrained by past
Sound	Daring
Safe	Risky

(Source: adapted from McHale and Flegg (1986), after Gryskiewicz)

Adaptors often have a poor opinion of innovators, and innovators can view
adaptors as boring, as Kirton (1989) points out:

> Innovators are generally seen by adaptors as being abrasive and insensitive,
> despite the former's denial of these traits. This misunderstanding usually occurs
> because the innovator attacks the adaptor's theories and assumptions, both
> explicitly when he feels that the adaptor needs a push to hurry him in the right
> direction or to get him out of his rut, and implicitly by showing a disregard for
> the rules, conventions, standards of behaviour, etc. What is even more upsetting
> for the adaptor is the fact that the innovator does not even seem to be aware of
> the havoc he is causing. Innovators may also appear abrasive to each other,
> since neither will show much respect for each other's theories, unless of course
> the two points of view happen temporarily to coincide. Adaptors can be viewed
> pejoratively by innovators, suggesting that the more extreme types are far more
> likely to disagree than collaborate. Innovators tend to see adaptors as stuffy and
> unenterprising, wedded to systems, rules and norms which, however useful, are
> too restricting for their (the innovators') liking. Innovators seem to overlook
> how much of the smooth running of all around them depends on good
> adaptiveness, but are acutely aware of the less acceptable face of efficient

bureaucracy. Disregard of convention when in pursuit of their own ideas has the effect of isolating innovators.

Activity 5.5

If a group of adaptors and a group of innovators were set the same problem in a training session, how would you expect the solutions from the two groups to differ?

Groups with different profiles tackling the same task generally produce solutions in keeping with their styles. For example, in a group with several innovators – who are often as intolerant of each other's ideas as they are of those of adaptors – the innovators may argue with each other and fail to complete the task as set; or they may come up with several original solutions. A group of adaptors would probably produce a single conventional solution worked out in more detail than any offered by the innovators.

Communication

Problems can arise when adaptors and innovators try to work together. McHale and Flegg (1985) quote an example in which an innovator in a group of adaptors in a training session made a suggestion which met with 'immediate resistance and hasty rejection, on the grounds that it would take time away from the task as set, and a strong urging that the conventional approach be adopted'. The innovator then withdrew from debate, preferring to listen to the others' opinions. In a later intervention the innovator drew attention to the interesting points that were emerging, once again to be cut short by the others, who wanted to get on with the task. The innovator was left bemused as to why the other group members should consider an arbitrary training exercise as so important, and they in turn were irritated by the innovator's 'irrelevant' interruptions. McHale and Flegg (1986) also cite an example of an innovative R and D manager in danger of being disregarded by her adaptor boss partly because of her tendency to attempt to convey why she was excited about an idea rather than concentrating on the procedural aspects that were of more interest to her boss – for instance, what was to happen, when, who would be involved and what resources would be needed.

Activity 5.6

Think of the team of people with whom you work most closely. Which of them would you classify as adaptors and which as innovators? (Hint: adaptors attend to detail and stick to the task while innovators address wider issues and raise further possibilities.) Do you need to modify the way you present to them to capitalize on your understanding of the implications of their style preference?

Technique preference

Adaptors and innovators may well react differently to creativity techniques. Quality circles may be seen as an essentially adaptive exercise, aimed at creating improvements and generating a consensus, which is unlikely to appeal to innovators. Our experience working with thousands of Open University MBA students and managers on training courses in creative problem solving suggests that adaptors may prefer more structured and conventional techniques, such as matrices, morphological analysis and nominal group technique, whereas innovators may prefer the less conventional techniques, such as those that draw on metaphor. We have anecdotal evidence to suggest that high-scoring innovators may react against the more structured techniques. Vollmer (1990), as reported by Kirton, made a follow-up study on the use of brainstorming several months after introduction of the technique. The study showed that low-scoring innovators were using brainstorming while adaptors were not, but that the highest-scoring innovators were not using the technique – on the grounds that they had always done this kind of thing.

Foxall (1989) presents evidence to suggest that the purchasing behaviour of adaptors and innovators with regard to new products may be different. Adaptors tend to be the first to purchase new improved products, and innovators, the early adopters, tend to lead to the purchase of radically new products.

Level

Kirton emphasizes that creative style is unrelated to the capacity, level or ability for creativity. A person might be a very capable creative adaptor or a not so capable creative adaptor or, similarly, a capable creative innovator or a not so capable creative innovator.[25] Kirton has helped clarify the distinction between style and level of creativity, and has drawn our attention to the neglected area of adaptive creativity. We are all aware of the grand innovations that changed the world, but less aware of the adaptive improvements. The adaptive approach to creativity may tie in with the notion of incremental creativity, in which many small changes build on each other and which may account for a large part of the art of realizing innovation.

It is important to remember your cognitive style only indicates a preference for the way you find it natural to undertake tasks. This is not to say that any given individual will act one way in all environments. With effort, an innovator in an adaptive environment may modify his or her style. However, Kirton suggests that under pressure people tend to revert to their natural style. Furthermore there is some evidence that the openness personality dimension is related to adaption and innovation (see discussion of the 'big five' personality traits). The implication is that you are not likely to change your preferred style much over the years, although you may become more adept at adopting a persona to fit in with an environment that favours a style at odds with your own.

---

[25] The evidence for the view that the ability level of creativity is completely unrelated to style has been contested in some quarters (Isaksen and Puccio (1988) offer a discussion on this point). Bartram *et al.* (1995, pp. 125–126) point out that the median interrelation between the KAI inventory and traditional tests of creativity (which tend to focus round divergent thinking) is .36, whilst granting that these tests may confound creative style and ability.

KAI Inventory

The KAI Inventory is a short inventory designed to assess adaption–innovation preference. (Innovation is normally scored higher than adaption.) Kirton suggests scores are normally distributed around a mean of 95. The UK, European and US managers' average appears to be around 97, but more adaptive scores have been found for African and Indian male (but not female) managers (Kirton, 1987, 1989, 1994). Samples from both Japan and Hong Kong have produced a mean score of 95. Scores tend to be relatively stable over time, as do problem-solving preferences. A score of 90 may be ideal for one problem but too adaptive or innovative for others.

A feature of AI theory is that perceptions are *relative*, and therefore how your score appears depends on the people that you are with. A score of 90 could appear quite innovative to someone scoring 60 and very adaptive to someone scoring 120. Kirton predicts communication difficulties and possible conflict where there is a 20-point difference between individuals.

Relative

Activity 5.7

Different occupational groups tend to score differently on inventories such as KAI.

If you had to rank the following occupations in order of members' average score on the KAI, in which order would you place them?

Bank managers, civil servants, maintenance engineers, marketing managers, MBA students, personnel managers, production managers, R and D managers, and teachers.

Compare your thoughts with the average score for members of each of these occupations given in Table 5.17. The range for each occupation is wide.

Table 5.17 KAI group norms	
Civil servants	80
Maintenance engineers	85
Production managers	90
Bank managers	90
Teachers	95
MBA students	100
R and D managers	102
Marketing managers	105
Personnel managers	105

(Source: adapted from Kirton, personal communication, 1990, 1999; see also Kirton, 1987)

Activity 5.8

Which dimensions of the MBTI and the 'big five', if any, do you think are correlated with the KAI?

After what you have read above, it will probably come as no surprise to you that there is a moderately high correlation between the KAI and the MBTI intuition/sensing (0.4) and perception/judging (0.5) scales, with a positive relationship between innovators on the KAI and intuition and perception on the MBTI. KAI innovators and MBTI intuitives like solving new problems and are impatient with detail, while adaptors and sensors work well with routine and are more realistic. KAI is also related to the 'big five' trait of openness. Correlations between the KAI and the MBTI thinking/feeling scales are negligible (Carne and Kirton, 1982). Some studies show a low correlation between extraversion and the KAI (Gelade, 1999).

Further reading

M.J. Kirton, 'Adaptors and innovators', in Henry (2001).

5.5   LEARNING STYLE

In addition to the KAI and MBTI, many other inventories serve to point out how humans differ in style and approach. For example, you may be familiar with Kolb's or Honey and Mumford's measures of learning style, or with related derivatives.[26,27]

Kolb's (1984) learning style inventory (LSI), outlined in Figure 5.1 below, describes four types: divergers, assimilators, convergers and accommodators. Honey and Mumford's LSQ (1985) refers to reflectors, theorists, pragmatists and activists, Basadur (1990) to generator, conceptualizer, optimizer, and implementer, and Herriman (1996) to rational, experimental, safekeeping and feeling selves.

Table 5.18	Related factors in learning and problem-solving inventories			
MBTI	**IF**	**IN**	**ET**	**ES**
Kolb	Diverger	Assimilator	Converger	Accommodator
LSI[27]	Reflectors	Theorists	Pragmatists	Activists
Basadur	Generator	Conceptualizer	Optimizer	Implementer
Herriman	Feeling	Rational	Safekeeping	Experimental

[26] The fact that a measure is psychometrically questionable does not, of course, negate the theory it relates to. Honey and Mumford (1985) drew on Kolb's theory in producing their English version of the LSI, which has superior psychometric properties to Kolb's original version.

[27] Honey and Mumford's scheme is in fact a slightly transposed version of Kolb's scheme; Kolb's types more properly fit between the Honey and Mumford types, as the LSI is based on the axes on which Kolb based his types. A high score on two axes leads to a Kolb type.

In Kolb's scheme, the *divergers* are imaginative, able to view situations from many perspectives, to sense opportunities, to recognize problems, to generate alternatives and generally to be open to experience. People who are highly divergent are often full of imaginative ideas, but not so good at following through, and may even become paralysed by all the alternatives that are so obvious to them. By contrast, *convergers* are good at practical application, at selecting from alternatives, at making decisions and at evaluating plans. However, their possible weaknesses include directing effort to solving the wrong problem. *Assimilators* are theorists who are brilliant at building models and comparing alternatives, but may produce ivory-tower schemes with no practical application. *Accommodators* are more action-oriented. They can be relied upon to carry out plans, are very adaptable, are willing to take risks and are able to commit themselves to schedules. Their weakness may be a tendency towards tremendous accomplishment in the wrong area.

A deficiency in any of these abilities leads to a corresponding weakness. A low divergent thinking ability may mean difficulty in recognizing problems and opportunities; a low assimilator ability may mean a lack of theoretical underpinning in work and difficulty in learning from mistakes. Those weak in the area of convergence tend to lack focus in their work and may fail to test theories; and those with little of the accommodator in them may fail to complete work on time and not direct work that is done towards goals.

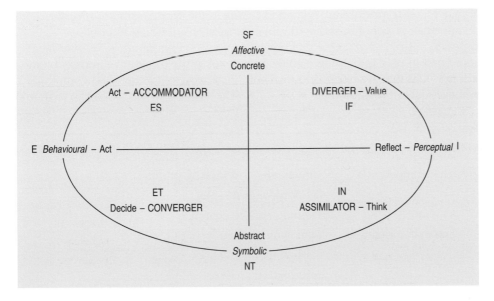

Figure 5.1 Kolb learning styles and competencies compared to the MBTI types

It is said, only partly in jest, that reflective divergers and assimilators think before they act – if they ever act at all; while the active accommodators and convergers act before they think – if they ever think at all!

You will see from Figure 5.1 that Kolb's experiential learning theory suggests that these types can be derived from two dimensions: first, a preference for reflection versus action; and second, a preference for concrete experience versus abstract conceptualization. Combinations of these preferences produce the four types. Thus accommodators favour active experimentation and focus on concrete experience, whereas assimilators are more concerned with abstract conceptualization and reflective observation.

There is overlap between the qualities categorized by the MBTI and LSI. Jung's theory of psychological types, on which the MBTI is based, provided the inspiration for Kolb's typology, hence the MBTI and the LSI are related. Accommodators are closest to extravert sensors, divergers to introvert feelers, convergers to extravert thinkers and assimilators to introvert intuitives.[28]

Activity 5.9

Have you come across any other measures of learning style? Can you relate these styles to the dimensions shown above?

Kolb *et al.* (1991) describe competencies that correspond to these preferences: a *perceptual* competency, which entails being able to see a situation from different perspectives, related to *reflection*; a *symbolic* competency of conceptualization, related to *abstraction*; a *behavioural* competency of taking initiative and responsibility, related to *acting* in the world; and an *affective* competency of being sensitive to others, related to attending to *concrete experience*. Kolb *et al.* argue that education in such competencies should have some part to play in helping managers to develop the integrative and problem-solving skills that are needed to deal with increasing environmental complexity and consequent uncertainty.

Activity 5.10

Kolb *et al.* (1991) list 12 managerial competencies:

Affective competence	Influencing and leading others
	Working with people
	Helping and delegating
Perceptual competence	Managing ambiguity
	Gathering information
	Information analysis

---

[28] Kolb (1984) quotes a study of 220 managers and MBA students as showing a 0.45 correlation between his LSI and the MBTI.

Symbolic competence	Planning
	Quantitative analysis
	Computers and technology
Behavioural competence	Goal setting
	Implementation skills
	Entrepreneurial skills

(a) Rate yourself on a scale from 1 to 5 for each of the 12 competencies.

(b) In which of the four areas – perceptual, symbolic, behavioural, affective – are you strongest and in which weakest?

(c) Where would you like to develop greater competence?

Kolb *et al.* (1991) take the argument one stage further and suggest a hierarchy of competencies corresponding to the increasing complexity of managerial jobs – from operational concerns in the immediate environment over the next few days to strategic concerns in the wider environment over a period of years. They assume that the competencies required at the highest level are integrative and require an adaptive flexibility that entails constant creation.

> In resolving the dialectic conflicts between value and fact, meaning and relevance, integrity is the master virtue ... wisdom the protector of fact and meaning, justice the protector of fact and relevance, courage the protector of relevance and value, and love the protector of value and meaning. These ... virtues ... instruct us to *create*, not adjust. *Wisdom* dictates that we do not blindly follow the implications of knowledge but that we be ... responsible in the use of knowledge. *Courage* tells us to push forward when circumstance signals danger and retreat. *Love* requires that we hold our selfish acts in check until we have viewed the situation from the perspective of the other – the Golden Rule. And *justice* demands fair and equitable treatment for all against the expedience of the special situation.
>
> *(Kolb, 1984, pp. 227–8)*

Given that people with different styles have different approaches to learning, different development needs, and incline to different approaches, you need to take the responsibility for selecting those that will be useful to you.

Further reading

D. Kolb, *Experiential Learning* (Englewood Cliffs, NJ: Prentice-Hall, 1984).

5.6   REVIEW

This chapter has explored style through the medium of personality inventories. Inventories provide one means of highlighting the ways in which different cognitive styles lead to different approaches to creativity, communication, problem solving and decision making, and emphasize the extent to which such differences can affect perception, strategy and behaviour. We have attempted to show that all styles have their strengths and weaknesses. A fuller appreciation of the extent to which these differences guide behaviour generally leads to more tolerance for others with different cognitive habits. Thus we can begin to recognize and understand patterns of behaviour that previously irritated us, as merely representative of styles that are different from our own, and can alter our presentation to take account of the different concerns of others. We may realize the benefit of working with colleagues with the strengths of a style in opposition to our own, as compared to the ease of working with sympathetic colleagues of a similar persuasion.

The inventories and activities also highlight our own strengths and weaknesses. At this point we have a choice. Do we try to make good our deficiencies, or build on our strengths? There are usually limits to the extent to which we can change our natural style, and most of us need to build on our strengths, remember our weaknesses, and adopt the strategy of working with someone who has the skills we do not have. We may even marry them!

Further reading

A. Furnham, *Personality at Work* (London: Routledge, 1992, 1995).

6 ROLES

One consequence of natural differences in cognitive style is that people tend to favour some roles more than others. Though people play many different roles at work, they normally prefer one or two roles that fit their cognitive style. Here we discuss team roles, and the many different roles entailed in bringing an innovative product or service to fruition.

6.1 TEAM ROLES[29]

Belbin's theory of team roles was developed after many years of observation and research into management team skills using personality tests and behaviour analysis[30] (Belbin, 1981). People were observed working in a group or team and the categories of behaviour they used were recorded. An analysis of these results shows that people do not use all the categories equally, and that their behaviour seemed to fall into a limited number of roles.

Belbin found that managers behave in one predominant role, even though they act in other roles as well. Belbin acknowledges that the preferred role is linked to reasoning ability, personality characteristics, personal values, learned behaviours, and the priorities and processes of the manager's job. The roles identified by Belbin are given in Table 6.1 below. They are taken from his revised ideas which identify nine roles, rather than the original eight (Belbin Associates, 1988). The weaknesses of each role are given in parenthesis. (See Table 6.1.)

Successful groups

One of Belbin's most interesting observations concerned successful groups. One might suppose the best team would be composed of the 'best' people, but Belbin noted that groups which consisted solely of striving, ambitious, high-flyers were not successful; they rarely got beyond what Tuckman (1965) called the 'storming' stage of group development. The high-flyer group members spent most of their time trying to establish dominance over each other and get their own ideas accepted rather than working on the solution to the problem for the common good. These groups were usually out-performed by groups of ordinary people who worked as a team and got down to solving the problem.

---

[29] This discussion draws on Beadle (1993).

[30] Rackham and Morgan (1977) developed a form of behaviour analysis which is useful in looking at group processes. They found that it was possible to categorize people's verbal behaviour in groups (i.e. what they said) into one of 13 categories. These categories are: proposing; building; supporting; disagreeing; defending/attacking; blocking/difficulty stating; open behaviour; testing understanding; summarizing; seeking information; giving information; shutting out; bringing in. Most people have a preference for a particular pattern of usage, and each person is different.

Table 6.1	Belbin's team roles
Plant	Creative, imaginative, unorthodox, solves difficult problems (Poor in communication and managing ordinary people)
Resource Investigator	Extravert, enthusiastic and communicative, explores opportunities and develops contacts (Loses interest once the initial enthusiasm has passed)
Co-ordinator	Mature, confident and trusting, a good chairperson, clarifies goals, promotes decision making (Not necessarily the most clever or creative member of the group)
Shaper	Dynamic, outgoing and highly strung, challenges, pressurizes, finds ways round obstacles (Prone to provocation and short-lived bursts of temper)
Monitor-Evaluator	Sober, strategic and discerning, sees all options, judges accurately (Lacks drive and ability to inspire others)
Team Worker	Social, mild, perceptive and accommodating, listens, builds, averts friction (Indecisive in crunch situations)
Implementer	Disciplined, reliable, conservative and efficient, turns ideas into practical action (Somewhat inflexible, slow to respond to new possibilities)
Completer	Painstaking, conscientious and anxious, searches out errors and omissions, delivers on time (Inclined to worry unduly. Reluctant to delegate)
Specialist	Single-minded, self-starting and dedicated, provides knowledge or technical skills which are in short supply (Contributes only on a narrow front)

(Source: Belbin Associates, 1988 and Beadle, 1993)

An effective team will be made up of a range of people who can perform a variety of roles. In the real world managers usually have to build teams from the people they have at their disposal. Managers have to encourage people to take on a variety of roles and become more flexible. Belbin's work enables managers to understand what strengths and weaknesses they and their teams have and take appropriate action to rectify potential problems.

Team role inventories

Belbin's team role inventory was not formally developed, but has caught on because it has face validity and the roles it described are recognized by managers (Belbin, 1993). The DIY origin of the inventory is obvious in the original version which had only 56 items which generated the original eight roles. Best practice suggests that at least 15 items per role or dimension are necessary. Furnham *et al.* (1993) reviewed the Belbin team role inventory: they commended Belbin on his 'substantial' contribution to team role theory but found little evidence for the reliability or the validity of the role preferences obtained, using either the original inventory or the later, extended version.

Belbin (1993) recognizes the limitations of the inventory and states that it was never designed to be a free-standing psychometric test. He also confirms that:

> Line managers are usually wary of using self-reporting measures when reaching crucial decisions about people. That reservation is seldom connected with technical issues of test construction but more with the recognition that people are subject to illusions about the self and are also tempted to distort their responses once they believe that their answers affect job and career prospects.

Margerison and McCann have produced the Team Management Index (TMI), a scheme with many similarities to that of Belbin, but with evidence of its reliability and validity (McCann and Margerison, 1989). The cost of an assessment using this system is correspondingly higher. The Margerison and McCann team role categories are:

Creator Innovator

Explorer Promoter

Assessor Developer

Thruster Organizer

Concluder Producer

Controller Inspector

Upholder Maintainer

Reporter Adviser

Linker.

These roles are related to the MBTI dimensions.

6.2 INNOVATION ROLES

In organizations, creative endeavour is almost invariably a team effort involving a series of different roles. In this section we will look at the characteristics associated with the different roles entailed in bringing creativity and innovation to fruition. (For an Eastern perspective on the relationship between knowledge creation and innovation see Nonaka and Takeuchi in Henry, 2001.)

Stages

Traditionally people have thought of innovation as a staged process, which can be considered as comprising three main stages:

1 identifying an idea – invention

2 developing the idea into something tangible – innovation

3 introducing the product or service to the market – entrepreneurship.

These three stages are each associated with a different role. First the *inventor* – the 'ideas' person who comes up with the new idea, product or service; second the *innovator*, who is gifted with a talent for transforming something from a brilliant idea into a tangible product or practice; and finally the *entrepreneur* who exploits new products or services by successfully bringing them to market. ('Intrapreneurs' fulfil a similar role inside the organization.) See Table 6.2 below.

Of course, this is a simplified picture. In larger companies several other roles seem to be critical to successful innovation – notably the technological or market gatekeeper and idea or product champion; in large companies there may also be a business sponsor. (Maidique, 1990, and Roberts and Fusfield, 1981, identify similar roles in technological innovation.)

Table 6.2 Stages and roles in new product development		
Stage	**Roles**	
Idea	Inventor	Gatekeeper
Product	Innovator	Champion
Market	Entrepreneur	Sponsor

Roles

The technological *gatekeeper* (Belbin's resource investigator) keeps abreast of new developments and acts as an information gatekeeper for the organization.

Often a new product needs a *champion* to sponsor it through the organizational jungle (Schon, 1963). A champion may be needed to draw the project to the attention of a business sponsor with the power and influence to provide the necessary resources. An example is the development of Post-it™ pads. In addition to Spence Silver's discovery of not very sticky glue, and Art Fry's prototype of a machine to apply the glue to one side of the paper, the marketing manager's championship of the project played a critical role in ensuring the product continued to receive support after its first market test failed (see Nayak and Ketteringham, 1991, for a fuller account).

The various innovation roles tend to be more prominent at certain stages and in certain types of research than in others. For example, *scientists* with good ideas are clearly critical in exploratory research in pharmaceutical companies, and big development projects like the tilting train need technological *gatekeepers* who are up to date with information. Products in search of applications like smart cards and not very sticky glue need product *champions* and sponsors. Spin-offs are particularly dependent on good *project leaders* to deliver the project fast to market before someone else beats them to it. See Table 6.3.

Table 6.3 Relationship between type of innovation and innovation role	
Exploratory research	Idea generators
Development engineering	Gatekeepers
Application seeking	Champions
Spin-offs	Project leader

Each of these roles may appeal to rather different personality types. One person may have a range of behaviours that enables them to adopt several roles successfully, but it is more common to prefer, or excel at, one role and one stage of the process. Some exceptional individuals can fulfil more than one role and migrate from role to role as a project moves forward. The inventor and innovator roles, for example, are sometimes found in the same person.

In small companies it is common for the technological brains behind the a new product to act as its entrepreneur and become MD of the company based round it. As the company grows, such owner-managers typically find it difficult to begin to relinquish control and to learn to delegate. Those with a technical orientation often find it difficult to forgo their technical involvement, and it is rare to find an inventor who possesses sufficient management skills to run a large company successfully. However, there are exceptions. Dyson (the 'Dual Cyclone' bagless vacuum cleaner inventor and entrepreneur) is an example of someone who has made the transition; so too is Bill Gates, chairman of Microsoft.

Activity 6.1

Think of the introduction of a new product or service that you have been associated with (or, failing that, know something about). Can you identify people who played the parts of inventor or ideas person, innovator, entrepreneur, champion or gatekeeper there, or among those you have worked with or come across in your working life?

What characteristics do you notice in each of these people? Compare the qualities you identify with those given below as we look at each of these roles in turn.

Technological obsolescence

'Maybe you can do good technological work for 10 years, if you work hard at it, but after that the younger guys are better prepared. It's a question of technological obsolescence.'

(R. Noyce, co-inventor of the integrated circuit and chairman of Intel, quoted in Maidique, 1988, p. 575)

One role or many?

Inventor

Curiosity
Independence
Risk-taking

The word 'inventor' may conjure up a picture of an eccentric genius working in an attic: just the kind of person who is unresponsive to rules and timetables and the bane of a manager's life. Creative research scientists are generally characterized as curious, risk-taking, independent thinkers ruled by intrinsic rather than extrinsic motivation. For example, Shapiro's (1966) review of the characteristics of creative scientists lists among key traits: curiosity, dedication to work, lack of inhibition, intuition, introversion, sensitivity, radicalism and showing initiative. Amabile and Gryskiewicz's (1988) industrial research scientists singled out the following personality characteristics as favourable to creativity: persistence, curiosity and energy, self-motivation, problem-solving abilities and risk orientation. Characteristics found unfavourable to creativity were lack of motivation, lack of experience, inflexibility and requiring external motivation.

Edison

An inventors or ideas person need not be concerned with new products or technological innovation. They could be a copywriter in an advertising agency or a social inventor working in the community, as much as a scientist in a research and development department.

Idea generators in organizations are generally motivated intrinsically, i.e. they work for personal job satisfaction more than financial gain. Thus appropriate company rewards for these people include the opportunity to publish and gain recognition from peers through attendance at conferences and symposia. Zeneca argue that financial rewards to research scientists are best given to individuals for their personal contributions, not shared among a team.

Innovator

Freedom
Flexibility
Initiative

The term 'innovator' is used in several ways. One refers to people who like to turn ideas into practical possibilities, and have the technical ability to do this. The term is also used in a more general way to cover entrepreneurship as well. We will discuss the narrower sense of the term, before considering 'entrepreneur' as a separate role.

Activity 6.2 _____

Think of five creative ideas that you or someone else at work have raised, and position them on the matrix in Figure 6.1. Rate each idea on a three-point scale, high, medium or low, first for attractiveness and then for feasibility. Your feasibility criteria might include commercial, technical, marketing and resource implications.

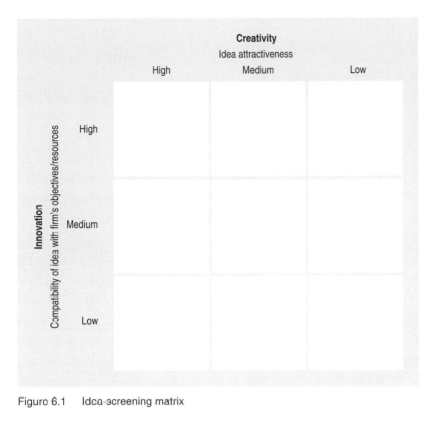

Figure 6.1   Idea-screening matrix

The best ideas score high on creative appeal and innovative feasibility.

Successful innovation seems to require a good measure of freedom and flexibility so that people can use their initiative. In addition, innovators like to see their ideas realized, so their attention is focused on the processes involved in achieving this. McPherson (1967) offers a description of creative engineers which portrays them as adopting conformist clothing to keep society at bay and ensure that management does not bother them too much: 'childlike and uninhibited in seeking ideas for testing, rigorous and scientific at other times. They have the guts to handle obstacles put in their way. They find autonomy and privacy for themselves and use it. They have their own way of communicating and getting information.' Art Fry, the 3M chemist and amateur mechanic, is an example. The company said it was not possible to build a machine to coat paper with Post-it™ glue, but Art disagreed. After working at home on the project for two years, he brought back a working prototype that led to the introduction of Post-its™.

Generally the kind of people who turn out to be innovators often work outside the system; they are mavericks who seem to value independence more than the respect of their peers. They can be quite resistant to pressures to conform. Innovators would appear to be part visionary and part autocrat, driven by single-minded obsessions. Their convictions give them persistence and stamina, but not necessarily the right kinds of skill for conventional management.

Innovations depend upon commercial or social success and wide diffusion. Davis (1991) argues that what unites the dozens of examples of innovators that he cites is their great enthusiasm for new challenges, their refusal to be put off and put down. Honda is a case in point.

Innovator/ entrepreneur partnerships

Several prominent innovators seem to have done particularly well as part of a long-term *business partnership* comprising an entrepreneurial business manager and technical inventor/innovator: for example, Wozniak and Jobs at Apple, Honda and his business partner Fujisawa, and Anita Roddick and her husband. One wonders if the English innovator Clive Sinclair might have fared better had he had a similar long-term partnership with someone attending to the business side of things.

Entrepreneur

Achievement orientation

Risk-taking

Opportunism

The entrepreneur is the person who takes the steps necessary to turn an innovative product into a marketable commodity. Richard Branson and Alan Sugar are classic entrepreneurs. Most entrepreneurs are achievement-oriented, and extrinsically motivated. Some identify strongly with particular business values, while others are much less particular about what they sell provided it offers the promise of high returns. Studies suggest that the entrepreneur's qualities include persistence, an ability to take risks and an opportunistic mentality. The entrepreneur has a strategic orientation and is proactive. Collins *et al.* (1964) suggest that the entrepreneurial personality is unwilling to submit to authority and needs to escape from it. (Kets de Vries (1977) has suggested that entrepreneurship may result from a home background where both parents were rejecting but one was controlling and the other not, leaving the individual self-sufficient but not well socialized, and hence unhappy working in large organizations and happier running his or her own business.)

Studies of entrepreneurial start-ups show that many small business owners value their independence so much that they are uninterested in growing into a larger firm for fear of losing their independence through the additional responsibilities of managing extra staff (Gray, 1997; Westhead, 1994). Colour House Graphics is a case in point (see Box 6.1).

BOX 6.1   COLOUR HOUSE GRAPHICS

This card and print business is run by the managing director and his wife. The business has grown from nothing in 1990 to a turnover of half a million pounds sterling in 1999, by working in partnership with independent sales agents. By 1998 their home was swamped with ever increasing numbers of boxes of cards and prints and they reluctantly outsourced card and print despatching. By 1999 the company had gained substantial orders with major sellers such as John Lewis in the UK and Pier 1 Imports in the US. Recently a presence at major trade fairs for two years has led to additional distributors in Europe, the Middle East, Asia and the Americas.

This was an obvious point at which to appoint an assistant to help with administration and invoicing, or a manager to oversee the day-to-day running of the business, so as to leave the husband more time to commission new work and open new markets. However, after much thought the couple decided against expanding further than they could manage at home.

The fact that many small business owners have no desire to expand beyond a certain point has implications for government policy. Several commentators have suggested that government support for new businesses might be better aimed at established small businesses (and the small proportion of small business entrepreneurs who desire growth beyond the start-up phase) rather than directed so much towards the initial start-up phase (Storey *et al.*, 1987).

Champion

Management literature is full of tales of excellent ideas that did not get taken up or inventors who had to struggle under obscurity for years before being recognized. At best the route from idea to innovation seems to be a struggle. In organizations good ideas often need champions to defend them against an apparently immovable status quo. Even in a company like 3M that is renowned for management support of creativity and innovation, it took Spence Silver, the inventor of the not very sticky glue in the ubiquitous Post-it® pads, years to find champion Geoff Nicolson who would back his development. Without this backing Art Fry might never have thought of applying the glue to little pads of paper for use as markers (Henry and Walker, 1991). Grossi (1990) suggests that champions and sponsors need three qualities: bravery, because going against the tide is necessarily risky; vision, so that the idea can be 'introduced coherently within the company's principles and strategies'; and realism, to counteract any tendency to wishful thinking. Schon (1963) suggests that champions primarily work through informal rather than formal channels.

Bravery
Vision
Realism

Activity 6.3

Think of an idea, practice or product that you might wish to introduce in your workplace. Who could you ask to support or champion this scheme? How might you set about enlisting this support?

Post-it® champions

Rewards

The individuals who occupy the different innovation roles can have different motivations and therefore need different sorts of resource and forms of recognition. Their managers might be well advised to consider different sorts of performance measures and rewards for these different roles, as Table 6.4 illustrates.

Table 6.4 Contribution of different innovation roles and appropriate organizational response

Role	Contribution	Reward
Idea generator	Quality ideas	Publishing opportunities Recognition from peers through conference presentations
Gatekeeper	Technical and market knowledge	Acknowledge role Increase autonomy Allow travel/journal budget
Innovator	Working prototype	Team rewards
Champion	Ideas carried through	Resources for project
Entrepreneur	Make new things happen	Make funds available High financial reward
Project leader	Meets project deadlines	Recognition Increase status

6.3   REVIEW

This chapter has looked at team and innovation roles and the parts played by plants, shapers, resource investigators, completer finishers, inspired inventors, maverick innovators, boundary-crossing entrepreneurs and committed champions. We have seen how these different roles may appeal to individuals with different styles and motivations, differences that successful teams can build on to advantage and managers need to allow for.

Further reading

M. Belbin, *Team Roles at Work* (Oxford: Butterworth-Heinemann, 1993).

J. Tidd, J. Bessant and K. Parvitt, *Managing Innovation* (London: John Wiley, 1997).

J. Henry and D. Mayle, *Managing Innovation and Change* (London: Sage, 2001).

PART 4
VALUES

This part looks at cultural and historical values and their impact on management, organization and development; including management style, how particular industrial sectors come to dominate in particular nations, and the way we set about learning and development.

7 CULTURE

Management is increasingly a global activity and one that often brings us into contact with people with different values and styles to our own. National stereotypes point to the rule-bound German, the uptight English and laissez-faire Brazilian. Studies of values in various countries show some fundamentally different approaches to life which underpin very different management practices.[31] This chapter looks at the effect of national values on management practice and expectation, and the way industry develops in particular cultures. It also examines the role of social capital.

7.1 NATIONAL VALUES[32]

National cultures are based on long-established shared values. One of the best-known management studies of differences in national values is Hofstede's (1984, 1991). He studied the effects of national culture on attitudes to management. Hofstede surveyed thousands of IBM employees from over 50 countries and, after analysis, concluded the work-related value differences he found were underpinned by four dimensions:

Power-distance – the extent to which inequality in decision making is seen as an irreducible fact of life, relating to closeness versus distance between subordinates and superiors

Uncertainty avoidance – the degree to which ambiguity is tolerated and formal rules needed, which relates to attitudes to risk

Individualism/collectivism – the degree to which people are concerned for themselves as individuals as opposed to the priorities and rules of the group to which they belong

Masculinity/femininity – the extent of emphasis on work goals and assertiveness as opposed to concern with personal goals (such as a friendly atmosphere) and nurturing.

Hofstede's work-related value differences

He rated each country as either high or low on each of these dimensions.

Activity 7.1

Taking Hofstede's four variables, how would you rate yourself, in relation to what you know about managers of other nationalities? Rate yourself as high/medium/low on each one.

---

[31] In this chapter 'culture' refers to national and regional differences in cultural values.

[32] This chapter includes material previously jointly authored by G. Jones and J. Henry in *Management and Culture* (Open University Press, 1998).

- Power–distance

  low   close, more acceptance of local discretion

  high   distant, more paternalistic and autocratic

- Uncertainty avoidance

  low   risk-takers, less need for rules

  high   risk-avoiders, more anxious about the future

- Individualism

  low   collectivist, concerned with group

  high   individualistic, concerned with self and own goals

- Masculinity

  high   assertiveness, task orientation

  low   nurturing

Compare your results with the discussion below.

Groupings of cultures

Hofstede went on to group together countries with similar ratings on the four variables, and produced the seven culture groupings shown in Table 7.1.

Culture clusters

		Power–distance	Uncertainty avoidance	Individualism	Masculinity	
I	More developed Latin	high	high	high	medium	Argentina, Belgium, Brazil, France, Spain
II	Less developed Latin	high	high	low	a range	Chile, Colombia, Mexico, Peru, Portugal, Venezuela, Yugoslavia
III	More developed Asian	medium	high	medium	high	Japan
IV	Less developed Asian	high	low	low	medium	Hong Kong, India, Philippines, Singapore, Taiwan, Thailand
V	Near-Eastern	high	high	low	medium	Greece, Iran, Turkey
VI	Germanic	low	high	medium	high	Austria, Germany, Israel, Italy, Switzerland, South Africa
VII	Anglo	low	low/medium	high	high	Australia, Canada, Ireland, New Zealand, United Kingdom, USA
VIII	Nordic	low	low/medium	medium	low	Denmark, Finland, Netherlands, Norway, Sweden

Table 7.1   Hofstede's country clusters and their characteristics

Note: The ratings on the individualism/collectivism and masculinity/femininity dimensions are based on the individualism and masculinity poles, e.g. low individualism = high collectivism. The table is based on Hofstede's original survey.

By and large these groupings bring together nations with geographical, historical and linguistic links (with the exception of Italy[33] and Yugoslavia). For example, Protestant cultures seem to have lower power-distance and Asian and Latin countries have high power-distance (though it is the less culturally homogeneous Latin, Germanic and Near-Eastern countries that show high uncertainty avoidance). Japan has relatively high anxiety, highest 'masculinity' and medium individualism/collectivism and power-distance.

Managerial characteristics

Hofstede's classification excluded developing countries, Eastern Europe and Arab nations. Hickson and Pugh (1995) include these in their seven-fold classification of groups of managerial characteristics based on national cultures.

Northern Europeans, e.g. Germany, Sweden, Finland, Switzerland (plus Israel)

Anglos, e.g. Britain, the United States, Canada, Australia, New Zealand

Latins, e.g. France, Italy, Portugal, Brazil, Argentina, Mexico, Peru

Asians, e.g. Japan, China, Hong Kong, Taiwan, Indonesia

Developing Countries, e.g. India, Africa, South-East Asia

Arabs, e.g. Saudi Arabia, Egypt, Bahrain, Kuwait

East-Central Europeans, e.g. Russia, Poland, Ukraine, Latvia, Bulgaria.

(Source: Hickson and Pugh, 1995, pp. 20–46)

Broadly speaking, the three groupings containing *European* national cultures are *lower on the power-distance* variable than the rest. This means generally that there is a higher expectation in those countries that individual and *local discretion* is favoured over more autocratic and paternalist patterns of power – except for France, which is in the unique position of having higher power-distance and higher individualism.

Latins and *Asians, Arabs* and those in the *Developing Countries* group are postulated to be more *collectivist* than the *individualist Anglos* and *Northern Europeans*. However, *Northern Europeans* except Germany are said to show high *femininity* (emphasising nurturing rather than assertiveness). Latin countries, led by Greece, are said to show higher *uncertainty avoidance* (meaning a higher anxiety about the future, or perhaps less optimism that anything can be done about it) compared to Anglos and Northern Europeans.

Work by other researchers (e.g. Hampden-Turner, 1993) has identified further factors on which national cultures differ, including attitudes towards managing authority, managing relationships, managing oneself, managing uncertainty and managing time (Hickson and Pugh, 1995). For example Westernized cultures show more time-consciousness than the rest, but Americans are said to value time and to look to the future more.

---

[33] The Italian respondents were from Northern Italy, e.g. Milan. People's expectation and stereotype of Italian values are perhaps more associated with the culture of Southern Italy.

Asian collectivity: Mitsubishi workers

Anglo individualism

Chinese and UK cultures compared

Hofstede's work was undertaken by a Westerner. A group of Chinese researchers used Chinese informants' descriptions of values that were important to them to generate a questionnaire subsequently given to students in 23 countries (Chinese Culture Connection, 1987). Interestingly, this survey also found four dimensions. Three of these parallel Hofstede's: integration, human-heartedness and moral discipline, which align with Hofstede's collectivism, femininity and high power-distance. But their important fourth dimension was different: they termed it Confucian work dynamism. It implies a forward-looking persistence, thrift, stable relationships and shame in disturbing or failing to observe order. Hofstede argued that those high on this value take a long-term perspective and those low on it focus more on the present and past. Interestingly, Confucian work dynamism rather than individualism correlated best with economic growth in the last quarter of the twentieth century.

The Chinese researchers did not identify Hofstede's fourth dimension, uncertainty avoidance. Perhaps both this and Confucian work dynamism are less universally accessible values than the other three.[34]

Fron Trompenaars, a Dutch consultant, has also investigated differences in cultural values. He administered research questionnaires to over 15,000 managers from 28 countries (Trompenaars, 1993). On the basis of these studies he proposed five dimensions, dealing with sense of social obligation, personal and group orientation, attitudes to relationships and to power and status.

The UK managers in the sample seem to exhibit a high sense of social obligation coupled with individualism and a neutral and specific attitude to relationships. This could be compatible with an emphasis on personal achievement rather than, say, family background in organizations. In contrast, data for China appears to place more emphasis on a sense of obligation, but more affective and diffuse relationships. An emphasis on family ties would

Confucian work dynamism

[34] Schwartz and Bilsky's study of values (1990) also found dimensions which can be related to individualism/collectivism, power-distance and masculinity and femininity.

accord with this and with a high level of ascription, meaning seeing the world as more powerful than individuals. Table 7.2 shows some of the contrasts found between the UK and Chinese managers.

Table 7.2 Cultural contrasts between UK and Chinese styles of management	
UK management	**Chinese management**
Legal-rational – terms specified	Relational-mutual – room for change
Unambiguous communication	Ambiguous communication
Individuality, self-interest	Communitarianism, social concern
Separate mental categories	Fused mental categories
Rights and entitlements	Obligations
Private gain and personal fulfilment	Group learning and national development

(Source: adapted from Hampden-Turner, 1994, p. 85)

In Hong Kong and China family-owned firms with a hands-on management style present a contrast with the Western emphasis on professional management and planning (though more convergence is seen in large multinationals).

Entrepreneurial Chinese family businesses build networked organizations typical of overseas Chinese companies (Weidenbaum, 1998). Rather than establishing a large single corporation of the type we might find in the US or Japan, entrepreneurs in Taiwan and Hong Kong, for example, have established large empires of privately owned medium-size companies interrelated through complicated networks, initially established through family clans. Networking through kin-based clans has provided an important route for business development in Chinese cultures. The Open University Business School *Management in Chinese Cultures* video (Henry, 1999c) illustrates this way of doing business.[35]

---

[35] 'Management in Chinese cultures', *Creativity, Innovation and Change* Video 4, and the accompanying Media Book notes elaborate. See also M. Weidenbaum, 'The Chinese family business', *California Management Review* (1996).

7.2 IMPLICATIONS FOR MANAGEMENT

Cultural differences: training Russian tax inspectors in Moscow

Organizational practice

Cultural values have a number of implications for organizations. For example, in high *power-distance* cultures (such as India or the Philippines) inequality is accepted, trust may come less easily, and employees expect managers to make decisions (and may be afraid to express their own views). In low power-distance cultures, such as Austria or Israel, employees express views and expect to be consulted.

France has high power-distance relative to Germany. French organizations tend to be more bureaucratic and to trust only their senior staff to define orders and procedures. In contrast German organizations rely more on the professional expertise of their better trained junior employees. Pay differentials also tend to be greater in France. These differences are reflected in the different education systems in the two countries. Top managers in France are quite likely to come from the elite alumni of the *grandes écoles*, whereas German managers are often promoted from within the company.

Contrasting values in France and Germany

In countries that prefer to *avoid uncertainty* (such as Portugal) employees tend to be more rule-abiding, whereas in those with weak uncertainty avoidance (such as Denmark) people are easier-going and prepared to change the rules. In *individualist* cultures the emphasis is on personal initiative and taking care of yourself and your immediate family. Collectivist cultures lay greater stress on belonging to a group, and at work people value group decisions. They have a tighter social (usually family-based) network whose members are loyal to each other.

Hofstede's findings suggest that management practices are unlikely to converge, since cultural differences lead to different understandings about the nature of organizations and the best approaches to problem-solving.

One implication is that workers in the less developed *Asian* countries (with high power-distance and low uncertainty avoidance) find it natural to turn to a leader or father-figure to sort out problems, and implicitly subscribe to the metaphor of the organization as *family*. The *Germanic* group (with low power-distance and high uncertainty avoidance) incline to using rules and procedures to sort problems, in keeping with the metaphor of the organization as a *well-oiled machine*. The *Anglo* group (low power-distance, low uncertainty avoidance) probably look to communication to resolve difficulties, in line with the organization as a *village market* metaphor. *Latin* and *Near-Eastern* cultures (with high power-distance and high uncertainty avoidance) are more likely to have prescribed work processes and subscribe to the metaphor of an organization as a *pyramid*. Table 7.3 summarizes these differences.

Table 7.3	Culture, problem-solving style and organizational metaphor	
Culture	**Problem resolution**	**Organizational metaphor**
Asian	Senior staff	Family
Germanic	Rules and procedures	Well-oiled machine
Anglo	Communication	Village market
Latin	Prescribed processes	Pyramid

Moreover, the different meanings and understandings that are brought to a workplace may result in inappropriate managerial behaviour. Box 7.1 offers a couple of examples.

BOX 7.1   CULTURAL ROOTS OF MANAGERIAL DIFFERENCES

A considerate supervisor

Smith and Bond (1993) surveyed leadership behaviours in electronic assembly plants in the USA, Hong Kong, Japan and the UK. Supervisors who were considerate towards members of the work team were positively evaluated. The focus of the study, however, was on what the supervisor has to do to be perceived as considerate. Workers in the plant were asked to indicate how often their supervisors performed a variety of different behaviours. It was found that 'considerate' supervisors have to do rather different things in each country in order to earn that label. For example, one question asked what the supervisor might do if a member of the work team is experiencing personal difficulties. Workers in Japan and Hong Kong responded that to discuss the matter with other members of the work team in the person's absence would be a considerate behaviour. In contrast, workers in the USA and the UK evaluated such public discussion as inconsiderate. The study illustrates how a specific action may have quite different meanings attributed to it, depending on the cultural context within which it is performed. In Japan and Hong Kong greater value is attached to indirect communication as a form of tactfulness, whereas in the UK and USA higher value is given to directness.

Polite criticism

Sam Heltman, head of human resources for Toyota Motor Manufacturing in Kentucky (USA), explained how American managers initially misinterpreted the behaviour of the Japanese managers they worked with:

'Initially some people thought that the Japanese managers were picking apart their proposals and even perhaps being overly critical. But what we didn't realise at the time was that if you go to Japanese managers and ask them their opinion about a proposal you've given them, if they don't give you something, they're going to feel that they haven't done what you've asked of them. So even if they have to struggle to think of something, they'll come up with a suggestion.

As a manager, I was more accustomed that if someone brought me a recommendation and if I was 95% OK with it, I bought it just to make them feel good. It's just the opposite for them. If they didn't say something, they would think that you would feel that it wasn't important to them.'

(Source: quoted in Hoecklin, 1995, p. 3 and p. 7 from Jones, 1998)

Attitudes to work

As one might expect, attitudes to work of Japanese and American managers can be very different, as the cartoon overleaf illustrates.

Even within Europe attitudes differ. Table 7.4 shows differences in British and Italian ICI staffs' attitudes to work, differences that are reminiscent of Kirton's adaptors and innovators. In this case both sides came together in workshops, designed to work on the positive images each side had, with a view to integrating their strengths. One year later both groups believed they had made real gains.

Differing attitudes to work

BOX 7.2 THE COMMUNITARIAN HERO

The Communitarian Hero

A heated argument between Kudo, the communitarian hero, and the villainous individualist, Tsugawa, exponent of American ideals. Tsugawa wants to ditch the subcontractors to those Japanese auto producers who must now relocate abroad. Kudo fights back with the organic images typical of Japanese communitarian attitudes. The politicians advise the community to build an amusement park, but Kudo, assisted by a wise elder with contacts at the highest level, opts for a new high-tech centre. The subcontractors will all be re-employed at enhanced levels of knowledge-intensity and a more complex collectivity will be formed.

Cartoons taken from *Japan Inc: Introduction to Japanese Economics.*

Table 7.4 Differences between British and Italian attitudes at ICI	
UK	**Italy**
Doing things the right way	Doing the right things
Working to protocols and standards	Encouraging flexibility
Establishing procedures to get things done	Building relationships to get things done
Providing essential information	Providing context
Diplomacy	Directness
British perception of Italians	**Italian perception of British**
Excessively flexible	Obsessed with rules and procedures
Entrepreneurs	Inflexible
Creative	Formal
Rely on people not structures	Avoid confrontation
Emotional	Inhibited/hide emotions
Undisciplined	Disciplined
Never meet deadlines	Good planners
Not very time-conscious	Suspicious
Averse to planning	Slow and ponderous

(Source: Hoecklin, 1995, p. 19 in Jones, 1998)

Not all cultural clashes of values have such a happy resolution. The following quote is from an American (French-speaking) manager working in a French company.

French and American attitudes in conflict

> Even experienced Euromanagers, the hardened veterans of the international job circuit, are pulled up short by some of the contentious conduct in the workplace in France. Trust does not come easily to the French. Relations with most colleagues are suspicious, wary, watchful. Only among family and long-standing friendships, preferably dating back to childhood, are these hesitations overcome. [...]
>
> From the outside, it takes a while to realise that the very concept of management in many French companies is different. The British or American manager sees his [sic] role as a co-ordinator of resources and activities. He judges it useless or even harmful to be more competent than his subordinates in their own activities. Each member of the team is invited to contribute a separate skill or expertise, making the combination more than the sum of its parts.
>
> The French executive, in contrast, considers it important to have precise answers to any questions that subordinates might have about the work they're doing. Implicitly, he [sic] bases his authority more on a superior degree of knowledge and competence than on his talent for co-ordination and management, says one academic study. The French manager does everything better, most of all giving sharply defined orders. The result, in a word, is centralisation in France and decentralisation in the USA. The scene is thus set for basic misapprehensions.

The American manager asked his French colleagues to utilize their network of contacts to deliver a PR attack against a competitor and was surprised that they failed to collaborate with each other to mobilize such a network. Such misunderstandings and entrenched attitudes eventually led the American to leave the company (Hoecklin, 1995, pp. 12–13).

Ideas

Cultural values also affect attitudes to management ideas, as illustrated by a European survey on attitudes to managing knowledge carried out by researchers at Cranfield University (Tate, 1997). In France, more than anywhere else in Europe, nearly a quarter of business leaders believe you can't create any processes to help you manage knowledge. It is simply a matter of 'management ability'. Almost a third believe knowledge about management is unimportant. In Germany, on the other hand, more than four out of five companies already consider themselves to be good at encouraging staff to share knowledge and bring forward new ideas, and are more likely to explicitly reward their efforts. The UK managers see the issue more as a method of exploiting and controlling the massive amounts of knowledge they believe they already have. Almost a quarter of UK firms say creating new knowledge is not a key priority, compared to only 1% in Germany. UK companies are also the most cynical about knowledge, with 27% regarding knowledge management as just a fad. Japan, on the other hand, believes its knowledge-creation processes are the key to its export success (Jones, 1998).

Activity 7.2

Can you relate any of the practical examples given above (or those you have encountered as a manager) to the cultural value differences identified by Hofstede, Hickson and Pugh or Trompenaars? For example, how does the considerate supervisor from Box 7.1 relate to Hofstede's dimensions?

7.3 CULTURE AND ECONOMIC DEVELOPMENT

The broad differences in the role of management in different economies, and in the type of activity it embraces, are at least partly accounted for by differences in national values.

Trompenaars and Hampden-Turner (1993) have tried to relate national values to particular sorts of economic success. They looked at seven different cultures of capitalism – the USA, the UK, Japan, France, Germany, Sweden and the Netherlands – and examined how the different values in each society have contributed to their economic performance. They consider why it is believed that, for example, Germans are particularly good at building infrastructure whilst Americans are good at invention and Japanese at innovation. They relate these stereotypes to variables such as universalism. They argue, for example, that Americans aim at the widest possible popular appeal for their products combined with a manufacturing process that is capable of being reduced to simple steps, so that the parent company can manufacture where costs are lowest and sell to as many people as possible.

Thus it is no surprise that the USA excelled early at mass manufacture and mass marketing. And should we be surprised that, as markets became more customized, more fragmented, more oriented to unique requests, America's difficulties have mounted? This is especially true of competition with nations such as Japan and France which are culturally oriented to heterogeneity, variety and particularities – customized goods, haute cuisine and haute couture.

(Hampden-Turner and Trompenaars (1993), in Hoecklin, 1995, p. 77)

Early versus late development

Hampden-Turner (1994) suggests that certain values (e.g. Protestant individualism) favour early industrialization and others (e.g. communitarianism) later industrialization, and that the logic of catching up is different from the logic of being a pioneer. The differences are summarized in Table 7.5. Of course communitarianism is not the only factor; if it were, South American and African countries would have industrialized as fast as South-East Asia.

Individualism and communitarianism

Table 7.5 Differences between old and newly industrialized nations		
	Early industrializers **UK, US, Australia**	**Later industrializers** **Germany, Japan, Hong Kong, Taiwan, S. Korea, Singapore**
Development strategy	Innovate piecemeal	Follow selectively
Government role	Ignorant about technology, foolish about business	Well informed on world technological trends
Intervention and social policies	Referee – regulate and reform after the fact	Coach – manage and facilitate before the fact
Education	Stress pure knowledge, subsequently applied	Stress successful technology and industrial process
Orientation	Competitive individualism	Co-operative communitarianism
Labour relations	Poor, because wages under pressure from other nations	Good, because wages rising
Development	Laissez-faire, empirical	Managed competition
Transition from agriculture	Slow	Fast: whole villages move
Identity	People form relationships	Relationships form people
Finance	High returns for huge risks over short term	Low-interest loans with lower risk over longer period

(Source: adapted from Hampden-Turner, 1994, p. 65)

7.4 SOCIAL CAPITAL

Francis Fukuyama argues that national differences in economic performance and business and governmental organization are related to deeply held cultural values.

Social capital

He singles out attitudes to trust and norms of reciprocity as critical. Trust takes a long time to establish but unfortunately can disappear very quickly. The degree of trust or social capital in a society or organization has profound implications for management. Box 7.3 outlines the main points of Fukuyama's social capital thesis which are elaborated in Fukuyama's book entitled *Trust* (1996).[36]

BOX 7.3   FUKUYAMA'S SOCIAL CAPITAL THESIS

The main points are as follows.

Modern economic activity requires a high degree of social co-operation and effective institutions such as property rights.

The economic cost of such co-operation is minimized where social capital and trust supplement such institutions.

Social capital includes family and kinship relationships and social groups such as religions and craft guilds.

Familistic societies with low trust among non-kin went through a period of strong political centralization when social capital was depleted.

Societies with high degrees of trust never experienced a prolonged period of centralized state power.

Societies with high spontaneous sociability are able to build large organizations which can exploit economies of scale.

Societies with low levels of trust can either rely on the state to promote large-scale organizations or seek foreign investment and joint ventures to do so. Both these routes have a number of potentially serious drawbacks for indigenous economic development.

Cultural factors such as spontaneous sociability are only one element of GDP growth and may not be the most important. Macro-economic issues such as fiscal and monetary economic policy, international conditions, barriers to trade, etc. remain the principal determinants of long-term GDP growth.

Sociability determines the number and importance of large corporations in an economy and thus in what kinds of industry it is able to compete. These factors may also make a difference to the degree and extent of innovation that takes place, although the advantages of small versus large companies may change in the future.

Network structures may offer the best of both.

Respect for education, a work ethic and the role of the state are common ingredients throughout East Asia but the extent of non-kin trust has been influential in the differing degrees of economic success and prospects for the future.

[36] See F. Fukuyama's article in Henry (2001).

> Rational economic liberalism is insufficient to account for why successful economies prosper. The degree to which people value work over leisure, their respect for education, attitudes towards the family and the degree of trust they show toward their fellows all have a direct impact on economic life.
>
> Source: G. Jones, 1998, p. 18

Activity 7.3

How convinced are you that Fukuyama's thesis is valid? Why?

Fukuyama argues that social capital is necessary for economic success. He applies these ideas to countries and regions. He points out that social capital seems to be important to the development of certain industries such as IT. For example, the success of the Silicon Valley IT firms over those around Route 128 in Boston has been put down to the freer exchange of information across social networks in Silicon Valley (Fukuyama, 1999). Fukuyama accepts there is convergence between countries' economies, values and practices throughout the world, but argues that countries like the US need to ensure their social capital is renewed in order to remain competitive.

In addition Fukuyama argues that *once social capital is destroyed, it cannot easily be replaced*. This has implications for economies with increasing social discord. For example, it follows from Fukuyama's analysis that Russia, with a weak state, its social capital destroyed and its economy prey to Mafia gangs, *will not* be able to build a flourishing economy in the near future unless either the state gets strong again or foreign investors flood in. The same argument can be applied to organizations, and implies that managerial change programmes should take great care to maintain trust; and that managers need to pay attention to creating and sustaining trust in their part of the organization. This analysis emphasizes just how important trust is, the danger of destroying trust within an organization, and the difficulty of building up trust again.

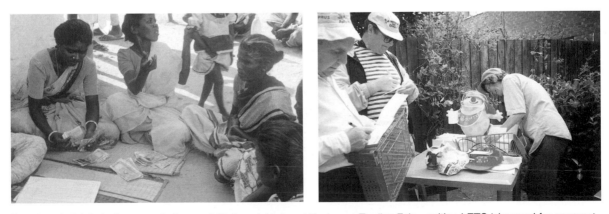

Social capital: left: India women's finance initiative; right: Local Exchange Trading Fair – writing LETS 'cheques' for payment

The social capital thesis suggests local, regional and national bodies need to make a point of building and maintaining social capital. Programmes involving national governments and community associations have been introduced in the US and parts of Europe in an attempt to counter urban deprivation, with mixed success. Rebuilding trust is not easy, and societal change programmes generally take at least a generation to come to fruition, so the prospects for doing anything dramatic in the short term seem bleak. Jones (1998) describes the long-term effect of Italy's introduction of a new regional tier of government. In the North, where civil society was strong, the new tier of government was successful in securing greater participation rates and voter satisfaction. But in the South, where civil society was weak, the sense of voter alienation was unaffected over a twenty-year period. It has been argued that it might take 30 years of consistent behaviour to re-establish trust sufficiently to change attitudes.

Not everyone accepts Fukuyama's thesis. In the 1990s, high-trust East Asian economies suffered a serious economic crisis. It can be argued that trust was one of the problems here. The Japanese system, for example, has produced some notoriously corrupt politicians. Sceptics argue that one person's trust may be another's lack of accountability. In addition social capital is only one of the factors that affect economic success; levels of investment, the roles of the state and of the banking system, and labour relations are also important. It may be that social capital is of more importance in some systems of capitalism than others.

7.5 REVIEW

Fundamentally different values are found in different parts of the world and these affect attitudes to, and the practice of, management. Managers are well advised to take account of different cultural values and their effect on expectations about the practice of management, when dealing with staff from other cultures.

Cultural values also play a part in determining the way business develops in different cultures. Each country tends to develop a form of industry and system of management in keeping with its values. The timing and speed of its development also appears to be affected by cultural values. Social capital appears to be a key ingredient in economic success.

Further reading/Viewing

D. J. Hickson and D. Pugh, *Management Worldwide* (London: Penguin, 1995).

J. Henry, 'Management in Chinese cultures', *Creativity Innovation and Change* Video 4.

F. Fukuyama, 'Technology, networks and social capital' in Henry (2001).

F. Fukuyama, *Trust* (New York: Free Press, 1996).

8 DEVELOPMENT

In addition to cultural values we inherit a raft of historical assumptions that channel the way we do things. Western thought has been dominated by three assumptions in particular – the tendency to linear thinking, abstraction and a reliance on rational approaches to learning. This chapter highlights some of the ways in which these patterns of thought have influenced the practice of development personally, professionally and globally.

8.1   LINEAR THINKING

Our approach to development is influenced by the tendency for Western thought to favour explicit thinking and employ rational, linear analysis (Nonaka, 1993). The tendency to think linearly partly accounts for the traditional conception of an organization as a hierarchy, and talk of the top and bottom of the organization.[37]

Stages

It perhaps also accounts for the Western tendency to conceptualize development as a sequence of linear stages. Organizational, team and individual development, problem solving and product development are all traditionally pictured this way by Westerners, as shown in Table 8.1.

Stages

[37] The tendency to think linearly is often dated roughly from the time of Descartes, i.e. about 300 years ago. (Others argue it has an older heritage, recognisable in classical Greece.)

Table 8.1	Developmental phases	
Individual	**Team**	**Organization development**
Explore	Form	Pioneer
Consolidate	Norm	Differentiate
Renew	Perform	Integrate
Problem-solving	**Innovation**	**Organization transformation**
Problem exploration	Invention (idea)	Vision (leader)
Idea generation	Innovation (product)	Strategy (champions)
Implementation	Entrepreneur (market)	Nurture (managers)

Most Western theorists have conceived of personal development as a series of stages, each building on the preceding one. Examples include Piaget (1929) and Perry's descriptions of cognitive development in childhood and adulthood, Maslow's (1962) hierarchy of needs, Erickson's (1959) stages of man, and Kohlberg's stages of moral development. Likewise Levinson's (1986) map of the evolution of individuals describes early adulthood as a time to explore, learn and dream, the thirties as a settling-down period in which to consolidate goals, and a mid-life phase in which inner values resurface as a time for the resolution of conflict and renewal.

A team is also assumed to go through well-recognized phases (Tuckman, 1965). First, there is a process of forming and storming in which members establish their identities. Later, the group establishes agreed norms and practices. Only after people feel recognized and norms are agreed is the group likely to perform well.

The common assumption is that, as organizations grow, the small pioneering enterprise, run by an entrepreneur, gradually expands to become a large depersonalized bureaucracy with specialized units, and – hopefully – then moves on to being an integrated learning organization, based round divisions, embarking on joint ventures with other organizations.

Problem solving too is normally thought of as a staged process, that elaborates to varying degrees the basic sequence of: problem exploration, idea generation, and implementation. (A five-stage version of this runs: analyse the situation, define the problem, develop options, select a strategy, develop an action plan.) In reality problem solving is much more of an iterative process than the stages idea implies.

The process of innovation (introducing a new product or service to market) has also traditionally been conceptualized as a sequential relay race: moving from the idea or invention through a working prototype, and on to market, via R and D, development engineering, production, marketing and sales. However here conceptions have changed: the need for overlapping phases and a multi-disciplinary input up front is acknowledged, and new product development now normally entails parallel, not just sequential, development.

Not all cultures think of development and growth in this linear way. Hindu thought stresses cyclical development more and Chinese cultures the role of balance. Western conceptions are also changing and now seem to have a greater appreciation of the role of relationships and networks in development.

Cycle

The idea of development as a cycle has a long history in the East. In India the root metaphor of *cycle* plays a prominent role in understanding how things work. This follows naturally from the Hindu cyclical conception of the universe's history. It seems to have led to notions of personal development which place greater stress on self-acceptance and forbearance than the idea of fixing and changing oneself implied in the West's notion of personal growth as transformation.

Cycle

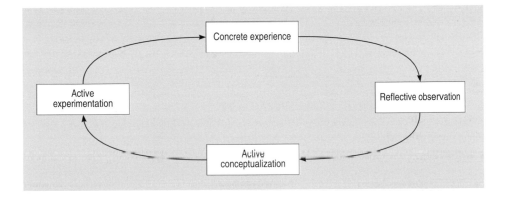

In the late twentieth century the idea of development as a cycle is becoming more commonplace in Western vocabulary. Kolb (1984) offers a cyclical conception of experiential learning and problem solving, entailing successive rounds of experience, reflection, generalization and testing out. We also see the idea of cycle in the notions of product and life cycles, 'cradle-to-grave' manufacturing, sustainability and Leonard-Barton's (1995) cyclical picture of knowledge creation in organizations.

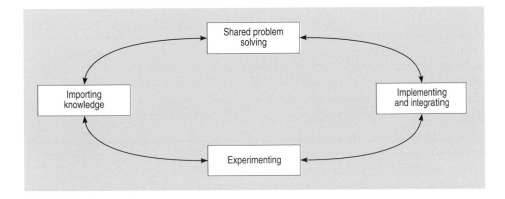

153

Balance

Another metaphor for development is *balance*. We find this metaphor used in nutrition (healthy eating is balanced eating), and in the idea of homeostasis and the thermostat. In China the idea of balance and harmony is probably the key metaphor for personal development. The Chinese notion of balance also accepts the inevitability of paradox, as shown in the intertwined figures of yin and yang, symbolizing passivity and action respectively. As a consequence it is more natural for the Chinese than the Western mind to appreciate the interdependence of apparent opposites, such as the destruction entailed in creativity, or the need for both innovation and stability.

Relationship

A fourth view of development sees it more as a matter of *relationship*. This perspective takes greater account of the surrounding context and interactions among participants on the way things develop. For example, rather than merely charting the rise of inner-city deprivation, this could be seen in relationship to suburban wealth, rural gentrification, international mobility of capital and out-of-town shopping and the like: other trends that intimately impact on inner cities.

Currently the ideas of network and partnership have taken hold of the management imagination. Commentators now look at informal interactions and relationships between members of organizations, not just the task or the plan. And organizations themselves have embraced the idea of alliance and partnership with sister organizations.

Activity 8.1

What metaphors for development dominate thinking in your organization – for example, growth as expansion or as partnership?

Imagine if development was more a matter of relationships, iterative cycles or balancing forces. Pick one of these, and think of one or more policy implications that arise from viewing development this way.

8.2   APPROACHES TO LEARNING

Personal, professional and organizational development are big business these days, as companies seek to develop their employees and transform their organizations to keep pace with the ever-changing world. In the UK there is now even an organizational kite mark, in the form of Investors in People (IIP), which publicly recognizes an organization's espoused practices in this area.

In a world in which physics students may find that the information they study for their degree is out of date by the time they graduate, and individuals can expect three or four different occupations in a lifetime, we cannot afford to stand still; it is not surprising that 'lifelong learning' has become popular rhetoric. Handy (1991) argues that organizations will have to place much more emphasis on *learning*, in terms both of organizational learning and of fostering learning among their employees.

Activity 8.2

Note down three of the most important learning experiences of your adult life, i.e. the experiences that have taught you the most.

Handy suggests that these are usually precipitated by new and unexpected challenges and crises. Many educational studies have found that people judge their most significant learning to have come from informal (everyday life), not formal (school or college) learning. Did you find this?

The formal approach to learning is conditioned by long-standing patterns of thought deeply embedded within our psyches. In particular it tends to be dominated by an information-processing model of knowledge acquisition: learning is assumed to be about inputting the missing competencies into our heads.

Information

In the West we tend to conceive of knowledge primarily as bits of information and skills, and learning to be the process whereby this data is instilled in people's brains to be stored until required. This is essentially a *top-down* and passive concept of education. Experts disseminate correct knowledge and information which mere mortals have to soak up.

Currently the idea of *competency* has a central hold on the way professional development is conceptualized and conducted. The competencies approach assumes knowledge can be bundled up in packages, passed between people and generalized to other settings. Management development generally makes the assumption that managers' skills in one area can be transferred to another. By and large, scientists studying knowledge have come to a different conclusion. They find that most *knowledge is situated*, i.e. the knowledge you possess is very much bound up with a particular area; so a car mechanic is unlikely to be a good boat mechanic and, by implication, someone from the private sector may lack the necessary public-sector management knowledge.

Competencies

Scientists who study how we learn are clear that we are not passive recipients of information and skills that are new to us. In fact we are *active* recipients of all the knowledge that comes our way, and to assimilate this knowledge we have to recreate our understandings and the connections between them. We do not just take in information onto a blank slate; instead we store it within and alongside our existing schemas, normally reconceptualizing the area(s) under scrutiny. In addition our brains are plastic, i.e. they store information in idiosyncratic ways, peculiar to ourselves, that reflect the particular schemas and interconnections we have laboriously built up over our lifetime. So the way we store knowledge is entirely personal, and my map of an area may be quite different from your map of the same area.

In the fields of personal and professional development (and for that matter counselling and coaching) the idea of active involvement is recognized in the emphasis placed on *active reflection*. For example most training courses ask

Reflection

participants to reflect on what the learning points have been. Counsellors ask counsellees to reflect on their experiences, actions and feelings. This entails asking participants to make explicit previously tacit knowledge, for example to acknowledge feelings that might not previously have been given much attention and reflect on what brought them about. However, Chapter 3 has explained how explicit learning lags way behind tacit knowledge, and that people are often unable to articulate what they know, especially where this is complex learning that has been grasped tacitly; so explicit reflections may never articulate our deepest understandings.[38]

Unlearning

The new paradigm of postmodernism encourages a form of analysis known as deconstruction. This draws attention to those elements we neglect in our dominant assumptions. What if we thought not in terms of forcing information into our brains, but concentrated instead on the idea of *unblocking* it? (And less on explicit competencies and more on tacit knowledge.)

Maybe learning is also about removing unnecessary assumptions. The psychodynamic tradition believes so. A small group of writers have adopted this very different approach to management and organizational development (Bion, 1968; Argyris, 1994). They conceive of learning as not so much a matter of inputting ever more explicit knowledge into our brains, but of unlocking the tacit assumptions that prevent us from seeing the way forward, learning and moving on. Their approach focuses on tacit assumptions and emotional tone, as a route to reframing our perceptions. The article by Gabriel in *Creative Management* (Henry, 2001) elaborates on this tradition. The article by Argyris in the same book explains why ignoring the emotional aspects of communication can prevent learning in organizations.

However, the *psychodynamic* approach's recognition of the place of the unconscious is a minority tradition. Generally, Western personal and professional development practice, and therefore privileges, a rational approach to development based round insight and reflection, thereby neglecting the role of the unconscious and tacit knowledge.[39] This orientation is in keeping with the rationalistic ethos that has held sway in the West for some centuries now. It has led to education and training that are very largely cognitive enterprises, and which give little attention to the body, affect or the unconscious. Similarly, professional development has embraced the idea of rational categorization and acquisition of relevant competencies, plus reflection on explicit learning points, as their route to development.

Modelling the best

Personal and professional development also tend to operate within a frame that is concerned with making good deficiencies, rather than modelling the best. We aim to input missing competencies, and solve problems through rational reflection. Managers have also tended to be reactive, oriented to solving

[38] Reason's article in Henry (2001) elaborates on action learning, a participatory approach to learning that aims to develop actionable local knowledge which takes account of the participant's deepest desires and is both meaningful and useful.

[39] By privilege I mean concentrate on (in this case) rational approaches to personal development at the expense of other alternatives (which in the case of personal and professional development includes the support of friends and colleagues, and hands-on experience gaining knowledge tacitly through osmosis rather than through reflection).

problems more than following their visions. However, management thinking is waking up to the idea of modelling the best, for example in benchmarking key competitors, and the use of forward-looking visions.

Interestingly, relatively little personal and professional development work derives from studying the habits of successful people. (Exceptions include Covey's 1989 *The Seven Habits of Successful People*, Csikszentmihalyi's 1996 work on flow and the approach taken by Neuro-Linguistic Programming.)

Studies of well-being suggest that contented people live life to the full, are actively absorbed in challenges they have some chance of completing, where they get feedback on their progress, and are supported by a social network to which they feel they belong (Argyle, 1987; Csikszentmihalyi, 1996; Haworth, 1997). Two other routes to happiness are humour and exercise. If personal and professional development were modelled on the practices found among adults who are functioning particularly well, we might spend rather more time encouraging employees to pursue their interests actively, have fun and develop their support network, rather than asking them to reflect on their problems, skill deficiencies and learning points. Interestingly, successful creative people are also known to pursue activities they enjoy.

Appendix A provides a series of activities you could use to identify and explore your own development goals.

8.3 LOCAL KNOWLEDGE

Western thought has also tended to privilege abstract thinking, where problems are broken down into elements and these elements are analysed (as in time and motion studies or science). This kind of fragmented thinking concentrates on the parts rather than the whole. It follows that this mode of thinking can easily neglect holistic aspects of a problem.

Vandana Shiva (1993) argues that standard accounting systems illustrate the Western capacity to fragment thinking. Such systems tend to recognize only unidimensional measures of productivity; hence they stress the yield of a few commercial crops and neglect to take account of social and other benefits. Thus standard accounting systems can rate rail transport as more expensive than road transport, whereas rail's proponents argue that taking the total health and environmental costs of road transport into account reverses the road/rail cost-benefit arguments in their favour.

Of course it is difficult to develop measures that take account of less tangible factors like intellectual capital, and social and environmental costs and benefits. Some commentators suggest, however, that one reason we have failed to attempt to measure social, environmental and intellectual benefits and costs, at least until very recently, is that the fragmented pattern of thinking we have inherited in the West makes it seem natural to us to analyse elements separately, in a way that would be unnatural in a traditional society with a more integrated world view.

Does a higher standard of living make you happier?

In 1955 one-third of Americans claimed to be happy with their lives, exactly the same proportion as in 1991, despite the fact that the standard of living (productivity and consumption) had doubled over this period.

(A. During, 1991, quoted in Russell, 1994, p. 9)

Fragmented thinking

In Box 8.1 Shiva (1993) argues that the West has exported its fragmented thinking and partial accounting to the Third World in a way that has been detrimental to people living there.

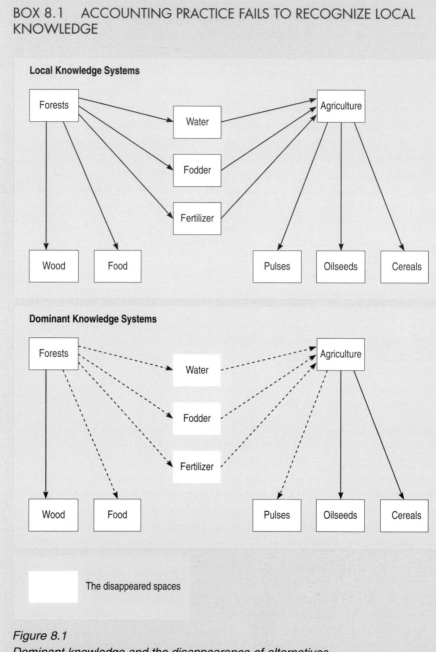

BOX 8.1   ACCOUNTING PRACTICE FAILS TO RECOGNIZE LOCAL KNOWLEDGE

Figure 8.1
Dominant knowledge and the disappearance of alternatives

(Source: Shiva, 1993, p. 13)

Vandana Shiva (1993) argues that the Western assumption that their approach to thinking is universally applicable fails to recognize the merits of local systems of knowledge. She attributes this problem to long-standing biases in Western thinking.

Shiva points out that local economies and their corresponding knowledge systems are based round integrated agricultural and forestry systems producing many outputs, few of which are measured by standard accounting systems. She argues that one reason why external solutions are advocated to solve third-world problems is because the quantitative measurement systems imported by experts, and used to analyse the situation, fail to recognize outputs locals value.

Shiva argues that, because Western thinking has tended to linear abstraction, it seems natural to a Westerner to categorize forestry as producing only the commodity of wood, and agriculture as producing food. This means that Westerners can easily neglect the food-bearing potential of the forest, since this is not what they associate with the term. Rather forests are conceived more like a timber mine, so to the Western forestry expert the fodder, fibre, herbs, and tubers of the forest are forgotten waste. Given this mind-set, it seems natural to the foreign expert to clear the native species and replace them with reputedly quicker-growing pine or eucalyptus monocultures (even if these lower the water table faster and deplete the soil).

Perhaps another part of the problem has been the way in which Western experts have tended to use science to generalize. The specialized knowledge of economics and forestry held by a few experts has been applied in areas other than those where it developed. As a consequence, the social, local and particular elements in knowledge can be hidden and forgotten.

The contrast between modern agriculture and traditional farming systems is stark. Though modern agriculture is efficient in the few dimensions measured by Western accounting systems, it requires external inputs such as fertiliser and antibiotics to function at all, since monocultures are easily prey to pests and disease. Monocultures are also centrally controlled and planned, and the crop is often sold abroad with no benefit to local people. In contrast, many traditional farming systems are sustainable, require no external inputs, are based on a decentered, self-regulating system; and the mixed growth and crop rotation systems leave the farm, and the animals and plants within it, more resistant to pests and disease. (Conventional theorists point out that the yield from 'modern' farming is higher, but Shiva contests that this is the case when and if accountants measure all the output from traditional systems and all the costs in Western-style conventional farming.)

> The implication she draws is that the traditional systems offer sustainable ways of conserving biodiversity and meeting the local population's needs, while modern monocultures require expensive fertilizer (imported from outside the local area), degrade the soil, and take no account of conservation, i.e. they are essentially non-sustainable short-term solutions.[40]

This analysis suggests that the problem is one of fragmented thinking that fails to take account of local knowledge. Shiva's article in Henry (2001) elaborates.

Another problem is perhaps undue faith in science and technology (Postman, 1993). The Western tendency to abstract analysis has led to great success in science and technology, which relies on an explicit system of knowledge that can be generalized to a range of situations. Knowledge about particular fields is held by specialist experts, who feel justified in applying their expertise the world over. In consequence it has seemed natural to agencies like the World Bank, International Monetary Fund and non-governmental institutions to look to outside experts to advise them how to improve and cure problems in the developing world.

In the past these outside experts have often advocated large-scale technological solutions, which in the course of time have often proved to be expensive failures. One of the reasons these, often inappropriate, schemes are accepted is perhaps because people have great faith in technology, and men, in particular, delight in it. The male's enthusiasm for gadgetry means is often easier to get governments to back hi-tech than low-tech solutions.

Ethiopia

The state wanted farmers to plant a new sorghum seed with a much higher yield, and educated the male farmers in its benefits. Nothing changed. A study showed this was because the women were not convinced of the benefits. A large part of their day was spent grinding the seed, and more output would be more work for them. Subsequently women were included in the development programme. Now people are beginning to use the new seed.

Fortunately attitudes are now changing. The powers that be have recognized that the expensive large-scale technological solution is not always the best for the recipient or the donors. Most activists working on the ground appreciate the need to consult and involve locals. Many not-for-profit organizations now practise participatory action, involving local communities in the design and execution of any scheme that affects them.[41]

8.4   REVIEW

The chapter has endeavoured to show how the Western approach to personal, professional and global development has been framed within deeply rooted cultural orientations that privilege rational, abstract, linear, top-down, short-term thinking over intuitive, relational, inclusive, participative and sustainable approaches. It has illustrated how these assumptions have affected Western

[40] The conventional perspective assumes that the enhanced productivity brought about by the 'green revolution' has been beneficial to the local population. Shiva and others seek to contest this perception (Shiva, 2001). (The green revolution in India entailed growing new Western-developed varieties that required more fertiliser and water but promised higher yields.)

[41] 'Developing participation', *Creativity, Innovation and Change* Audio 8 (Bell and Henry, 2001) illustrates the participatory way in which many development organizations now work in developing countries.

approaches to professional and global development and led to the neglect of intuitive learning and local knowledge. As we saw in Part 2 these patterns of thought are beginning to change, with the paradigm shift in thinking that is underway in management and Western thought more generally, as we move from the modern to the post-modern era. In respect of development, a more participative and individualized approach is beginning to come into play.

Further reading/Listening

V. Shiva, 'Monocultures of the mind', in Henry (2001).

R. Bell *et al.*, 'Developing participation', *Creativity, Innovation and Change'* Audio 8.

Y. Gabriel, 'Psychodynamics and organizations', in Henry (2001).

P. Reason, 'Learning and development through action research', in Henry (2001).

PART 5
SUSTAINABILITY

This part looks at the way organizations can respond to environmental and community concerns so as to develop businesses that are economically, environmentally and socially sustainable. Chapter 9 takes up the vexed question of sustainable development and its relationship to organizational growth. Chapter 10 looks at how organizations are aiming to be more socially responsible.

9 SUSTAINABILITY

Global companies have no future if the earth has no future.

(Ryuzaburo Kaku, Ex-President and Chair of the Board, Canon)

There are many crises facing the planet today, including the growth in population and growing resistance to antibiotics, but perhaps the potentially most serious issue is environmental problems. There is increasing consensus that global warming – seen in the recent degree-a-year temperature increases worldwide – is the result of human activity, and that business ought to take more preventative measures to rectify the situation. As a result there is growing recognition that business needs to start operating according to principles of sustainable development that do not mortgage the earth's future. This chapter discusses why and how business might have to change if it were to become truly sustainable.

9.1   GROWTH VERSUS SUSTAINABILITY

Industrialization took off in the nineteenth century, and Western conceptions of business development have been strongly influenced by notions of growth prevalent at that time. Organizations borrowed their ideas about development from the economic and biological growth they were surrounded by.

Growth
Competition

The nineteenth century was the time of the industrial revolution and expanding empires, a period of tremendous economic growth for many European nations. It was also when Darwin introduced the idea of evolution and the idea that nature advanced through survival of the fittest. This implied that competition was inherent in nature and necessary for survival. Industrial rhetoric borrowed this idea as a metaphor for economic life. The route to growth was to compete, conquer, and control people and markets as well as nature: hence the command and control model of managing and supervising staff was deemed appropriate. This approach still permeates much of our thinking about organizations and development. In some ways the modern commercial enterprise has been driven by a mind-set that evolved in the nineteenth century.

The idea that organizational development implies ever-expanding *growth*[42] is deeply embedded in the Western psyche. Given the historical heritage where economic expansion paralleled the geographic expansion of the nineteenth century colonisers, it is perhaps understandable that up until now economic growth has been undertaken as if the world were an open system, with unlimited resources and new areas to conquer, where it was legitimate to enter a new territory, take resources and leave.

---

[42] Though personal and organizational development in the West conceptualize improvement as growth, when thinking of individuals we tend to associate maturity with wisdom (at least ideally), whereas organizational maturity is normally regarded as synonymous with large size.

At the beginning of the twenty-first century, with no terrestrial territories left to conquer, we can no longer afford to maintain the fiction that we live in an open system where unbridled growth is possible. We now recognize that not only are markets global, but that all parts of the planet are interdependent. We live in a closed system where an action in one part can affect the balance elsewhere. As Herman Daly, previously head of the World Bank, says:

Growth in a finite world

> It is obvious that in a finite world nothing physical can grow forever. Yet our current policy seems to aim at increasing physical production indefinitely.
>
> *(Daly and Cobb, in Russell, 1994)*

The pressures of the next quarter's figures have also added to a tendency to focus on the short term at the expense of long-term thinking. Traditional cultures often plan for a longer time span, as Willis Harman illustrates:

> The Iroquois tradition was to make decisions having in mind the welfare of those who will live seven generations hence. Contemporary decisions – profoundly affecting the future generations and people around the globe – are guided by the next quarter's bottom line, or the way the next electorate will perceive the state of the economy.
>
> *(Russell, 1991, p. 24)*

Sustainable development

In the late twentieth century the female Norwegian Prime Minister Gro Brundtland gave the world another metaphor for development: that of 'sustainable development', i.e. growth that does not mortgage the future in any way. Many environmentalists argue that business must re-orient to take account of the this principle of *sustainable development*. This principle heralds a radical switch in organizational thinking and business values, from an ethic of *growth*, *competition* and *profit* to one of *sustainability, co-operation* and *responsibility*. It requires new methods of measurement and means of production. This concept embodies within it a concern for future generations. This notion of *sustainability* conveys the idea of developing in a way that does not mortgage the future – such as forestry that replants a tree for every one felled, and third-world governments permitting only industries that do not lower the water table. It implicitly acknowledges that we live in an interdependent world; a fact that is hard to deny in the age of the Internet and global pollution.

Sustainability

Table 9.1 contrasts traditional business beliefs with those espoused by advocates of sustainable approaches to development.

Table 9.1	Contrasting environmental beliefs
Traditional beliefs	**Emerging beliefs**
Felling forest supplies more agricultural land	Denuded forests lose topsoil and lead to infertile land
Fishing further from land increases the catch	Fish stocks need to be conserved
Chemical fertilisers increase food output	Overuse of fertiliser and antibiotics leads to pollution and immune system problems
Plentiful energy is necessary	Energy conservation saves money
Economic growth benefits all and can continue	All development needs to be sustainable
Economic criteria are sufficient for business	Economic, social and environmental criteria should inform business decisions
Species disappear naturally	Serious reduction in biodiversity could threaten the planet's stability

Figure 9.1   Sustainable ways of working: establishing a contour hedge to prevent erosion and tree-planting in Scotland

9.2 ENVIRONMENTAL PROBLEMS

Figure 9.2   Environmental problems (ozone hole depletion, burning forests and acid rain)

The average Westerner consumes 100 times the resources of their counterparts 200 years ago. The population has increased by a factor of ten over the same period. It is expected to double by 2025.

(Russell, 1994, p. 7)

In the process of obtaining and developing resources, industry has chiefly looked to the short term and, until recently, paid little heed to the environmental damage caused. In many areas we now have impoverished soil, polluted land, sea, air, livestock, and fisheries; the energy expended has fuelled the greenhouse effect, the chemicals involved have depleted the ozone layer. Human endeavour has been very largely responsible for this unprecedented environmental crisis.

It has been suggested that, if businesses had to factor in the true environmental cost of their enterprises, few if any would have made a profit in the last hundred years (Porrit, 1999). Box 9.1 outlines some key environmental problems.

BOX 9.1   ENVIRONMENTAL PROBLEMS

Environmental problems affect the planet's land, water and atmosphere plus its inhabitants.

Air

- increasing emissions of greenhouse gases (caused largely by CO_2 emissions) exacerbate global warming
- which leads to climate change (the eleven warmest years since records began over 100 years ago have occurred in the last twenty years)
- diminishing ozone layer (through CFC and related product use) leads to increases in cancer and could eventually blind insects vital for pollination. This will take hundreds of years to rectify even if we stop releasing CFCs now
- airborne pollution causes acid rain to kill forests

Water

- rising sea levels (caused by global warming) could flood many parts of the world including Bangladesh, some Pacific Islands and low-lying regions of East Anglia. For example, Cambridge, England, could become a seaside town
- climate change may lead to the collapse of the Gulf stream leaving the UK and Northern Europe much colder than at present
- leached fertiliser encourages toxic algal blooms
- widespread pollution (from pesticide leakage and cattle slurry, for example) can kill or maim fish and many other species

Land

- lowering the water table and climate change are leaving insufficient water in many parts of the world
- soil erosion, desertification and salinization are undermining food security
- diminishing wood, metal and other finite natural resources
- diminishing biodiversity that might leave us more vulnerable to pests, viruses and bacteria

Animals

- collapse of fish stocks in many parts of the world through overfishing
- increased bacterial and pest resistance to antibiotics, pesticides and herbicides leading to the untreatable versions of diseases such as malaria and TB
- pollution is affecting many species (including *homo sapiens*, e.g. declining male sperm count)
- leached antibiotics (e.g. from fish farming) are affecting animal immune systems adversely

Excessive *greenhouse gases* build up and prevent radiated heat from the sun leaving the earth. We are now experiencing the fastest rate of atmospheric change for 10,000 years. Environmentalists warn that greenhouse gases, with their potential to increase global warming, are potentially life-threatening. This is not just because the increased temperature could melt the ice cap, raising the sea level substantially, so that many low-lying regions and islands will be under water, but because reduced rainfall in places like the Mid-West (America's grain belt) may cease to make agriculture viable there. A one metre rise in sea level could leave 200 million people homeless. We have already lost half the polar ice cap. The average thickness of the Arctic ice cap is six feet, and we are losing four inches a year. If this continues it will be gone in 20 years. Kiribati, the Pacific island that was first to see in the year 2000, is expected to be under water in 50 years (Lovejoy, 2000).

Greenhouse gases

Carbon dioxide *emissions* account for half the global warming effect, with methane, CFCs and nitrous oxide accounting for another third. Industry produces over half the carbon dioxide emissions, a major source being the burning of fossil fuels. Intensive livestock farming is the single largest source of methane, accounting for a quarter of emissions.

The depletion of the *ozone layer* has led to an increase in skin cancers in New Zealand and could restrict plant growth. The depletion is caused principally by CFCs, which are used in refrigerators and air-conditioning systems, in cleaning, aerosols and foaming agents. People in developing countries now naturally want the goods those in developed countries have long enjoyed, which – for example in the case of refrigerators for a billion Chinese – will exacerbate the problem unless environmentally friendlier designs are used.

Ozone hole

The Antarctic ozone hole has swollen to an all-time record of 10.5 million miles, which is larger than North America, according to the National Aeronautics and Space Administration and National Oceanic and Atmospheric Administration.

(*Herald Tribune*, 8 October 1998, p. 3)

Ammonia from animal excrement contributes to *acid rain*, which has been killing forests and aquatic life in Northern Europe and America. Much wildlife and virgin forest is under serious threat; rain tends to wash away nutrients from newly cleared rainforest which can leave the land largely infertile in a short time. Fish stocks are already dangerously low in many areas; the quadrupling of the fish catch over the last 50 years has left eleven of the world's fifteen major fisheries on the point of collapse.

For these reasons few informed people now believe companies can continue to grow in line with population levels at current energy levels and sustain the planet. There are those who believe that there are, or soon will be, technological or biological solutions to the world's problems, and there is no doubt that great strides have been made. Others argue a more fundamental change in expectation and lifestyle is required, and many of this group doubt we can mobilise the change in mind-set needed to generate the will power to carry out policies that might reverse the existing damage to the planet. Meanwhile companies continue trying to grow in a sustainable way where they can afford it or it is easy to do so, and in unsustainable ways where they cannot (Henry, 1999d[43]).

The Natural Step movement offers three principles which organizations can try to follow in their attempts to operate sustainably, as explained in Box 9.2.

BOX 9.2   NATURAL STEP

The Natural Step aims to encapsulate in three key principles the conditions necessary for sustainable development, as described below. It was founded in Sweden by Dr Karl-Heinrik Robert, a leading cancer specialist. Dr Robert was inspired to develop this partly due to the increase in childhood leukaemia he observed. The principles were developed by a process of iterative consensus that entailed successive drafts, first involving 50 scientists and subsequently all Swedish households and schools. The conditions are:

1   Stored deposits: decrease dependence on fossil fuels and extracted metals and minerals

The earth cannot sustain a systematic increase of substances extracted from the earth's crust. This means that in a sustainable society the burning of fossil fuels, and metal and mineral mining, must not occur at a greater rate than the threshold at which the earth's biosphere can accommodate the resultant substances without harm.

The implication is that society needs to take up mineral and metal recycling programs as an everyday part of industrial processes and substantially reduce its dependence on fossil fuels; also cut back on nuclear fuel. Recycling alone is insufficient as, even with say cadmium batteries where 95% is recycled, the remaining 5% escapes into the environment, adding to the build-up.

2   Alien substances: decrease use of persistent synthetic compounds

Substances should not be produced at a faster pace than they can be broken down and rebuilt. This means sustainable societies should avoid generating the substances which persist in the environment such as PCBs (polychlorinated biphenyls), freons and numerous other man-made substances. PCBs have an adverse effect on predators such as man and freons deplete ozone which increases the risk of cancer. Society needs to find ways to reduce dependence on such persistent manufactured substances.

---

[43] 'Sustainability', *Creativity, Innovation and Change* Audio 3, offers a debate on whether industry's attempts at cleaning up its act are sufficient, whether further incentives are necessary, or a more fundamental attitude change is required that accepts a changed lifestyle.

3   *Eco-systems: increase attempts to ensure any encroachment on a natural system is minimized and temporary*

Humans should avoid taking more natural resources than they can replenish. For instance we should not take more fish from the sea than can be replaced, or cut down forest where that leads to desertification.

Resources should be used fairly and efficiently by all. This means finding ways of organizing life such that the use of resources becomes more efficient in all countries. The bottom line is that you must not consume more resources than you can put back.

In moves to becoming more sustainable companies can audit themselves against these principles. A number of organizations have tried to produce goods in line with Natural Step principles. For example IKEA produces a line of furniture which has no metal parts, avoids glue that persists in the environment and uses wood from a sustainable source.

A feature of the Natural Step ethos is that the people involved are best placed to find creative solutions to environmental problems. Natural Step consultants do not judge, but go to individual organizations and ask staff what they could do to work more in line with the Natural Step conditions described above.

Activity 9.1

How could you apply these principles in your organization? For example, what steps could your organization take to reduce its dependence on:

large amounts of energy and resources?

mined metals and minerals?

fossil fuels?

persistent synthetic substances?

encroaching on productive ecosystems?

What steps is it taking?

9.3   DRIVERS FOR CHANGE

Many businesses are opting to change and work in ways that take greater account of the environmental consequences of their actions. The motivation for 'going green' varies and includes the following:

- Business case
- Environmental regulation
- Consumer demand
- Ethical values
- Public image.

Business case

Recently companies have woken up to the fact that more energy-efficient manufacturing processes and waste minimization strategies offer substantial cost savings. In addition increasingly rigorous legislation is forcing companies to adopt greener policies. Consumers are also demanding that corporations produce products in environmentally friendlier ways. For these and other reasons many companies are beginning to adopt environmental concerns as part of corporate social responsibility.

Legislation

Legislation

Whether or not industry wishes to be green, regulation is increasingly forcing it to be more so. Industry is by far the biggest polluter, and consumers and governments increasingly look to industry to make amends. Global concern for the environment is forcing governments to bring in legislation to ensure that industry takes 'green' issues into consideration: for example, phasing out the use of various hazardous chemicals and dumping of sewage at sea, and cutting sulphur and nitrogen dioxide emissions. The shift to the 'polluter pays' principle, waste, packaging, health and numerous other environmental regulations are now a part of business life in the advanced world (and increasingly in the developing world). Since the 1970s green legislation has been getting steadily tougher. For example the European Union has committed itself to stabilizing carbon dioxide emissions and phasing out CFCs, and the UK has introduced environmental policy standards such as BS7750. Many forward-thinking companies, including Norsk Hydro and AEG, have voluntarily reduced emissions and/or resources used to a level much less than that required by law.

Various air and water quality regulations have assisted environmental change in many countries. The London smogs of the fifties are long gone. However, not all regulations are so effective: for example, high fuel prices in the UK do not appear to have reduced the consumption of petrol or diesel. And the problem of introducing a carbon tax (like the fuel price hike imposed on the UK road haulage industry) is that it can damage firms unless there is a level playing field with neighbouring countries. Hence the need for regional (e.g. European) and global co-ordination of policies.

Furthermore, the current environmental threats do not sit happily with traditional economic values. Drucker (1991) has argued that transnational action and law is required to deal with global ecological concerns, drawing an analogy with the coalition of nations that rid the Western world of institutionalized slavery two centuries ago. The nations of the world have indeed come together in Rio, Kyoto and The Hague, in attempts to agree protocols that will cut damaging emissions and curtail energy consumption. One success was the ban on CFCs, a product which clearly depletes the ozone layer around the planet. A depleted ozone layer raises ultraviolet levels, and could do so to a point which destroyed mankind. This is because it will not only increase skin cancer, but could kill plankton, which have no skin to protect them but are the base of the food chain on which fish and their predators depend. Raised UV levels could also blind bees, making it difficult for them to pollinate plants, and prevent plants reaching maturity by destroying the DNA in their growing tips (Russell, 1994 p. 11).

Unfortunately the bans agreed are far from universally altruistic. For example methyl bromide, which is used to kill pests, and is known to be a major ozone depleter, was left out of the initial voluntary ban because heavy users, such as Israel, Brazil, Greece, Spain and Italy, blocked its inclusion. Unless one has absolute faith that a technological solution to the world's climatic problems will emerge, these countries' refusal to ban chemicals that could play their part in devastating climatic changes seems remarkably short-sighted and insular. However, it is a psychological fact that people often make decisions for short-term gain and neglect the longer-term consequences. (Hence, it is argued, people continue smoking and have unwanted pregnancies as the undesirable effect is some way off.)

The World Trade Organization (WTO) is the body that sets global trading rules. It is currently enforcing a policy based on the principle of free trade. Up to now their rules have tended to favour the interests of multinationals and paid scant attention to the resources that are critical to the economy of the poor. For example the global shrimp industry entails a factory-farming process that salinates the surrounding soil and water, depletes ground water, and so prevents local people from growing traditional crops. In addition the resulting pollution destroys local fish, forcing local people out of a sustainable way of living (Shiva, 1999).

Consumer concern

Social pressure is an important driver for change and, in some instances, consumers are forcing change without any intervention by government. The growing number of green consumers (albeit 'light green'!) are demanding environmentally friendlier products that do less damage to the planet and its inhabitants, and come from sustainable sources. European consumer objections to genetically modified food are a case in point. By 2000 virtually all UK supermarkets had ceased to use GM products in their own-label food, and a number had ceased to stock genetically modified food altogether, due to consumer pressure; and the British Government has been obliged to introduce a labelling scheme.

Consumers are increasingly aware of the impact of greenhouse gases on the biosphere and of the undesirable effects of pollutants on the earth and its inhabitants. They can see for themselves changing weather patterns; doctors report an increasing incidence of child asthma; and scientists wonder about the cause of the declining male sperm count found in many countries. Few citizens can have escaped environmental problems of one kind or another, from toxic algae in swimming pools as far afield as New Zealand and the Mediterranean, acid rain-damaged trees in the UK and Scandinavia, to smog warnings in Los Angeles and Tokyo, and increased flooding across the globe.

There is an increase in consumer demand for more ethically produced products, from free-range meat and eggs to ethical investments. For example, it is consumer demand that led to more humane tuna-fishing methods, stopped the dumping of the Brent Spar oil plant at sea and, until recently, had all but killed the market for fur coats. Ethical investment has also been growing substantially, in the UK, from £280 million in 1990 to £1000 million in 1996. Companies have learnt that being seen to be environmentally friendly appeals to staff and customers – and can have a positive effect on share price.

In several countries the government, or the industrial sector concerned, have introduced green badges to help consumers sort authentic from misleading environmental product claims. Germany has Blue Angel, Japan Eco-mark and Canada Environmental Choice eco-labelling, for example.

Staff too are often happy to do what they can to help their company become greener. In the Berol paint company in Sweden a number of employees found the external pressure for a cleaner environment at odds with the profit-oriented strategy of the company. A deep conflict arose over this issue. One faction had the goal of making Berol the 'cleanest chemical company in the world'; the other faction saw this as 'financial suicide'. Despite the wide variance of views there emerged a common core belief expressed as 'I cannot put my hand on my heart and say I am proud to earn my salary in the chemical industry'. Staff went on to form teams to investigate ways of producing more environmentally sound products (Evans and Russell, 1991).

9.4 ORGANIZATIONAL RESPONSE

4Rs
reduce
recycle
replace
reuse

But how can a company respond? Environmentalists argue for the four Rs – *recycle, reduce, replace, reuse*: for example, recycling waste, reducing the amount of energy and materials used and emissions produced over the life of the product, replacing damaging chemicals like CFCs and reusing materials.

All this seems to demand a *responsibility* from industry that is not obviously compatible with the traditional business values of growth and profit.

Nevertheless, considerable progress has already been made in minimizing waste, using energy more efficiently, cutting emissions, and redesigning processes to take account of environmental impact across the product life-cycle. And a shift to these more environmentally friendly processes often leaves businesses financially better off.

In the UK the privatisation of utilities such as electricity seems to have generated a new era of environmental innovations, such as increased interest in combined heat and power and solar energy, that had previously been suppressed.

Recycling

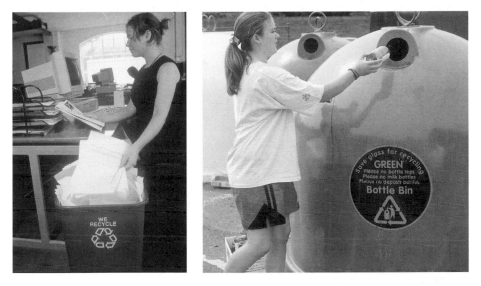

One of the most common ways to begin responding to environmental concerns is to *recycle waste*. Many countries have embarked on major recycling programmes for paper, metal, glass and plastic. Most European manufacturers mark plastic packaging with letters such as PET, PP and PETE that indicate its constituents, to aid recycling. British local authorities make varying efforts to recycle paper, aluminium, tin, glass and certain plastics, and have been set recycling targets by the national government. Intercontinental Hotels tries to recycle food, glass and paper. The food recycling is organized by staff at the hotel. Intercontinental Hotels has not made much financially from these recycling schemes, but they are liked by staff. Many companies find environmentally friendly policies contribute to a feel-good factor in the company.

Recycle

Eighty-five per cent of aluminium cans are recycled in Sweden.

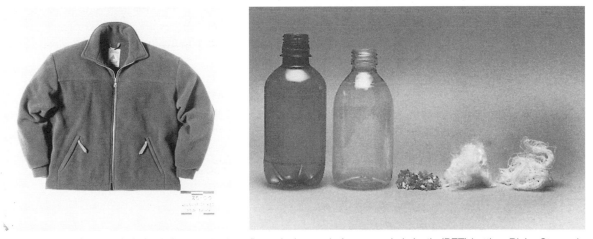

Figure 9.3   Left: Recycled plastic jacket: Karrimor fleece jacket made from recycled plastic (PET) bottles; Right: Stages in recycling PET bottles into yarn

Many camera companies now recycle lightweight single-use cameras. DuPont also recycle their film. This has given them the incentive to research better film. They now make thinner and stronger film for which customers are prepared to pay more than for conventional film.

Waste management

Reduce

Recycling is only the tip of the iceberg. A number of companies have also tried to reduce their use of unnecessary materials. Most businesses can cut costs, reduce waste and pollution by:

- improving wall and roofing insulation
- using more energy-efficient lighting and heating, coupled with automated controls
- using waste heat that would otherwise be lost
- using low-energy-consumption equipment
- using recycled paper
- using e-mail instead of paper
- encouraging teleworking.

Incentives and simple guidance could encourage more businesses to move in this direction. Implementing environmentally sound programmes can cost money, but most businesses find *waste* management programmes offer substantial savings. Dow Europe cut paper flow by 30% in six weeks merely by discouraging unwanted information (Lovins *et al.*, 1999). Johnson Wax saved hundreds of thousands of pounds by reducing waste and scrap from around 3% to 1% (Henry, 1991b). For highly polluting processes like aluminium production, the conscious attempt to cut *emissions* can bring substantial benefits. Norsk Hydro's environmental reports enabled them to show that emissions were cut by about 90% in the 1970s and 1980s.

Many other companies have saved money by anticipating potential sources of pollution and eliminating them early on, so saving on raw materials, waste and pollution charges. We see the results of these changes all around us, for example buildings that put in automatic light switches to save money.

Environmental audit

Organizations have begun to use *environmental audits* to see how environmentally efficient they are, in areas such as waste management, energy conservation and pollution emission.

A typical environmental audit would look at the following areas:

Waste management	Hazardous materials
Energy conservation	Pesticides and herbicides
Product purchase	PCBs
Water	Storage tanks
Air emissions	Laundry and cleaning
Noise	Community actions

An audit may suggest replacing certain items that were previously in use for environmental reasons. Johnson Wax was an early innovator in this respect. It phased out its most popular aerosol deodorant (US) in 1975, because of concerns over the effects of CFCs. Like most innovators, it was not popular among its peers for this move. It has also brought recycling into the manufacturing process, though early attempts to use recycled plastic packaging were hampered by the lack of security of supply of recycled plastic. Interestingly, this idea was suggested by an employee.

Replace

Companies that have adopted the notion of environmental responsibility as a key business value (such as Body Shop) may insist on auditing their suppliers as well: checking, for example, that hardwoods come from a sustainable source. Nowadays bids and tenders increasingly require an environmental impact statement and many organizations, including major players like British Airways, produce an annual environmental report.

Cradle-to-grave manufacturing

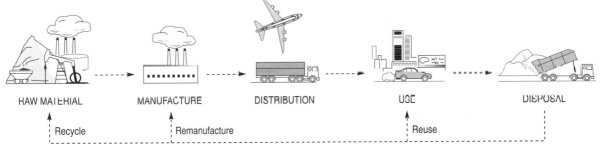

RAW MATERIAL — MANUFACTURE — DISTRIBUTION — USE — DISPOSAL

Recycle   Remanufacture   Reuse

Figure 9.4   Life cycle analysis chart

Until quite recently the standard business response to environmental issues normally consisted of attempts to clean up after the product had been made, for example adding catalytic converters to cars. Environmentalists are now encouraging organizations to take account of the total life cycle of the product, as illustrated in Figure 9.4. Companies such as AEG and Ford have begun to design manufacturing processes on the 'cradle to grave' principle, that takes account of the environmental costs of manufacture, distribution, use and disposal of their product.

Reuse

Disassembly

German manufacturers have developed impressive *disassembly* technologies where all parts are marked and can be recycled once the machine has finished its natural life.

In the early 1980s AEG made a policy decision to adopt a 'green' approach. They introduced washing-machines using 75 litres of water compared to the average UK model's 110. They adopted the 'cradle to grave' concept in which the manufacturer takes responsibility for the disposal as well as manufacture of the materials in his or her product. AEG now manufactures and assembles its washing-machines in such a way that the plastic can be recycled when the

The Chinese chose an inefficient Japanese fridge manufacturer. While this gave them cheap fridges, these fridges use more power to run, so from an ecological perspective they might have done better adopting a dearer but more efficient refrigerator manufacturer.

customer has finished with the product. AEG found that its moves towards more environmentally friendly processes spawned related concerns amongst employees who insisted on further changes: for example, a demand to bring back reusable rather than disposable cutlery and crockery – a practice now adopted by a number of airlines.[44]

Car manufacture and use

Car manufacturers are beginning to consider ways of reducing the serious pollution caused by current car design. Roy *et al*. (1996) explain that cars are made largely of steel, other metals such as aluminium, plastics and glass. Extracting and processing these materials involves consuming large amounts of energy and water, and producing various emissions and substantial quantities of solid waste. During car manufacture there is further consumption of energy, water and other inputs, which in turn produces unwanted air emissions and solid waste. US manufacturers have tended to focus on reducing emissions during the manufacturing phase, for example using water-based paints. Volvo has a relatively clean factory.

During *use* the car not only consumes substantial quantities of finite petrol or diesel but produces CO_2, carbon monoxide, unburned hydrocarbons and nitrogen oxides, which are harmful to health and/or the environment. Reducing emissions during use, through lead-free petrol and catalytic converters, in turn reduces the output of lead, carbon monoxide, hydrocarbon and nitrogen oxides. Saab cars have relatively clean engines and exhausts. At least 80% of cars' environmental impact is generated during use, due to their consumption of non-renewable fossil fuels and exhaust emissions. Thus fuel-efficient designs entailing lighter more aerodynamic bodies and smaller cars are likely to be more environmentally friendly. Honda and Citroën have produced more fuel-efficient cars (Roy *et al*., 1996).

Some car manufacturers have attempted to introduce more plastic parts which are readily identified and easier to remove for recycling. Though plastic saves fuel, as it makes the car lighter, it is more expensive to recycle. German car manufacturers have tried to design cars so that an increasing proportion of the car can be recycled. About 75% of current car design is steel, which is already generally recycled, but that leaves about a considerable quantity of other materials. Volkswagen has made further progress than most. Nearly 100% of the plastic they use during production can be recycled. All parts are now marked. A pilot project disassembling old cars has led the company to favour clips over screws in the newer designs. They accept Golfs for recycling at the end of their life. BMW aim to recycle 100% of their cars through a design that takes account of disassembly.

Whilst the redesign of products can often reduce environmental impact by 50%–75% this is hard to achieve with cars, as about 80% of the environmental impact is caused during car use, not manufacture.

---

[44] Sometimes the environmental equation is not straightforward. Once you take into account the environmental cost of manufacturing and washing ceramic cups, surprisingly disposable crockery can be environmentally preferable in certain circumstances.

CITELA – CITROËN'S PROTOTYPE ELECTRIC TOWN CAR
Neg. No. 651

Figure 9.5   Electric vehicles: Left. Citroen Citela; right: Camden Community Transport minibus

Electric cars afford less local pollution, but at the expense of increased pollution at the power stations producing the electricity, unless this comes from renewable energy such as hydro-electric, solar or wind power.

Lovins *et al.* (2000) point out that present car design is not at all efficient. The Hypercar reduces fuel consumption by 85% and the materials used by 90%, through four innovations based on existing technologies. First, using a carbon fibre polymer reduces the weight by two-thirds and this, together with improved aerodynamics, substantially reduces resistance which cuts fuel use by about two-thirds. A small clean, hybrid electric drive based on a fuel cell reduces fuel consumption by a further third. Finally, much of the hardware such as the transmission is replaced by electronics. These vehicles offer 80 to 200 miles per gallon.

Increased efficiency

Most manufacturing organizations can introduce more environmentally friendly policies, and often in such a way as to cut costs, by adopting one or more of the strategies summarized in the table below.

Table 9.2 Environmental manufacturing strategies		
Environmental goal	**Strategy**	**Example**
Reduce energy	Energy efficient	Lean-burn engine
	Conservation	Thermostatic radiator valves
	Renewable	Solar water heater, wind turbine
Reduce materials	Use less	Rechargeable batteries
	Recycled	Packaging from recycled plastic
	Renewable	Furniture from sustainably managed sources
	Reuse	Computers designed for upgrading
Reduce pollution, waste	Reduce hazardous materials	CFC-free fridges
	Pollution control	Vehicle catalytic converter

(Adapted from R. Roy, 1994)

Zero emissions

Some manufacturers have gone further and are aiming at zero emissions. For example Xerox now have the goal of zero landfill. They have already saved 80 million dollars through product reprocessing, and landfill is down to less than 9% of solid material. Ecover, the environmentally friendly cleaning materials company, has gone further than most towards this end (see Box 9.3).

BOX 9.3   ECOVER

Ecover is a Belgium-based company manufacturing phosphate-free cleaning materials in a conscious attempt to do less damage to the environment. The factory is made of pine from renewable forests, and clay sawdust and coal-mining waste bricks which are lighter and better insulated than their conventional equivalents. Waste water is recycled through a reed meadow. There are no airborne emissions. The factory also boasts a grass roof which acts as an effective heat and sound insulator in summer and winter. Though construction costs were double that of a conventional building, the factory recouped that additional cost in three years through reduced power and water bills. Employees get a travel allowance of 15 Belgian francs a kilometre if cycling to work, 10 for a trip by motorcycle and only 5 for a car journey, though those in a car pool can each claim the allowance (Carvel, 1992; also www.ecover.com).

However, Ecover still produce some emissions albeit far less than the industry norm. The altruistic Gunter Pauli, previously Ecover's CEO, wanted to do better and is now engaged in producing products which involve zero emissions. For example using sludge from a brewery to grow Shitake mushrooms, using the leftovers from this for cattle feed and using methane from the cattle dung to fuel the brewery.

But Gunter Pauli is an exception. Many people argue that the only way environmental problems are ever going to be addressed on a sufficiently major scale is to fundamentally alter the way we think about business.

Natural capitalism

The Natural Capitalism movement, championed by Hunter and Amery Lovins (Hawken *et al.*, 1999) of the Rocky Mountain Institute in Colorado, argues that the way forward for business is to mimic nature as this is often very efficient and environmentally friendlier. For example, abalone (an edible marine mollusc) converts sea water into a shell twice as tough as the best ceramics, and trees convert sunlight, water, air and soil into cellulose, which is stronger than nylon. Fifteen per cent of Wisconsin's cattle farms have now turned to a system, long used in New Zealand, whereby cattle graze intensively in an area for a short time and then move, mimicking the action of large herds of buffalo. This produces clearly superior returns on traditional methods.

The proponents of Natural Capitalism point out that mimicking nature in this way is often good for business. *Leasing* rather than selling is an example of a change in mind-set that can support the move to a better environmental balance without compromising the balance sheet.

Interface is a carpet company that offers a carpet leasing service. In reframing the nature of the carpet business from selling to leasing the incentives change. If you are selling carpet, the incentive is to offer cheap carpet that does not last long and that customers need to replace more often, which in turn increases the use of landfill. The company gains through leasing by offering better carpet that needs less maintenance and, as it lasts a long time, one that has to be replaced less often. Furthermore only certain areas of carpet get worn, so by using carpet tiles the company can replace only about a fifth of the total square footage in most offices. This avoids the need to move office furniture when replacing carpet, thus minimizing cost and disruption; and because less carpet has to be produced and disposed of, the use of energy, materials and landfill is cut correspondingly. The company has invented a new type of long-lasting carpet (Solenium) that uses less material, is chlorine-free, virtually stainproof, does not have mildew, can be cleaned with water and looks good. All these are moves in the right direction from an ecological point of view, whilst giving the customer a better deal and making the company money.

Natural capitalism

Leasing

181

Through emphasizing service rather than sales, Interface has increased profits by 200%, doubled their revenue and tripled employment. Replacing carpet squares can take more staff than replacing a whole carpet; but, since it is natural not human resources that are in short supply these days, an increase in staffing is beneficial as it provides employment. This is a social service in an era where unemployment is pandemic: in the UK, for example, one in five households has no one in work (Darling, 1999).

A number of other firms have seen advantages in reframing their business as leasing rather than selling. These include Schindler the elevator company, and Dow Chemical which leases dissolving services rather than selling solvents (as they can reuse the solvents). United Technologies Carriers division leases air-conditioning, and is now in partnership with building firms to develop more efficient buildings using less or no air-conditioning. Their clients pay for an agreed comfort level, not the means of achieving it. Lovins *et al.* (1999) argue that in this way the service economy has the potential to be good for the environment and for business (Lovins *et al.* in Henry, 2001).

Activity 9.2

What drives decisions in your organization? Is it short-termism, or do the decision takers take account of the long-term consequences of their actions?

Do you believe that managers and organizations are becoming more environmentally responsible, or is this just green tokenism?

Has your organization responded to ecological concerns in any way?

What would you like it to do?

What can you envisage happening in your organization in the near future that would represent a move towards greater ecological responsibility?

9.5 REVIEW

Organizations can do a lot to improve the environmental balance sheet in ways that make business sense. They can reduce waste and pollution, improve energy efficiency, recycle, introduce cradle to grave manufacturing, design for recycling and reuse, and switch to renewable resources. Others argue, however, that more fundamental change is needed if we are to avert potential environmental disaster, and that this requires leadership from senior industrialists and politicians. Cradle to grave manufacturing, natural capitalism and zero emissions are steps in the right direction.

Further reading/Listening/Surfing

J. Henry *et al.*, 'Sustainability', *Creativity, Innovation and Change* Audio 3.

Lovins A. *et al.*, 'Natural capitalism', in Henry (2001).

Your Business and the Environment: An Executive Guide (London: Business in the Community, 1991)

Hypercar website: http://www.hypercar.com

Ecover website: http://www.ecover.com

10 RESPONSIBILITY

> Some are sceptical of the trend towards accountability and corporate citizenship – claiming that businesses only do it because they see benefits for themselves. That's precisely the point. It's good common sense for business to implement corporate citizenship.
>
> *(Sir Christopher Harding, Chairman, United Utilities (BIC, 1998b, p. 3))*

It has been suggested that sustainable ways of doing business will not happen until business considers the social as well as the environmental consequences of their actions alongside economic concerns (e.g. Shiva, 1999).

Fortunately there seems to be a trend towards taking social concerns more seriously. For example a MORI poll of 100 UK captains of industry found the percentage who agreed that 'Industry and commerce do not pay enough attention to their social responsibilities' increased from 28% in 1997 to 44% in 1998.

A number of business gurus, including Charles Handy and Rosabeth Moss Kanter, stress that companies will have to pay greater attention to their ethical image in the future (Handy, 1999). The argument is that, in an increasingly portfolio-based world of work, people will opt to work for organizations whose values they share. A number of surveys have shown people are attracted to working for companies they believe to be socially responsible. In addition values have become a key element of corporate branding.

There are a number of different ways in which organizations can be socially responsible.[45] These include:

- donating goods and services
- staff volunteering
- social marketing
- ethical investment
- social auditing.

Traditionally companies have merely offered token support for the local community in the form of cash handouts to worthy causes, like local hospital equipment or national sponsorship of sport. In either case the company usually had their eye on the publicity. Nowadays, in addition to cash, companies are increasingly providing goods or services. There is also growing interest in the idea of involving staff more directly, for example as community volunteers, or developing education projects in areas allied to the company's expertise.

---

[45] 'Organizations in the community', *Creativity, Innovation and Change* Audio 4, illustrates various approaches to social involvement – including volunteering, helping the local community, the problems facing fair trade organizations and the processes entailed in conducting a social audit through interviews with staff from Boots, Body Shop, the Co-operative Bank and elsewhere.

The benefits of a socially responsible approach include the following:

- people in the community benefit
- community projects enhance a feel-good factor in the organization
- good staff like to work for socially responsible organizations
- community projects offer excellent ways of developing and training staff and team building
- consumers like to buy goods from socially responsible companies
- community projects also build good relations with the local community.

In addition there is a legislative trend towards encouraging if not enforcing more responsibility towards stakeholders.

In 1992 Whitbread allocated a fifth of their community investment to charitable giving and an increasing proportion (currently three-quarters) of this is being handled regionally rather than centrally.

10.1   COMMUNITY INVOLVEMENT

Volunteering

A number of companies allow staff at any level a s*mall amount of time* off work to act as community volunteers. For example Body Shop allows staff half a day a month. Volunteering is not for everybody; though now aiming for 100 per cent participation, in the early 1990s Body Shop found about a third of their staff opted to take part. IBM Edinburgh has half of their 180 staff involved in community initiatives. Boots, who have been assisting their local community for many years, now offer many different kinds of project, including some where whole departments shut down for a day to complete a community task. Regardless of the type of volunteering, staff usually value the experience very highly.

Fifty-one per cent of UK adults volunteer and most do so regularly.

(National Council for Volunteering Survey quoted on BIC webpage)

Boots and Marks and Spencer are two of many companies that make a point of helping their *local community*. In past years Marks and Spencer has set aside over £5 million to support the communities in which it operates. Three specialist sub-committees deal with health care, the arts and community services and education. Boots head office has a policy of helping Nottingham, the area from which it recruits its headquarters staff and in which it is the largest employer. One project entails Boots staff helping with literacy projects in schools, a project with a potential long-term payoff, as the schools are those from which future Boots workers may be recruited. A number of companies have given their staff more say in which projects they work on: Boots and IBM provide grants to support local community activities (such as clearing derelict land) suggested by groups of their employees.

Staff volunteers renovating a local windmill

Other companies send managers off on *longer* projects. For example Hindustanlever, the Indian branch of Unilever, sends young managers off to local villages for weeks or months. They find the local knowledge managers pick up pays off for product development, and is a prerequisite for opening up their market – as well as being an important educational and life experience for middle-class trainees unfamiliar with the privations of village life in the Indian subcontinent.

Training and development potential

We have stopped seeing our activity as philanthropic and manage the process more professionally, ensuring the company as well as the community receive a direct return on our investment.

Ian Henderson. (Corporate Community Involvement, Whitbread. (BIC, 1998, p. 13)

Many organizations now realize the potential of volunteering for staff *training and development*, and pick projects with this in mind. Indeed volunteering is increasingly popular as a form of management development. For example Marks and Spencer requires all store managers to take a leadership role in a community initiative. As well as helping the community, this type of volunteering is also an excellent way of team building and keeping staff in touch with customers. BP and Hewlett Packard, for example, have sent teams to work on community development projects in Africa. Whitbread claim that bringing staff from different divisions to undertake community projects – such as cleaning and decorating an all-weather shelter for the homeless – is better for bonding, networking and generating team spirit than more traditional approaches. Proponents also argue that completed employee-led projects have more impact than merely handing over a cheque, and lead to more goodwill from the community.

Social innovation partnerships

Some local authorities encourage public–private partnerships which link businesses with appropriate voluntary organizations. Thanet has matched 43 local businesses with 37 local voluntary organizations (BIC, 1998b).

Social innovation partnerships

A number of organizations have found *partnerships* with community and educational organizations useful in developing prototype products and services while helping the community. Companies engaged in such schemes work in areas that utilize their core competencies: for example IBM and computing, or Bank Boston and community banking. Bell and IBM have found partnering state schools a useful forum for developing IT innovations. For example IBM developed new drag and drop technology using the latest software features. Marriott and United Airlines are involved in welfare to work programmes employing people previously on benefit. More than two-thirds of Marriott's employees tend to be poorly qualified and the company has been plagued by high staff turnover. Their programme included supplying transport to work, offering a mentor and providing advice on non-work issues such as housing benefit. As a result they have ended up with a much more stable workforce, which pays for the programme costs through reduced turnover and absenteeism (Kanter, 1999).

Kanter claims that companies engaged in social partnerships with educational and community enterprises have a better chance of success if they have a clear business agenda and are committed to change; if both parties invest in the project and make staff commitments; if the project is rooted in the user community (as in IBM working with schools using their computers); and if the organization can involve other organizations where necessary, and has a commitment to sustain and where appropriate replicate any resulting improvements (Kanter's article in Henry, 2001 elaborates on this).

Social marketing

Social campaigning and cause-related marketing has been with us for a while. Few people can have escaped Benetton's 'designed to shock' advertising, or Body Shop's campaign against animal testing. Many companies involve themselves in projects related to their product, for example Flora margarine's health and fitness schemes.

Appropriate social marketing is proving very popular with customers. For example, after offering 'computers in schools' vouchers, Tesco handed over 30,000 computers to schools in 1997 (Buckby, 1998). Banks are now operating credit schemes in conjunction with environmental and other not-for-profit organizations whereby the recipient organizations retain a small percentage of the profits. Beneficial Bank operates such a scheme for the Open University which, amongst other things, has been able to offer hardship grants to many poorer students. Many retailers like the Body Shop, the Co-op and B and Q do-it-yourself also run in-store awareness campaigns on health, environmental and/or social issues.

The Tesco 'Computers in Schools' scheme

10.2   SOCIAL RESPONSIBILITY

Ethical investment

Some organizations and consumers take the question of social responsibility more seriously, and make a point of investing only in companies they believe to be ethical. Typically this involves excluding companies who are engaged in manufacturing weapons or whose products or processes can have a deleterious effect on health, such as tobacco companies, or the environment: for example, only backing forestry companies that practise sustainable forestry. The Co-operative Bank also refuses to invest in companies which extract and process fossil fuels, and those producing CFCs or undertaking unsustainable agriculture.

The UK market for ethical investment trusts, though still relatively small, is growing rapidly, suggesting consumer interest in this area is increasing.

Other companies' *raison d'être* is to be socially responsible. The various fair trade companies, such as Cafédirect, Green and Black chocolate and Traidcraft, exist to give producers in the developing world a fairer price for their goods. These businesses have to face economic realities like any other company, and normally charge the consumer a small

Percent club

Over 300 companies, including United Biscuit Holdings and Tate and Lyle, have committed themselves to donating 1% of dividends or 0.5% of UK profits to the community.

(Business in the Community Newsletter, 1999)

FINANCIAL ADVISER

REST ASSURED MADAM DE BEERS HAVE NOTHING TO DO WITH BREWING

premium to cover the more generous rates they are paying suppliers, a charge many consumers in the developed world are happy to pay.

Social audit

Doing well by doing good

The idea of a social audit is fairly new to the business community. It was first tried in the UK in the early 1990s. Ethically minded companies like the Body Shop, the Co-operative Bank, Traidcraft, Ben and Jerry's and Co-op Italia have led the way in attempting to demonstrate their ethical credentials through a social audit. A number of larger companies like Shell and BT have followed suit.

A study by the Centre for Environmental and Social Accountancy Research found major British companies had quadrupled their social reporting over the last twenty years (Zadek, 1998). At present this is largely voluntary, but the prospect of further mandatory social reporting is on the horizon. In the UK companies are already required to disclose charitable donations, employment data, pension fund data, employee consultation, employee share ownership, employment of disabled people and provisions for health and safety. Many companies also voluntarily report on environmental protection measures, energy saving, consumer protection, product safety, community involvement, health and safety, racial and sexual equality, redundancies, and employee training, and also include their mission statement (Gray, 1997).

Most social audits use a mix of qualitative and quantitative data. United Utilities suggested social, environmental and financial audits can be achieved through examining the conveniently alliterative 'five Ps' :

- Perception – how we are perceived
- Participation – scale and effectiveness of company action
- Partnership – satisfaction of community partners
- Processes – measuring effectiveness of planning, implementation and assessment
- Performance – actual benefits to business, employees and the community.

Stakeholders

Typically organizations use existing measures to indicate their social performance, coupled with survey data on *stakeholder's* views about how the company is performing in social terms. The stakeholders surveyed normally include staff, customers and shareholders plus representatives of the local community and, in some cases, suppliers. Traidcraft's 1998 social accounts cover customers, suppliers, funders and staff. Ben and Jerry's, the ice cream company, viewed their stakeholders as the communities in which they operate, their employees, customers, suppliers and investors. The Co-operative Bank also contacts past and future co-operators (members of the bank) and attempts to take account of the interests of the global community.

The problem is in deciding on *appropriate indicators* to represent the interests of different stakeholders and finding ways to measure them. Straightforward measures like financial performance data generally meet the shareholders' needs, and details of staff turnover, wage and training day comparisons cover some staff concerns. Benchmarks like price and profit and speed of payment can be used as indicators for suppliers, but the views of the local and global community can be harder to determine. Surveys of local opinion are one option, and using experts to comment on global impact offers another way forward. Surveys can be expensive, so companies may attempt to spread the cost by surveying different suppliers each year: thus Traidcraft approaches African suppliers one year and those in south-east Asia the next.

Another key feature of social audits is *external verification* at some stage(s) of the process. Organizations may ask one or more trustworthy third parties to suggest appropriate indicators, collect and provide data and/or comment on their social report. The object of the exercise is to reassure readers that this is more than a PR exercise. For example, Business in the Community, a NGO (non-governmental organization), suggested that the Co-op Bank investigate the social consequences of branch closure. The Co-op Bank then checked the nature of customers' concerns in areas where branches had been closed. About half of those contacted were concerned about staff losing jobs through branch closure and wished to be able to bank locally. The Co-operative Bank claim the audit enabled them to disclose that they had a policy of no compulsory redundancies and a deal with Post Offices enabling local banking. They claim this information met most of the customers' concerns.

External verification

Social audits can lead to *policy changes* by the organization concerned. Ben and Jerry's social audits have led to changes in formal parental leave and employee stock ownership. Traidcraft has identified as a future priority the need for it and its suppliers to reduce use of potentially harmful dyes and unnecessary packaging. Surveys of customer opinion have helped the Co-op Bank and American Express decide on their priorities (in the latter case, which charities to support). Cynics suspect that Shell undertook a social audit merely in an attempt to enhance their image after the Brent Spar public relations disaster, but the company claims the audit has helped the company understand what they need to do.

A feature of social audits is a warts and all approach. Even the most ethically minded companies, like the Body Shop and Ben and Jerry's, have been surprised to find that their social audits have thrown up criticisms of company policy. Nevertheless Ben and Jerry's argue that they have benefited from the *goodwill* brought about through their socially responsible attitude. And most companies who undertake social audits claim doing so increases understanding, enhances company and brand reputation, and builds trust with stakeholders.

KPMG, the large accounting consultancy, have bought out the Body Shop audit team, so perhaps social audits are on their way to becoming a growth area. It remains to be seen if social auditing represents a passing fad or a sea change in the type of information companies will be obliged to report.

Board representation
Most manufacturing and chemical companies have a board member responsible for co-ordinating environmental policies, but very few companies have an equivalent overseeing socially responsible activities.

Activity 10.1

What would you say are your organization's moral responsibilities to each of its stakeholders? How is the organization doing?

If it has one, does your organization's mission statement address a sufficiently broad group of stakeholders?

Citizen companies

RIGHT THEN, THAT'S UNANIMOUS. DAI'S BOSS AGAIN THIS WEEK.

Handy and Kanter argue that it is not sufficient to direct these good works to the community, but rather that businesses themselves will have to reorganize on more ethical lines. Handy (1998) suggests that we need to think of employees as citizens and give them the rights associated with citizenship. The right to a financial stake in the company, to be privy to information about the company, to participate in decisions affecting its and their future, to wear what they want, and have a lot of control over where and how they achieve tasks. Kanter envisages private-sector organizations becoming more like voluntary-sector organizations attracting good staff who share the company's values. If they are right about a move to more socially responsible business practice, organizations may be expected to increase their public engagement in dealing with the potentially devastating environmental and social issues currently facing the world, and to do so in a creative manner. (See Handy's article in Henry, 2001, for elaboration.)

10.3   REVIEW

There is an increasing recognition of the need to earn a 'licence to practise' through corporate citizenship. There has been a trend away from philanthropy towards undertaking activities that integrate socially responsible action with other aspects of the business; for example socially innovative public–private partnerships such as a multinational producing an education pack with a local authority. Some organizations now undertake social audits; these tend to incorporate principles of benchmarking, stakeholder dialogue, external verification, disclosure and continuous improvement.

Further reading/Surfing/Listening

J. Henry, 'Organizations in the community', *Creativity, Innovation and Change* Audio 4.

C. Handy, 'The citizen company', in Henry (2001).

R. M. Kanter, 'From spare change to real change', in Henry (2001).

Business in the Community website: http://www.bitc.org.uk

BOOK REVIEW

The book as a whole has addressed creativity, cognition, style, development and sustainability. Its main thrust has been to show how thought constrains action. It has illustrated how our assumptions about creativity influence the strategies we use to achieve it, and introduced ways in which creative endeavour can be enhanced in organizations. It has emphasized the importance of intuitive thinking, unconscious learning and tacit knowledge for managers dealing with uncertainty, and illustrated the cognitive constraints imposed by mind-sets and judgement biases. It has advocated the use of metaphor as a route to reframing different aspects of organizational life. In discussing style it has shown how individuals have strong tendencies to approach problems, communicate and make decisions in particular ways, and how these preferences may make them more suited to some organizational roles than to others. It has shown how management attitudes and behaviour, and organizational development, are framed through deep-seated cultural and historical values. It has suggested that the environmental crisis is bound up with long-standing patterns of thought, and that social responsibility is a quality the best companies are now keen to exhibit and the best employees keen to associate with.

This book has presented a picture of employees who have very different understandings of the appropriate way forward, and who need each other to grasp the whole story. Such an image leads naturally to a facilitative and participative style of managing which can build on the differences between individuals. This creative approach to management recognizes the importance of fostering individual development, empowering others, nurturing promising ideas and building an open climate. The book has attempted to convey some of the principles behind the open attitude that is the hallmark of managing creatively, such as the idea of challenging assumptions and considering different angles and alternatives through processes of reframing and empathizing with others' viewpoints, while acknowledging the constraining influence of cultural context on the possibilities perceived. In so doing, it has championed the importance of management by perception rather than analysis.

The practical consequences of these ideas for innovation and change management are explored in more detail in Henry *et al.* (2001) *Innovation, Climate and Change,* and the associated follow-up readings in Henry and Mayle (2001) *Managing Innovation and Change.*

REFERENCES

Agor, W. (1986) 'The logic of intuition: how top executives make important decisions', *Organisational Dynamics*, 14, Winter, pp. 5–18, also in Henry (1991).

Albery, N. and Yule, Y. (1989) *Encyclopaedia of Social Inventions*, London: ISS.

Amabile, T. (1998) 'How to kill creativity', *Harvard Business Review*, September–October, pp. 77–87, also in Henry (2001).

Amabile, T. (1983) *The Social Psychology of Creativity*, New York: Springer Verlag, also 2ndedn, *Creativity in Context* (1990).

Amabile, T. and Gryskiewicz, S. (1988) 'Creative human resources in the R and D laboratory: how environment and personality affect innovation', in Kuhn, R., *Handbook for Creative and Innovative Management*, New York: McGraw-Hill, pp. 501–24.

Argyle, M. (1987) *The Psychology of Happiness*, New York: Methuen.

Argyris, C. (1998) 'Empowerment: the emperor's new clothes', *Harvard Business Review* May/ June pp. 98–105, also in Henry (2001).

Argyris, C. (1994) 'Communication that blocks learning', *Harvard Business Review*, July/August, pp. 77–85.

Barron, F. (1968) *Creativity and Personal Freedom*, New York: Van Nostrand.

Bartram, D. (1995) *Review of personality assessment instruments (level B) for use in occupational settings*, Leicester: British Psychological Society.

Basadur, M. (1990) 'Identifying individual differences in creative problem-solving', *Journal of Creative Behaviour*, 24, 2.

Bayne, R. (1994) 'The "Big Five" versus the Myers–Briggs', *Psychologist*, January, pp. 14–16, also in Henry (2001).

Beadle, I. (1993) 'Different not better', in J. Henry (ed.) *Creative Management Readings*, Milton Keynes: Open University Press.

Belbin, R. M. (1993) *Roles at Work: a strategy for human resource management* , Oxford: Butterworth Heinemann.

Belbin, R. M. (1981) *Management Teams: why they succeed or fail*, Oxford: Heinemann, also 2nd edn (1988).

Belbin Associates (1988) *Interplace: Matching People to Jobs.* Cambridge, Belbin Associates.

Berreby, D. (1998) 'Complexity theory: fact-free science or business tool?', *Strategy and Business*, No. 10, pp. 40–50.

Berry, D. C. and Dienes, Z. (1992) *Implicit Learning*, London: Lawrence Erlbaum.

BIC (1998a) *Business in the Community: a Financial Times guide*, London: Business in the Community/Financial Times, December 3rd.

BIC (1998b) *Business in the Community Annual Report*, London: BIC.

BIC (1999) *Business in the Community Newsletter*, London: BIC.

Bion, W. R. (1968) *Experiences in Groups*, London: Tavistock Publications.

de Bono, E. (1984) *Lateral Thinking for Management*, Harmondsworth: Penguin.

de Bono, E. (1971) *Lateral Thinking*, Harmondsworth: Penguin.

Bohm, D. and Peat, F. D. (1991) 'Science, order and creativity', Chapter 4 in Henry (1991).

Briggs Myers, I. and McCaulley, M. H. (1988) *Manual: A Guide to the Development and Use of the Myers–Briggs Type Indicator*, Palo Alto, CA: Consulting Psychologists Press.

Briggs Myers, I. and Myers, P. (1989) *Gifts Differing*, Palo Alto, CA: Consulting Psychologists Press.

Brown, M. (1988) *The Dinosaur Strain*, London: Element.

Brown, M. (1971) 'Management's set solution', *Management Today*, April.

Buckby, S. (1998) 'Propping up the bottom line', in BIC (1998).

Burrell, G. (1996) *Pandemonium*, London: Sage.

Burns, F. T. and Stalker, G. (1961) 'Mechanistic and organic systems of management', Chapter 6 in *The Management of Innovation*, London: Tavistock.

Campbell, D. and Van Velsor, E. (1978) *The Use of Personality Measures in the Leadership Development Program*, Greensboro, NC: Center for Creative Leadership.

Carne, G. and Kirton, M. (1982) 'Styles of creativity: test–score correlations between Kirton adaption–innovation inventory and the Myers–Briggs type indicator', *Psychological Reports,* Vol. 50, pp. 31–6.

Chikudate, N. (1991) 'Cross-cultural analysis of cognitive systems in organizations: a comparison between Japanese and American organizations', *Management International Review,* Vol. 31, pp. 213–19.

Chinese Culture Connection (1987) 'Chinese values and the search for culture free dimensions of culture', *Journal of Cross-Cultural Psychology,* 18, pp. 143–64.

Clark, A. (1997) *Being There*, Cambridge, MA: MIT.

Claxton, G (1999) 'The innovative mind: becoming smarter by thinking less', in Henry (2001).

Claxton, G. (1997) *Hare Brain, Tortoise Mind: Why intelligence increases when you think less*, London: Fourth Estate.

Collins, J. and Porras, J. (1995) 'Building a visionary company', *California Management Review,* 37, 2, pp. 80–100.

Collins, O., Moore, D. and Umwalla, D. (1964) *The Enterprising Man*, Michigan State University.

Covey, S. (1989) *The Seven Habits of Effective People*, New York: Simon and Schuster.

Csikszentmihlyi, M. (1997) 'A systems view of creativity', in Henry (2001).

Csikszentmihalyi, M. (1996) *Creativity: Flow and the Psychology of Discovery and Invention*, New York: HarperCollins.

Cyert, R. and March, J. (1963) *A Behavioural Theory of the Firm*, Englewood Cliffs, NJ: Prentice-Hall.

Daly, H. and Cobb, J. (1991) *For the Common Good*, Boston: Beacon, quoted in Russell (1994).

Darling, A. (1999) quoted on 'Newsnight', BBC 2, 6th September.

Davis, J. (1991) *Greening Business: Managing for Sustainable Development*, Oxford: Blackwell.

Davis, W. (1991) *The Innovators*, London: Ebury Press. See also Chapter 14 in Henry and Walker (1991).

Deal, T. and Kennedy, A. (1982) *Corporate Cultures*, Harmondsworth: Penguin.

Drucker, P. (1985) *Innovation and Entrepreneurship*, London: Heinemann.

Drucker, P. (1991) 'Transnational ecology', in Henry (1991).

Ekvall, G. (1997) 'Organisational conditions and level of creativity', in Henry and Mayle (2001).

Ekvall, G. (1991) 'The organizational culture of idea management', in Henry and Walker, op. cit.

Elkington, J., Knight, P. and Hailes, J. (1991) The Green Business Guide: How to Take-up and Profit from the Environmental Challenge, London: Gollancz.

Erikson, E.H (1959) *Identity and the Life-Cycle*, New York: Norton.

Evans, R. and Russell, P. (1989) *The Creative Manager*, London: Unwin Hyman.

Evans, R. and Russell, P. (1991) 'Using the creative process to resolve a strategic conflict at Berol', in Henry and Walker (1991).

Foucault, M. (1980) *Power/Knowledge*, Brighton: Harvester.

Foucault, M. (1977) *Discipline and Punish: the Birth of the Prison*, London: Penguin.

Foxall, G. (1989) 'Adaptive and innovative cognitive styles of market initiators', Chapter 6 in M. J. Kirton, *Adaptors and Innovators*, London: Routledge.

Furnham, A. (1995) *Personality at Work*, London: Routledge.

Furnham, A., Steele, H. and Pendleton, D. (1993) 'A psychometric assessment of the Belbin Team-Role Self-Perception Inventory', *Journal of Occupational and Organizational Psychology*, Vol. 66, pp. 245–47.

Fukuyama, F. (1999) *The Great Disruption*, London: Profile.

Fukuyama, F. (1996) *Trust*, New York: Free Press.

Gabriel, Y. (1999) 'Psychodynamics', in Henry (2001).

Gelade, G. (1999)' Locating creative style in the personality domain: a meta-analysis of KAI and the five-factor model', unpublished.

Goldberg, L. R. (1993) 'The structure of phenotypic personality traits', *American Psychologist*, 48, pp. 26–34.

Goleman, D. (1998) 'How to be become a leader', in Henry (2001).

Gray, C. (1997) 'Small business growth and owners' motivation', in *Creative Management Readings 3*, Milton Keynes: Open University Press.

Gray, R. (1997) 'The practice of silent accounting', in S. Zadek, *Building Corporate Accountability*, London: Earthscan, pp. 210–17.

Grossi, G. (1990) 'Promoting innovation in big business', *Long Range Planning*, Vol. 23, No. 1, pp. 41–52.

Guildford, J. (1959) 'Trends in creativity', in Anderson, H., *Creativity and its Cultivation*, New York: Wiley.

Haley, U. and Stumpf, S. (1987) 'Cognitive trails in strategic decision-making: linking personalities and cognitions', *Journal of Management Studies*, Vol. 26, No. 5, pp. 477–97 (also in *Creative Management Readings*, Milton Keynes: Open University Press, 1991).

Hammer, M. and Champy, J. (1994) *Reengineering the Corporation: A Manifesto for Business Revolution*, London: Nicholas Brealey.

Hampden-Turner, C. (1994) *Corporate Culture*, London, Piaktus.

Hampden-Turner, C. and Trompenaars, F. (1993) *The Seven Cultures of Capitalism*, New York, Doubleday.

Hampson, S.E. (1999) 'Personality', *Psychologist*, 12, 6, pp. 284–88, and in Henry (2001).

Hampson, S. E. (1995) 'The construction of personality', in Hampson and Coleman (1995).

Hampson, S. E. and Coleman, A. M. (1995) *Individual Differences and Personality*, Harlow: Longman.

Handy, C. (1999) quoted in *Creativity, Innovation and Change* Audio 1.

Handy, C. (1998) 'The citizen company', in Henry (2001).

Handy, C. (1998) *The Hungry Spirit*, London: Arrow.

Handy, C. (1997) *Beyond Certainty*, London: Arrow.

Handy, C. (1993) 'Trust', *Harvard Business Review*, 40–50, also in Henry *et al.* (1999) *Creativity, Innovation and Change Readings 3*, Milton Keynes: Open University Press.

Handy, C. (1991) 'The age of unreason', in Henry (1991).

Handy, C. (1990) *The Age of Unreason*, London: Arrow.

Handy, C. (1989) *The Future of Work*, Oxford: Blackwell.

Harman, W. (1988) *Global Mind Change*, Indiana: Knowledge Systems.

Hawkin, P., Lovins, A.B. and Lovins, L. H. (1999) *Natural Capitalism*, London: Earthscan.

Haworth, J. (1997) *Work, Leisure and Wellbeing*, London: Routledge.

Henry, J. (2001) *Creative Management*, 2nd edn, London: Sage.

Henry, J. (1999a) 'Changing conceptions of creativity', *Proceedings Rural Creativity Conference*, Aberystwyth.

Henry, J. (1999b) *Creativity, Cognition and Development*, Milton Keynes: Open University Press.

Henry, J. (1999c) *Management in Chinese Cultures*, Video 4 and accompanying Media Notes, *Creativity, Innovation and Change*, Milton Keynes: Open University Press.

Henry, J. (1999d) 'Sustainability', *Creativity, Innovation and Change* Audio 3, Milton Keynes: Open University.

Henry, J. (1998) 'Organizational change processes', paper presented to British Psychological Society Annual Conference.

Henry, J. (1997) 'Creativity and policy', paper presented to British Academy of Management Conference, Westminster.

Henry, J. (1994) 'The nature and development of creativity', *Co-Design*, Autumn.

Henry, J. (1992) 'Visioning in action', in B882 *Creative Management Media Book*, Milton Keynes: Open University Press.

Henry, J. (1991) *Creative Management*, London: Sage.

Henry, J. (1991b) 'Sustainable responsibility', in J. Henry (ed.) *Creative Management Media Book*, Milton Keynes: Open University Press.

Henry, J. (1991c) *Perspective*, Milton Keynes: Open University Press.

Henry, J. and Mayle, D. (2001) *Managing Innovation and Change*, London: Sage.

Henry, J. and Martin, J. (1991) *Creative Management*, Milton Keynes: Open University Press.

Henry, J. and Walker, D. (1991) *Managing Innovation*, London: Sage.

Henry, J. *et al.* (2001) *Innovation, Climate and Change*, Milton Keynes: Open University Press.

Henry, J. *et al.* (2000a) *Creativity, Innovation and Change*, Audio 1, Milton Keynes: Open University.

Henry, J. *et al.* (1999) *Creativity, Innovation and Change Guide*, Milton Keynes: Open University Press.

Herriman, N. (1996) *The Whole Brain Business Book*, New York: McGraw-Hill.

Hickson, D. J. and Pugh, D. S. (1995) *Management Worldwide*, Harmondsworth, Penguin.

Hines, T. (1987) 'Left/right brain mythology and implications for management and training', *Academy of Management Review*, Vol. 12, No. 4, p. 606.

Hirsch, S. K. (1985) *Using the Myers–Briggs Type Indicator in Organizations: a resource book*, , Palo Alto, CA: Consulting Psychologists Press.

Hirsch, S. K. and Kummerow, J. M. (1994) *Introduction to Type in Organizations*, Oxford: Oxford Psychologists Press.

Hoecklin, L. (1995) *Managing Cultural Differences,* Wokingham: Addison-Wesley/ Economist Intelligence Unit.

Hofstede, G. (1984) *Culture's Consequences: International Differences in Work-Related Values*, Beverley Hills CA: Sage.

Hofstede, G. (1991) *Cultures and Organizations: Software of the Mind*, London, McGraw-Hill.

Honey, P. and Mumford, A. (1985) *The Manual of Learning Styles*, Maidenhead: Peter Honey.

Hurst, D. K., Rush, J. C. and White, R. E. (1991) 'Top management teams and organizational renewal', Chapter 18 in Henry (1991).

Isaksen, S. and Puccio, G. J. (1988) 'Adaption–innovation and the Torrance tests of creative thinking: the level style issue revisited', *Psychological Reports*, Vol. 63, pp. 659–70.

Isenberg, D. J. (1987) 'The tactics of strategic opportunism', *Harvard Business Review*, March–April, pp. 477–97 (also in J. Henry (ed.) *Creative Management Readings*, Milton Keynes: Open University Press).

Jay, A. (1987) *Management and Machiavelli*, London: Hutchinson.

Jelinek, M. and Schoonhoven, C. B. (1991) 'Strong culture and its consequences', Chapter 8 in Henry and Walker (1991).

Jones, G. (1998) *Management and Culture*, Creative Management Book 4, Milton Keynes: Open University Press.

Jones, G. (1997) 'Perspectives on strategy', Chapter 20 in S. Segal-Horn, *The Strategy Reader*, Oxford: Blackwell.

Jones, L. (1984) 'Barriers to effective problem-solving', *Creativity and Innovation Network*, April–June, pp. 71–4.

Kabanoff and Rossiter (1994), 'Recent development in applied creativity' *International Review of Industrial and Organizational Psychology* Volume 9, edited by C.L. Cooper and I.T. Robertson, John Wiley & Sons.

Kanter, R. M. (1999) 'Spare change, real change', in Henry (2001).

Kanter, R. M. (1997) 'Restoring people to the heart of the organization', in F. Hesselbein, M. Goldsmith and R. Beckhard, *The Organization of the Future*, Drucker Foundation Series, San Francisco: Jossey Bass (also in *Readings 3*).

Kanter, R. M. (1991) 'Change masters', Chapter 5 in Henry and Walker (2001).

Kanter, R. M. (1988) *The Change Masters: Corporate Entrepreneurs at Work*, London: Unwin.

Kaufmann, G. (1991) 'Creativity and problem solving', in Henry (2001).

Kets de Vries, M. F. R. (1977) 'The entrepreneurial personality at the crossroads', *Journal of Management Studies*, Vol. XIV, pp. 34–57.

Kirton, M. J. (1989) *Adaptors and Innovators: Styles of Creativity and Problem-Solving*, London: Routledge, also 2nd edn 1994.

Kirton, M. J. (1987) *Adaption–Innovation Inventory (KAI) – Manual*, 2nd edn, Hatfield, Herts: Occupational Research Centre.

Kirton, M (1984) 'Adaptors and innovators – why new initiatives get blocked', *Long Range Planning*, 17, 2, pp. 137–43, also Chapter 16 in Henry (1991).

Kruglanski, A. W. and Freund, T. (1983) 'The freezing and unfreezing of lay inferences', *Journal of Experimental Social Psychology*, Vol. 19, No. 5, pp. 448–68.

Kolb, D. (1984) *Experiential Learning*, Englewood Cliffs, NJ: Prentice-Hall.

Kolb. D. *et al.* (1991) 'Strategic management development: experiential learning and managerial competencies', Chapter 17 in Henry (1991).

Koestler, A (1969) *The Act of Creation*, Aylesbury: Pan.

Krackhardt, D. and Hansen, J.R. (2000) 'Informal networks', in Henry (2001).

Lessem, R. (1990) *Developmental Management*, Oxford: Basil Blackwell.

Lakoff, G. and Johnson, M. (1980) *Metaphors We Live By*, University of Chicago.

Levinson, D. (1986) 'A conception of adult development', *American Psychologist,* 41, pp. 3–13.

Locke, R. (1996) *The Collapse of the American Management Mystique*, Oxford: Oxford University Press.

Lovejoy, T. (2000) quoted during Reith Lecture, BBC Radio 4 , 19 April.

Leonard-Barton, D. (1995) *Wellsprings of Knowledge: Building and Sustaining the Sources of Innovation*, Boston: Harvard Business School Press.

Lewicki, P., Hill, T. and Crysweka, M. (1992) 'Non-conscious acquisition of information', *American Psychologist*, 47, pp. 796–801.

Libet, B. (1993) 'The neural time factor in conscious and unconscious events', *Consciousness*, Chichester: Wiley.

Lovins, A., Lovins, H. and Hawken, P. (1999) 'Natural capitalism', in Henry (2001).

Maidique, M. (1990) 'Entrepreneurs, champions and technological innovation', *Sloan Management Review,* Winter, pp. 59–76.

Majaro, S. (1988) *The Creative Gap,* London: Longman.

Makridakis, S. (1989) 'Management in the 21st century', *Long Range Planning,* Vol. 22, No. 2, pp. 38–9.

Mangham, I. L. (1990) 'Managing as a performing art', *British Journal of Management,* 1, pp. 105–15.

Mansfield, E., Schwartz, M. and Wagner, S. (1981) 'Imitation costs and patents: an empirical study', *The Economic Journal* 91, pp. 907–18, quoted in Pfieffer (1994).

Marcel, T. (1993) 'Slippage in the unity of consciousness', in *CIBA Symposium,* 174.

Martin, J. (1991) 'Play, reality and creativity', Chapter 5 in Henry (1991).

Maslow, A.H. (1962) *Towards a Psychology of Being,* Princeton NJ: Van Nostrand.

Mason, R. O. and Mitroff, I. (1981) *Challenging Strategic Planning Assumptions,* New York: Wiley.

McCann, R. and Margerison, C. (1989) 'Managing high-performing teams', *Training and Development,* Vol. 11, pp. 53–60.

McCaskey, M. (1982) 'Mapping: creating, maintaining and relinquishing conceptual frameworks', in *The Executive Challenge: Managing Change and Ambiguity,* Pitman 14–33, reprinted in Henry (1991).

McHale, J. and Flegg, D. (1985) 'How Calamity Jane was put in her place, or why teams don't pull together', *Transition Now,* November, pp. 14–16.

McHale, J. and Flegg, D. (1986) 'Innovators rule OK – or do they?', *Training and Development,* October, pp. 10–13.

McKim, R.H. (1980) *Experiences in Visual Thinking,* Belmont, CA: PWS Publishers.

McPherson, J. (1967) *The People, the Problems and Problem-Solving Methods,* Michigan: Pendell Midland.

Miles, R. and Snow, C. (1978) *Organizational Strategy, Structure and Process,* New York: McGraw-Hill.

Miller, W. (1987–8) 'Synergising total quality and innovation', *National Productivity Review,* Winter, pp. 34–44.

Miller, W. (1988) *Innovation, Intuition and Total Quality,* Mill Valley, CA: SAI Associates.

Mintzberg, H (1996) 'Ten ideas designed to rile everyone who cares about management', *Harvard Business Review,* July–August, Vol. 74, No. 2, pp. 61–70, also in Henry (2001).

Mintzberg, H. (1994a) 'The rise and fall of strategic planning', *Harvard Business Review,* Jan–Feb, pp. 107–114.

Mintzberg, H. (1994b) 'Rounding out the manager's job', *Sloan Management Review,* Vol. 36, 1, pp. 11–30.

Mintzberg, H. (1987) 'Crafting strategy', *Harvard Business Review,* July–August, pp. 66–75.

Mintzberg, H. (1976) 'Planning on the left and managing on the right', *Harvard Business Review,* Jul–Aug, pp. 49–58, also in Henry (1991).

Mintzberg, H. (1975) 'The manager's job: folklore or fact', *Harvard Business Review,* July–August, pp. 49–61.

Mintzberg, H. and Waters, A. (1989) 'Of strategies, deliberate and emergent', in Asch, D. and Bowman, C. (eds) *Readings in Strategic Management*, Basingstoke: Open University/ Macmillan.

Morgan, G. (1993) *Imaginization*, London: Sage.

Morgan, G. (1991a) 'Paradigms, metaphors and puzzle-solving in organizations', in Henry (1991).

Morgan, G. (1991b) 'Emerging waves and challenges: the need for new competencies and mindsets', in Henry (1991).

Morgan, G. (1989) *Creative Organization Theory*, London: Sage.

Morgan, G. (1986, 2nd edn 1997) *Images of Organization*, London: Sage.

Naisbitt, J. and Aburdene, P. A. (1990) *Megatrends 2000*, London: Unwin.

Nayak, P. R. and Ketteringham, J. M. (1991) '3M's little yellow note pads', Chapter 27 in Henry and Walker (1991).

Nonaka, I. and Takeuchi, H. (1995) 'Organizational knowledge creation', in Henry (2001).

Nonaka, I, and Takeuchi, H. (1995) *The Knowledge-Creating Company*, Oxford: Oxford University Press.

Nonaka, T. (1993) 'The knowledge-creating company', *Harvard Business Review*, pp. 80–94.

Ouchi, W. A. (1981) *Theory Z: How American Business can meet the Japanese Challenge*, Reading, MA. Addison Wesley.

Piaget, J. (1929) *The Child's Conception of the World*, New York: Harcourt Brace.

Pascale, R. (1999) Extract from Complexity and the unconscious, *Creativity, Innovation and Change* Audio 2, Milton Keynes, Open University. Also in J. Henry, *Creativity, Innovation and Change Media Book*, Milton Keynes: Open University Press, pp. 9–10.

Payne, R.L. (1987) 'Individual differences and performance amongst R and D personnel: Some implications for management', *R and D Management,* 17, pp. 153–161, quoted in Bartram (1995) p. 127.

Pearce, F. (1990) 'Last of the string and sealing-wax boffins', *Independent*, 24 June.

Pearson, G. (1989) 'Promoting entrepreneurship in large companies', *Long Range Planning*, Vol. 22, No. 3, pp. 87–97.

Pedlar, M. and Boydell, T. (1985) *Managing Yourself*, London: Fontana.

Pepper, W. (1942) *World Hypotheses*, Berkeley, CA, University of California Press.

Perkins, D. (1981) *The Mind's Best Work*, Cambridge, MA: Harvard University Press.

Peters, T. (1988) *Thriving on Chaos: Handbook for a Management Revolution*, London: Pan.

Pfeffer, J. (1994) 'Competitive advantage through people', *California Management Review*, Winter, pp. 9–28.

Polyani, M. (1958) *Personal Knowledge: Towards a Post-Critical Philosophy*, London: Routledge and Kegan Paul.

Porrit, J. (1999) quoted on 'In Business' BBC Radio 4, 5th September.

Postman, N. (1992) *Technopoly*, New York: Knopf.

Rackham, N. and Morgan, T. (1977) *Behaviour Analysis in Training*, Maidenhead: McGraw-Hill.

Roberts, E. B. and Fusfeld, A R. (1981) 'Staffing the innovative technology-based organization', *Sloan Management Review*, pp. 19–34.

Robbins, A. (1990) *Unlimited Power*, New York: Simon & Schuster.

Rosenthal, R. (1969) *Artefact in Behavioural Research*, New York: Academic Press.

Roy, R. (1994) 'The evolution of ecodesign', *Technovation*, Vol. 14, No. 6, pp. 363–80.

Roy, R., Wield, D., Gardiner, P. and Potter, S. (1996) *Innovative Product Development* (Block 4 of *Innovation, Design, Environment and Strategy*), Milton Keynes: Open University Press.

Russell, P. (1994) 'Who's kidding whom? Is Western civilisation compatible with sustainable development', *World Business Academy Perspectives*, 8, 1, pp. 5–21.

Schein, E. H. (1992) 'Coming to a new awareness of organizational culture', in G. Salaman *et al.*, *Human Resource Strategies*, London, Sage, 1992, pp. 237–53.

Schein, E. H. (1985) *Organization, Culture and Leadership*, San Francisco: Jossey-Bass.

Schon, D. (1963) 'Champions for radical new inventions', *Harvard Business Review*, March–April.

Schooler, quoted in Claxton (1997), pp. 86–7.

Schwartz, S.H. and Bilsky, W. (1990) 'Towards a theory of universal content and structure in human values', *Journal of Personality and Social Psychology*, 58, pp. 87–91.

Semler, R. (1996) *Maverick*, London: Arrow.

Semler, R (1994) 'Why my former employees still work for me', *Harvard Business Review*, also in Henry (2001).

Senge, P. (1991) *The Fifth Discipline: The Art and Practice of the Learning Organization*, London: Century.

Shapiro, E. (1966) 'The identification of research scientists', *Psychologica Africana*, pp. 99–132.

Sharma, D. (2001) 'The Green Revolution turns sour', *New Scientist*, 8 July, pp. 44–5.

Shiva, V. (1993) 'Monocultures and mind', in Henry (2001).

Shiva, V. (1993) *Monocultures of the Mind: Perspectives on Biodiversity and Biotechnology*, London/Atlantic Heights NJ/Penang: Zed Books.

Shiva, V. (1999) quoted in 'Organizations in the community', *Creativity Innovation and Change* Audio 4, Milton Keynes: Open University.

Shotter (1993) *Conversational Realities: Constructing Life Through Language*, London: Sage.

Sim, R. (ed.) (1998) *Icon Dictionary of Postmodern Thought*, Cambridge, Icon Books.

Simon, H. (1988) 'Understanding creativity and creative management', in Kuhn, R., *Handbook for Creative and Innovative Managers*, New York: McGraw-Hill.

Simon, H. (1960) *Administrative Behaviour*, London: Macmillan.

Simonton, D. K. (1988) 'History, chemistry, psychology and genius', in M. Runco and R. Mark, *Theories of Creativity*, Newbury Park CA: Sage Focus, pp. 92–115.

Smith, P.B and Bond, M.H. (1993) *Psychology Across Cultures: Analysis and Perspectives*, London: Harvester Wheatsheaf.

Stacy, R. (1996) *Complexity and Creativity in Organizations*, San Francisco, CA: Brett-Koehler.

Storey, D.J., Watson, R. and Wynarczyk, P. (1987) 'Fast growth small businesses: case studies of 40 small firms in North-East England', *Research Paper 67*, London: Department of Employment.

Taylor, W.G.K. (1989) 'The Kirton Adaption-Innovation Inventory: a re-examination of the factor structure', *Journal of Organizational Behaviour*, 10, pp. 297–307, quoted in Bartram *et al.* (1995), pp. 125–127.

Tidd, J., Bessant, J. and Parvitt, K. (1997) *Managing Innovation*, London: John Wiley.

Trompenaars, F. (1993) *Riding the Waves of Culture*, London, Nicholas Brealey.

Tuckman, B. W. (1965) 'Development sequences in small groups', *Psychological Bulletin*, Vol. 6, pp. 384–99.

Vickers, G. (1984) 'Judgement', in *The Vickers Papers*, Open Systems Group (eds) Paul Chapman, pp. 230–45, also in Henry (1991).

Vollmer, C. (1990) 'The effect of lateral thinking training on innovative–adaptive cognitive style', Masters thesis, University of Cape Town.

Wack, P. (1985) 'Scenarios: uncharted waters ahead', *Harvard Business Review,* Sep–Oct pp. 73–89, also Chapter 25 in Henry and Walker (1991).

Weick, K. E. (1998) 'Improvisation as a mind-set for organizational analysis', *Organization Science*, Sept–Oct, Vol. 9, 5, pp. 54—55.

Weick, K. E. (1979) *The Social Psychology of Organizing*, Reading, MA. Addison Wesley

Weidenbaum, M. (1996) The Chinese family business enterprise, *California Management Review,* 38, 4, Summer. Also in Henry *et al., Creativity, Innovation and Change, Readings 4,* Milton Keynes: Open University Press pp. 208–17.

Weisburg, R. (1986) *Creativity: Genius and Other Myths*, New York: W. H. Freeman.

West, M. A. and Anderson, N. R. (1996) 'Innovation in top management teams', *Journal of Applied Psychology*, Vol. 81, No. 6, pp. 680–93.

West, M. A. and Farr, J. (1990) *Creativity and Innovation at Work*, Chichester: Wiley.

Westhead, P. (1994) 'New owner-managed businesses in rural and urban areas in Great Britain: a matched pairs comparison, *Regional Studies*, 29, 4, pp. 367–80.

Westley, F. and Mintzberg, H. (1991) 'Visionary leadership and strategic management', Chapter 4 in Henry and Walker (1991).

Wheatley, M. (1994) *Leadership and the New Science*, San Francisco, CA: Brett-Koehler.

Whittington, R. (1993) *What is Strategy and Does It Matter?*, London: Routledge.

Witzel, M. (1998) 'Getting back to our management roots', *FT Mastering Management Review*, May, pp. 16–19.

Zadak, S. (1998) *An Overview of Contemporary Developments in Social Auditing*, London: New Economics Foundation.

Zimbardo, P., McDermott, M., Jansz, J. and Metal, M. (1995) *Psychology: A European Text*, London: HarperCollins.

APPENDIX A

LIFE GOALS

Know thyself

There is now appreciation of the need to develop individual members of staff if they are to learn to their full potential. A number of companies have appraisal and training schemes that ask employees to identify what qualities they wish to develop in themselves. We have seen that creative individuals spend more time problem-finding, checking that they are addressing a question that is really important to them. The following activities provide a means of reflecting on your goals.

The change process begins with a diagnosis of problems participants consider important.

(Argyris, 1990, p. 107)

These first few activities are concerned with problem-finding, identifying what you consider important enough to spend time on. The next few ask you to start exploring how you might begin tackling key issues.

Activity A.1

(a) Write down five qualities that you like about yourself. Ask five friends to offer a quality that they admire or enjoy about you.

(b) Think of five people who made a lasting impression on you. What characteristics do you think account for this?

(c) Write a brief obituary for yourself. Ask someone who knows you well to write one for you.

What characteristics and achievements do you wish to be remembered for?

Activity A.2

What has your path of development been?

(a) Take a piece of paper and draw a line (similar to the one in Figure A.1) that represents your life from birth to now, projecting into the future if you wish.

(b) Does your line go up or down or is it essentially straight? Most people point their lines upward.

(c) Where are the big peaks and troughs? This may tell you something about what really matters to you in life.

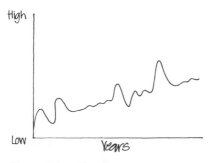

Figure A.1   Time line

Activity A.3

What is important to you at this point in your life?

(a) Write down the ten things you have enjoyed most in the past year.

(b) In each case note:

– whether you were alone or with others

– whether it was free or cost money.

(c) Which of the ten things was most important? (See Table A.1 below.)

The majority of people find that the things they enjoyed most were free.

Table A.1 Enjoyment table			
Things I enjoy	**Alone or with others**	**Cost**	**Last experienced**

Activity A.4

Imagine a typical working day (or a composite day if they vary).

(a) Write down the types of activity you actually do in your working day (*not* what you are supposed to do or what your job description says!).

(b) Estimate the percentage of time that you normally spend on each. Don't spend too long on this. Rough estimates will be fine.

(c) Note which of these activities you enjoy, perhaps marking them 'E', and which you think are important, perhaps marking them 'I'.

(d) Imagine an optimistic scenario at work, in which you could increase the percentages of time spent on activities you enjoy. Put these new percentages next to the old ones.

(e) Note the differences between the two percentages.

(f) Life is short. Start thinking about how you might minimize the discrepancies you noted in respect of the activities you enjoy and consider important.

Activity A.5

List two things you want to achieve:

- this week

- this month

- this year

- in five years

- in your lifetime.

THE PENALTY FOR
NOT KEEPING
IN TOUCH

IS
HAVING LESS
TO FEEL.

Visionary leaders often have an image of what they want to achieve. Anyone can attempt to create a positive vision to help gain a clearer picture of what they want and guide them towards it. There are several ways of doing this. One of the most effective seems to work quite illogically. You start with the very pleasant task of imagining yourself doing what you wish to achieve. For the imaging to work, it helps to imagine this in some detail.

Activity A.6

List several goals that you would like to achieve, writing them down 'as if you had already achieved them', e.g. 'I am...' or 'I have...'

Choose one goal and imagine it in as much detail as you can. Visualize the scene, the actions, notice how you feel and what you are thinking or saying. What colours, sounds, feelings, smells and tastes are there? Who else is there? How are you relating to them? Really enjoy this experience.

Imagine you are in a cinema and this picture is on the screen in front of you. When you can imagine it in detail and have explored it well, imagine the film winding back to where you are now, and as this happens notice how you reached where you want to be. You may well be surprised.[46]

Charles Dickens

[46] The *Creativity, Innovation and Change* Audio 5, 'Imaging', provides a further chance to try some imaging exercises.

Activity A.7

Issues. Choose five areas you would like to work on, perhaps to do with yourself, family, work, leisure, home or finances. In each case phrase the issue as a question: 'How can I ... ?'

Then complete the following.

(a) *Symptom.* 'How things are at the moment is ... .'

(b) *Intention.* 'How I would like them to be is ... .'

(c) *Alternatives.* 'What I could do about this is ... .'

(d) *Choice.* 'I am willing to ... .'

(e) *First steps.* 'I will take the first step of ... on ... .'

It does not matter if you complete statements (a) to (e) for each issue in turn or complete all the statements for one issue before moving on to the next.

(See Figure A.2.)

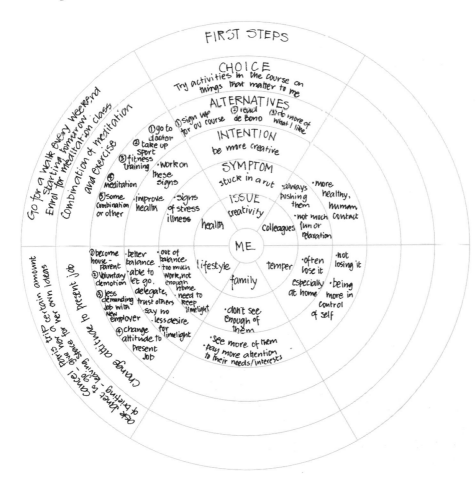

Figure A.2   Domain map (Source: adapted from Pedlar and Boydell, 1985, p. 41)

APPENDIX B

SOLUTIONS TO PROBLEMS

Earth–rope gap problem

You may recall the circumference (c) of a circle is $2\pi r$, i.e. 6.28 times the radius of the circle. So $2\pi r$, where r is the radius of the earth, is the circumference of the earth, and the circumference of the rope is $2\pi r + 200$ cm. The radius of the earth plus the gap between the rope and earth is therefore $2\pi(r+g)$ where g is the gap between the earth and rope.

$2\pi r = c$

$2\pi(r+g) = 2\pi r + 200$ cm

$2\pi g = 200$ cm

$g = 200/6.28 =$ approximately 32 cm

Remarkably, any circle adding 2 metres to the circumference will result in an increased radius of about 32 cm.

(Adapted from Claxton, 1997.)

Embedded pictures

Cowboy and man's bearded face images contained with embedded pictures.

Figure B.1

Figure B.2

Nine-dot problem

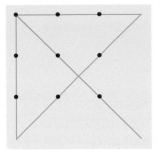

People often fail to solve the nine-dot problem because they assume the lines have to be kept within a square implicitly formed by the dots, even though the problem as stated does not present this as a constraint.

Inverted triangle

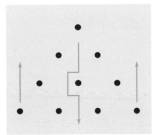

Move the dot at the top to the centre below the bottom row. Move the two outside dots on the row of four to the outside of the row with two dots, to complete the triangle inversion.

Animal enclosures

ACKNOWLEDGEMENTS

Grateful acknowledgement is made to the following sources for permission to reproduce material in this text:

Figures

Figure 3: © Tony Stone Images Ltd, Robert Brons/BPS; *Figures 3.2, 3.3, B.1 and B.2:* © Tony Stone Images, Robert Brons/BPS and Porter, P.B. 'Hidden man', from *American Journal of Psychology*, Vol. 67, 1954, p. 550. Reprinted by permission of the University of Illinois Press; *Figure 4.2:* Morgan, G. (1989) *Creative Organization Theory*, Sage Publications Inc.; *Figure 8.1:* Shiva, V. (1993) *Monocultures of the Mind: Perspectives on Biodiversity and Biotechnology*, Zed Books Ltd; *Figure 9.1 (left):* © Mark Edwards/Still Pictures; *Figure 9.1 (right):* © Mike Jackson/Still Pictures; *Figure 9.2 (top):* © NASA/Still Pictures; *Figure 9.2 (middle):* © Tantyo Bangun/Still Pictures; *Figure 9.2 (bottom):* © Chris Martin/Still Pictures; *Figure 9.3 (a) and (b):* Karrimor International Ltd; *Figure 9.5 (left):* © National Motor Museum, Beaulieu; *Figure 9.5: (right):* Courtesy of Stephen Potter.

Photographs/Illustrations

pp. 8, 29, 32, 68, 121, 204: Brilliant, A. (1985) *All I Want Is a Warm Bed and a Kind Word*, Woodbridge Press. Copyright © Ashleigh Brilliant; *p. 29:* Copyright © Mary Evans Picture Library; *p. 80 (top left and bottom right):* © Mehau Kulyk/Science Photo Library; *p. 80 (top right):* © Cambridge University Collection of Air Photographs, copyright reserved; *p. 80 (bottom left):* © Marcus Enoch; *p. 81 (right):* © Tony Stone Images Ltd; *p. 81 (left):* © Nacy Kedersha/Science Photo Library; *p. 130:* Reproduced by permission of Tony Remali from A. Mavromatis, *Hypnogogia* (London: Routledge & Kegan Paul, 1987); *p. 132:* © Thierry Boccon-Gibod; *p. 139 (left):* © Paul Harrison/Still Pictures; *p. 139 (right):* © Popperfoto; *p. 141:* © Associated Press; *p. 144:* Cartoons by Shotaro Ishinomori, from: *Japan Inc. Introduction to Japanese Economics.* © Regents of the University of California Press; *p. 149 (right):* © Courtesy of Michael Bull/DuckLETS, Aylesbury; *p. 151:* National Aeronautics and Space Administration (USA); *p. 175 (top left):* © Nick Cobbing/Still Pictures; *p. 175 (top right):* © Mark Edwards/Still Pictures; *p. 180:* © Courtesy of Ecover NV; *p. 185:* © Courtesy of The Body Shop; *p. 187 (top):* © Reproduced by courtesy of Tesco 'Computers for Schools' Press Office; *p. 204:* Reproduced by courtesy of The Dickens House, London.

INDEX